Power
and
Policy
in
the
Third
World

Power
and
Policy
in
the
Third
World

Robert P. Clark
Professor of Government
George Mason University

John Wiley and Sons
New York   Santa Barbara   Chichester   Brisbane   Toronto

Photo Research by Hildegard Kron
Photo Editor, Stella Kupferberg

Cover Design, Blaise Zito Associates, Inc.

Library of Congress Cataloging in Publication Data:

Clark, Robert P
  Power and policy in the Third World.

  Bibliography: p.
  1. Underdeveloped areas—Politics and government.
2. Comparative government. I. Title.

JF60.C553   320.9′172′4   77-25224
ISBN 0-471-02710-3

Printed in the United States of America

10 9 8 7 6 5 4 3

Preface

Today's world is a highly stratified political and economic system, with a very few nations clustered at the top of the scales of well-being and power, a few more in the middle, and the great majority near the bottom. With a few exceptions, such as the oil-exporting nations, the countries at the bottom of the world's lists of wealth and power lie in what is called the "Third World." Like poor and weak citizens in domestic politics, the developing countries either cannot uncover the secret for increasing their power and well-being, or they are prevented from doing so by the intervention of the system's wealthy and powerful members. Either way, the experiences of the past decade or two have not been especially promising for the Third World.

A generation ago, economists, political experts, and other social scientists believed that they found the secret of progress for the developing nations, depending on whether they were advocates of unrestrained *laissez faire* capitalism, or of welfare state socialism, or of centrally directed Marxism-Leninism. Since that early beginning in "political development," many of us who write about such matters, or who have been engaged in the practical business of trying to assist developing countries, have become much more chastened about our abilities to engineer development quickly, and more pessimistic about the capacity of many nations of the Third World to do so for themselves.

This book is an attempt to communicate to today's American college student my understanding of the obstacles that block the progress of the Third World toward increased material well-being and increased power over their own destinies (personal as well as national). The objects of my analysis are the developing countries of Latin America, Asia, Africa and the Middle East.

My approach is a mixture of things. It is comprehensive, in that it attempts to treat the Third World as an entity, while recognizing the special features of certain countries or parts of the world that cause them to resist easy generalization. It is also systematic. Through the first three chapters, I examine the historical, social, environmental, psychological, and economic context within which the Third World's developing effort must progress. The last four chapters examine how Third World political systems actually go about the business of politics: the allocation of certain key values (power, well-being, respect, and enlightenment). Thus, Chapter 4 discusses how individual and group participants attempt to steer developing polities toward their (the participants') preferred value distribution patterns; Chapter 5 assesses the institutions available in the Third World to distribute these values; Chapter 6 analyzes the policy process that can be brought to bear on value distribution in developing countries; and Chapter 7 looks at the level of political performance achieved by Third World states.

Finally, my approach is both integrative and comparative. I attempt to blend together the theoretical and the empirical, to make some sense of the political process, and to give the reader some feel for what politics is like at the level of the daily concerns of the average citizen in the Third World. In addition, I try to place the contemporary Third World experience in the context of the development, modernization, and industrialization records of the Western European and Marxist nations.

This book was written to take its place as one-third of a comprehensive comparative analysis of public policy problems. The larger book, titled *Comparing Political Systems: Power and Policy in Three Worlds,* includes as companion studies to my book, parallel treatments of the Western European democracies, written by David Wood, and of the Marxist systems, contributed by Gary Bertsch. It was our hope that the comprehensive study would add to a comparative understanding of policy problems encountered across political systems, regardless of their level of development or ideological base.

Above all, this book is meant to be sympathetic to the countries and to the peoples of the Third World. I sincerely wish them well, and direct my remarks to that end. I point this out now, because the bluntness of some of my later comments may obscure this attitude. When I first ventured in the field of the analysis of political development, nearly 10 years ago, it was easy to be both sympathetic and optimistic, or at least uncritical. Such is not the case today. After a generation or more of false starts, "failed revolutions," Great Power interventions, military coups, abuse of human rights, and illusory devices like "Decades of Development" or "Alliances for Progress," sympathy for the cause of development requires the saying of things that at times may sound unduly critical or even hostile. This is not my intent. I simply believe that I owe to my readers (who may include some Third World citizens) an analysis based on the philosophical proposition that I enunciated in my earlier book on the Third World:

> *Political development, like all social processes, can be subjected to human intervention and guidance. While we cannot dictate with certainty the path a developing state can take, we may certainly throw the weight of human intelligence into the scales to insure that some paths will be more likely than others. The challenge to behavioral science is to demonstrate how this is done, and to show what the costs and benefits of certain strategies may be.* *

In closing, I wish to thank two institutions for their material support during the preparation of the manuscript: the University of Tennessee at Chattanooga, for their financial support during a sabbatical year of research and writing; and the Brookings Institution, Washington, D.C., where I enjoyed an appointment as a Guest Scholar during the 1976–1977 academic year. Naturally, neither of these institutions bears any responsibility for the contents of this book.

Robert P. Clark

* Robert P. Clark, *Development and Instability: Political Change in the Non-Western World* (Hinsdale, Illinois: Dryden Press, 1974), p. vi.

Contents

Power
and
Policy
in
the
Third
World

INTRO-DUCTION

Studying Politics in the Third World

One day recently, while the manuscript for this book was being prepared, the Washington *Post* carried stories with the following headlines.

"Taiwan To Curb A-Role"

"Whites Doubt Rhodesia To 'Give In' Now"

"Chilean Bomb Victim Told FBI of Threats To Life, Friends Say"

"4 Leftist Guerrillas Killed in Argentina"

"Soviet Foothold Slipping in Shifting Sands of Mideast"

"Indonesia Says Coup Plot Thwarted"

"Panamanian Hits Zonians As Racists"

Although each story dealt with a unique historical event, they all have at least two things in common. Each event has the potential for affecting our lives in one way or another over the next few years, and each event took place in what is called the Third World—the developing countries of Africa, Asia, Latin America, and the Middle East.

This book is about the more than 100 independent nations that make up the Third World. As we read about the political struggles of many of these countries, we will learn about their historical background, the effects of the centuries-long colonial experience, the many social and economic problems that plague their governments, and the prevailing attitudes and modes of thinking that one is likely to encounter there. But, primarily, this is a book about politics: about the ways in which Third World political leaders organize themselves for collective tasks, how power is obtained, shared, transferred, and used, how policies and decisions are made and implemented, and how well the governments of the region are meeting the challenges of industrialization and modernization.

1

WHY STUDY THE THIRD WORLD? No doubt, as you glanced over the headlines from the *Post,* you were puzzled about what all of those events have to do with you and with your way of life. This is a normal reaction to news accounts of far-off happenings. After all, Taiwan is so far away, Rhodesia is so different from us, and Latin America is so out of our control that we have a tendency to close such matters out of our minds, preferring to consider things that are closer, more familiar, or more susceptible to our influence and control. Nevertheless, this book is based on the assumptions that what goes on in the Third World has effects on our lives far beyond what we may think at first, and that the events of Third World politics are actually much more familiar to things that we already know about than we may realize.

To begin with, only the most hardened isolationists would today deny the political and economic importance of many countries in the Third World. In 1974, more than half of the world's 4.3 billion people lived in countries in the Third World; rising population growth rates assure us that this percentage will increase over the coming decades. Not only is the Third World the home of half the earth's population, but it is also the location of crucial deposits of strategic raw materials, such as oil, uranium, copper, and bauxite, all of which the United States must import to feed our industrial economy. Think back to the energy crisis of 1973 and 1974. It was clear then, even if we have forgotten it since, that countries like Saudi Arabia and Venezuela possessed a good deal of influence over our government and our standard of living. But interdependence is a two-way street. Third World nations depend on America's farmers to produce a great deal of the wheat, rice, and soybeans that are consumed in developing countries; our farmers, in turn, depend on the Third World markets to absorb food surpluses that would depress the domestic market if they were sold here at home. Security issues, such as skyjacking and other forms of guerrilla insurgency and terrorism, can obviously affect Americans abroad as they visit unstable countries in the Third World. Famine, pollution racial discrimination, and other events in the turbulent developing countries can all affect our lives in one way or another.

We must go further, however, to stress the role of the Third World in the struggle for national security that has affected American politics for the last 30 years. Since the end of World War II, the United States has been involved in two major wars (both in Third World states), resulting in nearly 100,000 dead Americans. In addition, we have intervened in literally dozens of minor conflicts all around the globe, from Guatemala and Bolivia and the Dominican Republic, to Lebanon, to the Philippines, in order to achieve or preserve that elusive goal of national security. We have spent over $100 billion in foreign assistance since the Marshall Plan days of the late 1940s to improve (and influence foreign economies; and we spend currently each year over $100 billion on weapons and other military items to defend our nation. Finally, we have created an intelligence and surveillance network in the Central Intelligence Agency and the Federal Bureau of Investigation that has angered and shocked many Americans for what they feel are unwarranted intrusions into our private lives. Why have these things come about? What is it about the countries beyond our borders that makes some of them threats to us, others allies, and still others the cause of great concern because of their very weakness? To answer these and other questions about American politics, we must know more about the countries that make up the Third World.

In addition, the Third World countries are now the scene of an important struggle between the forces of authority and freedom, a struggle that will affect the fate of human rights throughout the world. For centuries, human beings have argued about the relative importance of equality, freedom, stability, and prosperity. Today, in the developing world, political élites have concluded that economic well-being is too important a goal to allow it to be eroded by policies that permit the free exercise of civil rights and liberties. As we will demonstrate later, in one country after another in the Third World, human rights are being systematically violated in order, some say, to achieve more rapid economic growth. Presently, fewer than one person in five of the world's population lives under democratic conditions. Respect for human rights is clearly ebbing, and in no area is this trend clearer than in the Third World. We must come to grips with the reasons for this trend in order to improve our understanding of its implications for our own country.

Fourth, the Third World is important to study for clues about traditional and modernizing politics that will help us to understand better what goes on in local and big city politics in the United States. The basis for studying politics comparatively is to enable us to apply lessons learned in one setting to the problems we confront in another. In this context, I would argue that developing nations are much like American urban centers in many ways. Both kinds of governments, Third World nations and American cities, suffer from a severe lack of adequate financial resources. Both political systems depend on outside sources for much of their income and food. Both social systems are beset by ethnic, racial, economic, linguistic, religious, or other kinds of strife that are only dimly appreciated by studying American *national* politics. In this sense, south Boston has more in common with Rhodesia or Uganda than it does with the federal government in Washington. Finally, both developing countries and America's cities are characterized by political and governmental institutions that are usually underdeveloped. Patron-client politics is common, as much in Chicago as in Mexico. What we call clientelistic politics in the Third World is really quite similar to machine politics in many American cities.[1] The obvious power and modernity of the American national political system often obscure from us the fact that America's local communities frequently constitute an entirely different kind of political system, one much more like those in the Third World. As we study politics in the Third World, we should try to apply what we learn to improve our understanding of our own communities, many of which will be more like the Third World than we had realized.

THE FUNDAMENTALS OF POLITICS IN THE THIRD WORLD

Politics and Human Values. Human values change, from one culture to another and from one historical period to another. Yet, it seems that human beings spend a considerable part of their time worrying about and trying to change the condition of their lives. For some, the principal problem may be tan-

---

[1] Henry Bienen, "Political Parties and Political Machines in Africa," in Michael F. Lofchie, ed., *The State of the Nations: Constraints on Development in Independent Africa* (Berkeley, Calif.: California, 1971), Chapter 9.

gible or material: enough food to eat, proper clothing or shelter, adequate medical care. For others, the unsatisfactory conditions may involve less tangible factors: education for themselves or for their children, the right to worship as they choose, permission to speak the language of their ethnic group. For still others, the major problem may be social: their acceptance by antagonistic groups, denial of rights by others, a feeling of racial or ethnic inferiority.

In earlier times, people were generally expected to cope with life's struggles as individuals, or as members of small, informally organized groups, such as families, clans, or tribes. Human problems were usually individual and private issues, not political and public ones. In recent decades, however, men and women the world over have looked more and more to government to help them to manage their lives and to overcome inadequacies in their conditions of life.

Each of the more than 100 governments in the Third World is organized to respond to what its leaders perceive to be the paramount challenges facing the country. Many of these challenges have to do with the conditions of human life in the nation. Each of these governments has achieved a certain level of response to these challenges, a certain track record of accomplishment in meeting the needs of their people. No government solves all of its country's problems immediately; no government can fail completely for long and remain in power. All governments fall somewhere in between the two extremes of total success and abject failure.

In the course of this examination of politics in the Third World, I will present two broad sets of questions and provide you with some information to help you look for the answers.

First, how do governments help people to achieve the things that they value? What do governments do to resolve human problems? How well do they accomplish their objectives? How can we measure and compare political performance or achievement in so many countries?

Second, what factors can we look for to explain these different levels of government performance? What difference do ideology or government structure make? What about political parties? Or interest groups? Or the media of mass communications? Are they important? Are constitutional freedoms crucial to enhancing human values, or do they just get in the way of determined governments? Perhaps other factors that are not political are more important in determining the ability of governments to solve human problems: the wealth of the country, its natural resources, the level of education of its people, its level of industrialization, its geographical location, its historical background, and so forth. In short, does government matter to people and to human values and, if so, how much and in what ways?

What Do People Want? For years, scholars from different fields of knowledge have studied what people value in different cultural and economic settings.[2] No one has yet developed a list of universal human values that is

[2] The literature on human values is extensive. The interested reader can begin with these. Hadley Cantril, *The Pattern of Human Concerns* (New Brunswick, N.J.: Rutgers University Press, 1966). Abraham Maslow, ed., *New Knowledge in Human Values* (Chicago: Regnery, 1970). Gunnar Myrdal, *Value in Social Theory* (Boston: Routledge & Keegan Paul, 1958). Milton Rokeach, *The Nature of Human Values* (New York: Free Press, 1973). Harold Lasswell, *A Pre-View of Policy Sciences* (New York: Elsevier, 1971).

acceptable to all scholars in all cultures and, at the same time is precise and capable of being investigated empirically. Therefore I must work here with a set of values that is derived from criteria other than that of universal scholarly consensus.

In order to organize my inquiry into political performance in the Third World, I will work with four values: *power, respect, well-being,* and *enlightenment.*

I do not claim that these four values are universal, or sacred, but only that they are a useful organizing principle to guide my work, that they tend to be the most important human values that are dealt with in a political context, and that they span the entire range of important values, from the inner needs of individuals to the public requirements of social groups.

Power is the key value in the political process, because power is the ability to change or influence policy choices. Power in the sense we use it here means the ability of one person to influence, shape, or alter the behavior of another. The extent to which power is distributed between élites and nonélites in a society will go far toward determining the range of policy choices in that society. The second basic value at stake in politics, well-being, involves the degree to which individuals and groups enjoy income, goods, services, wealth, health, safety, and comfort. Although there seems to be a universal desire for increased well-being, different political systems hold differing ideas about how the level of well-being should be raised and how its benefits should be distributed. Respect, the third fundamental value, has to do with human rights, affection, comradeship, loyalty, honor, and prestige; these are all elements of that broader concept, political community. Political community refers to the affective ties that bind together individuals who communicate, work well together, and understand one another. Without a strong sense of community, a political system will be faced with excessive conflict and turmoil. Finally, many politicians seek to distribute enlightenment, which means education, knowledge, and information, as well as (in some countries) religious and cultural preferences.

The four human values form a complex of individual and collective goals and objectives that varies from country to country and from epoch to epoch. From time to time, I will simplify my discussion of these values by referring to them collectively, by using the encompassing term, human dignity. Human dignity is an over-arching concept that reflects the specific mixture of values of power, well-being, respect, and enlightenment characteristic of any given culture or subculture.

In my view, human dignity carries with it the notion that each person is to be considered an end in himself or herself, and not a mere instrument to enhance the values of some "higher" entity, for example, the state, a party, or a dictator. Obviously, I cannot claim that all governments in the Third World follow policies designed to maximize this concept of human dignity. A glance through today's newspaper will probably provide ample illustrations of governments that deny their people many or even all of the four values. The approach of each government to meeting its society's problems will differ, depending on the relative weight it places on competing factors such as dissent and conformity, or the rights of the individual and the rights of the collectivity. The concept of human dignity gives us a measuring stick with which to evaluate and compare the performance of governments in the Third World.

Political System and Process. There are many different factors that influence how these four values are distributed. Some of the factors are clearly not part of politics in most countries, for example, the prevailing religious beliefs of a culture, and the way in which families are organized. But politics does make a difference in value distribution in every country in the world. As politicians go about the tasks of making decisions regarding value distributions, they are inevitably imposing some kind of cost on some group or individual. Political economists like to remind us of the old adage, "There is no such thing as a free lunch." All political choices bring both benefits and costs to the citizens of a country. In the Third World, leaders are acutely conscious of the dilemmas involved in the choice between growth (the increase of the absolute amount of economic product) and equity (the more nearly equitable distribution of that product).

The place where the political process unfolds is called the political system. The political system includes all of the functioning institutions within the formal governmental structure, but it also can embrace many nongovernmental institutions that enter the political process on an informal, unofficial, or irregular basis. In addition, the historical, geographic, and demographic characteristics provide a certain setting within which politics takes place; this, likewise, must be included in our analysis. Thus, the political system encompasses the individuals, both leaders and followers, who influence the making of public policy; the structures or institutions that surround these individuals and shape their behavior; and the environment that provides the inclusive background against which the political drama is enacted.

I have referred to the idea of the political process. A process is a related sequence of events, and so we are led to look for event sequences that involve the authoritative distribution of values. Actually, of course, the real world of human behavior does not divide itself neatly into discernable things called "events." For purposes of analysis and understanding, however, we must impose a certain degree of artificial structure on reality and give these phenomena labels. Thus, the political process begins with the selection of goals by a set of leaders.

All political systems seek to preserve their nation and their regime from threats, so these constitute the irreducible minimum goals in politics. Furthermore, virtually all political élites have set their countries on the path toward industrialization of their economic structures and modernization of their societies, in the belief that to do so will enhance the level of human dignity among their peoples. But the processes of industrialization and modernization have created as many tensions and problems as they have relieved; governments around the world must now cope with the adverse consequences as well as the benefits of these social and economic changes. To accomplish all of these objectives, each political system strives to increase its capabilities or its capacities to perform certain tasks: to regulate its citizens' behavior; to extract resources from society; to distribute these resources productively; to generate and transmit reassuring symbolic messages to its people; and to sense what the people want and respond to their needs. Once a political system's goals have been chosen, decisions must be made to implement policies that will bring these goals nearer to realization. This phase of the process involves actions to put ideas into practice.

The actions that a political system takes are determined not only by the system's goals, but by the capabilities of the government and by the ability and inclination of the citizens to cooperate with or resist the implementation of policies. As the actions of the state filter down through the society, certain things begin to happen. People's behavior changes; money is spent; troops are mobilized; land changes hands; and houses are built.

Yet the political process is not over. The third stage, then, is marked by an evaluation of outcomes. That is, political leaders need to know how successful (or unsuccessful) they have been in trying to cope with a specific problem. The information they gather about present performance (called feedback) will be helpful in correcting their mistakes and improving future performance. The entire process then begins again by returning to the setting of new goals and objectives, the implementing of new policies, the evaluation of new outcomes, and so on, literally forever.

If Third World political leaders are interested in evaluating the outcomes of their policy choices, so are we interested, as students, in evaluating and comparing political performance. Our analysis would not be complete without an opportunity to assess the relative levels of performance seen throughout the Third World. Do some regimes seem to do a better job of maximizing well-being, respect, or enlightenment? Do others do a superior job of distributing power? On the whole, are military regimes better at governing than democratic ones? Is restriction of human rights worthwhile in order to achieve higher rates of economic growth?

To answer these and other questions, we must evaluate political performance in four ways. First, we must assess system performance in absolute terms, that is, without comparison with any normative standards. What is the growth rate of the gross national product of Nigeria, for example? Second, we seek to compare one system with another under similar circumstances. Is Nigeria's GNP growth rate higher than that of Zaire? Third, we compare the system's performance with its own self-professed goals. Is Nigeria's GNP growth rate higher or lower than the goal established by the Nigerian government? And fourth, we compare the system's present or current performance with that of an earlier period. Is Nigeria's GNP growth rate higher now than it was in 1965?

After evaluation must come explanation. We are interested in knowing more than simply how well the government of Nigeria has managed to raise its nation's GNP. We want to know why it has succeeded (or failed), and why some nations may have done a better (or worse) job of the same task.

We find explanations at three levels. At the first level, we find the elements of the environment that influence political performance: historical background, socioeconomic structures, and natural resource endowments. At the second level, we will examine the individuals who are both the authors of policy and its objects. What kinds of leaders occupy positions of power in the Third World? How does charisma play a role in the struggle for power? The masses of the population must also be analyzed. What are prevailing levels of literacy in the general populace? What are the important personality or attitudinal characteristics of Third World citizens? Finally, we come to the structures, or institutions, within which political figures must work. Is the institutional network rich and flexible, or is it still relatively primitive and rigid? Are there adequate channels of communication to permit leaders to evaluate their policy outcomes or to sense the feelings of the masses?

THE PLAN OF THE BOOK. The organizational structure of this book is derived directly from the analytical framework just described. Chapters 1, 2, and 3 examine the environment within which Third World political systems operate. Chapter 1 is devoted to the historical background of the developing world, with special emphasis on the effects of the colonial experience. This chapter's findings lead directly into Chapter 2, which considers some outstanding social and economic problems faced by the Third World. We first discuss the special role of the international system as we examine the various aspects of the "dependence" theory as an explanation for poverty in the Third World. Also discussed in Chapter 2 are demographic problems, particularly the population explosion, and economic questions, such as unequal distribution of income and poor resource endowment. The chapter also includes a brief discussion of some salient social problems, including racial, ethnic, religious, and linguistic schisms in developing countries. In Chapter 3, I examine some important psychological aspects of modernization; I begin with the attitudes that are peculiar to traditional people and then follow these people through the modernization process to ascertain the psychological impact of such changes. This chapter also includes some material on public policies that are designed to accelerate the pace of psychological change in modernizing societies.

Chapters 4 and 5 consider the structural aspects of the political process. Chapter 4 is devoted to the special problem of channeling political participation in modernizing countries. We know that one of the supposedly irreversible developments in modernizing nations is the radical increase in the numbers of individuals who wish to gain access to the political system. One of the foremost challenges to developing countries is somehow to foster the growth of institutions—political parties, interest groups, peasant leagues, cooperatives, or neighborhood associations—that can facilitate that objective. Chapter 4 examines the record of the Third World in meeting this goal. Chapter 5 moves into the governmental sphere proper and discusses the primary official structures in typical Third World polities. The different attitudes held in the Third World toward the notion of "separation of powers" as a doctrine for organizing the public sector is presented first; then we will see the effects of these attitudes on actual governmental operations. Chapter 5 also introduces the patron-client systems that are so prevalent and so powerful in local politics in developing countries. Finally, Chapter 5 looks at the role of the civilian bureaucrats and the military regimes as each group tries to pursue economic development in their own way.

Many of the above observations are then brought together in Chapter 6, which discusses the policy-making process in the Third World in its entirety. How Third World governments typically set goals and why these goals are frequently unrealistic is examined. Prevailing methods of implementing public policy are noted, and some of the main reasons for failure are presented. The evaluation of outcomes is discussed, and some of the major reasons why Third World governments have so much difficulty learning from their mistakes are indicated.

Chapter 7 concludes the study by evaluating and analyzing Third World political performance in each of the four areas of value distribution: power, well-being, respect, and enlightenment.

In concluding this introduction, several *caveats* should be issued. First, be careful of applying very broad generalizations too closely. This book treats 112 self-governing political entities, each with its own historical background, socioeconomic structures, and sets of ruling élites. I have tried to select those features of Third World politics that appeared to be modal, that is, that appeared most frequently in the category. However, none of my observations can be applied to every single one of the countries simultaneously. Instead, the book paints a general picture about politics in the Third World that is accurate in describing most of the features of most of the 112 systems most of the time. The analysis should not be pressed to do more than that.

Second, beware of "hard" data. Empirical data from most developing countries suffer from one or more of the following flaws. In many cases, there are substantial intranation variations in the data. The spread of modernization reaches into different parts of the country at different rates, and a single indicator for an entire nation may mask considerable differences within the nation. In addition, data from the Third World may be highly unreliable, because the data gathering services are untrained, poorly staffed, or under-financed; they may be noncomparable, because different countries use different statistical constructs to identify the same concepts; or they may be deliberately manipulated by politically sensitive data gatherers, who seek to shape the data to support one or another kind of policy. In any event, statistical information from the Third World should only be regarded as indicative of general orders of magnitude, and not of narrow shades of difference.[3]

Third, avoid jumping to too hasty conclusions about the irrationality of some of the governance mechanisms we are about to discuss. Quite probably, a mixture of bizarre events or institutions and a certain degree of ethnocentrism will lead the average reader to conclude that Third World leaders and masses do not act in their own best interest. We should not forget, however, that these behavior patterns have emerged over centuries of dealing with a certain kind of political environment that was not always comfortable or trustworthy. When Third World leaders react to threat or impending crisis with what seems to us to be paranoia or apathy, remember that from their point of view this reaction may be completely rational, especially as their universe is defined.

Finally, avoid the notion that politics is a universal solution to all of humanity's problems. As a matter of fact, most governments came into being to solve only a relatively small fraction of their society's difficulties; the vast remainder were to be solved by individuals or institutions outside of the political process. All over the world, in Western industrial democracies, in com-

---

[3] I have discussed this problem further in *Development and Instability* (Chicago: Dryden, 1974), pp. 250–251. See also Ralph H. Retzlaff, "The Use of Aggregate Data in Comparative Political Analysis," *Journal of Politics* 27 (4) (November 1965), pp. 797–817.

munist states, and in the Third World, governments are being asked to perform near miracles in solving problems of pollution, social disharmony, and poverty. Very few of them manage to do their job so well that there are never complaints. It is no wonder that performance in the Third World suffers from these same flaws. After all, political outcomes in Africa, Asia, Latin America, and the Middle East are the product of ordinary people, who are working to solve human problems with incomplete information, too few resources, an inadequate institutional base, not enough time, and huge numbers of impatient people waiting for their answer. Many of them could do a better job than they are doing but, before we criticize them too sharply, let us at least have the compassion to understand what it is that causes their reach to so far exceed their grasp.

CHAPTER ONE

The Impact of Colonialism on Third World Politics

In all probability, historians of the next century will look back on the period from 1500 to 2000 as the time of one of the most remarkable and significant events in world history: the expansion of Europeans beyond their continent to explore, populate, and dominate the rest of the world, and to bring with them the ideologies, technologies, and institutions of modernity. The period of European domination of the globe was, historically, relatively brief. By 1776, less than 300 years after it began, the tide of European expansion began to ebb in the Western Hemisphere, first in the north, with the American Revolution, and then, 30 to 40 years later, in the south, with the breakup of the Spanish empire. The reversal of colonialism is lasting about as long as its launching, but the rapid dissolution of empire around the world since 1945 seems to establish the trend quite firmly. By 2000, it seems, most legal colonial relationships will be eliminated, and national self-determination will be worldwide.

Nevertheless, for all of its brevity, European colonial domination of less advanced peoples must be the point of departure in our journey to the Third World, since it was the European influence that initiated the spread of industrialization and modernization around the world. Without the colonial experience, most of the nations of the Third World would not even exist, at least in the form that we know them today; indeed, entire regions, such as Latin American and Indochina, would certainly carry different labels when we locate them on a map. The European colonial influence brought to the peoples of the Southern and Western Hemispheres the social, intellectual, and material inventions that had allowed Europe to break out of its own Dark Ages; the introduction of these cultural innovations would prove to have much the same effect on the so-called "backward peoples" of the globe. That the introduction of these inventions has not brought to the Third World similar levels of material prosperity and political progress as it did for Europe is due partly to the colonial experience itself, partly to its remnants, which still characterize Third World relationships with the industrialized West, and partly to the inability of Third World political élites to exploit the enormous value of European ideas.

THE COLONIAL PERIOD

By some accounts, pre-modern life was brutal, savage, unpredictable, and ignoble. The population was divided into two groups: the landed gentry, who controlled the only real source of

A small boy carries water to his home in a remote village in Ecuador. The boy's clothing, and the materials used in building the dwellings identify the village as traditional. Millions of citizens of Third World countries continue to live in similar villages despite the modernization of their country's major cities.

Enveloping all these communities (of peasants) there is a sense of life robbed of all significance. Man is both degraded and mocked. The peasantries are all haunted by the fear that the earth will lose its fertility.... They are obsessed by an almost panic concern to maintain the size of their populations. Surrounded by malignant demons and spirits, threatened by the unruly forces of nature and society, they were led to seek the intervention of occult powers whom they must try to propitiate or coerce by means of offerings, spells, worship, to protect their precarious though unchanging position in the natural and social order ... war, famine and disease desolated them, conquerors swept over them, tax collectors ... robbed them, but these villages remained unchanged and unaffected, always ready to resume the old burdens and to submit tamely to the same degrading routine.[1]

wealth, the land; and the peasants, who tilled the land for their masters. Traditional populations were uniformly rural, agrarian, ill-educated or illiterate, cut off from all external influences, and subject to the ravages of famine, pestilence, war, plagues, and natural disasters. Life spans were short, personal civility was lacking, the social order was shot through with suspicion and distrust, and there seemed to be little opportunity for members of the society to realize any of their higher ambitions, short of obtaining enough food to get through the day.

I. R. Sinai has painted for us a dramatic picture of the life of Asian peasants in *The Challenge of Modernization.*

By other accounts, life in pre-modern societies, although certainly hard physically, was stable and secure and provided people with what they needed most—a sense of belonging, a feeling of one's place in the universe. Society was divided into two classes, a poor majority and a wealthy élite. But the aristocracy cared for and looked after the peasants or serfs and managed their lives in a remarkably efficient manner, given the overall scarcity of goods for society generally. Furthermore, the fact that traditional society lived in extended families, spread out into clans, made it possible for individuals who suffered from some particular problem to be supported by the psychic resources of the entire community. According to this way of looking at things, pre-modern societies were internally consistent and logical and, above all, their system worked. Since their village political system was closely linked to their village social system, the two functioned in harmony. If food and shelter were not available in abundance, at least they were adequate

[1] I. R. Sinai, *The Challenge of Modernization* (New York: Norton, 1964), pp. 34–35.

to meet the needs of the villagers. Land was usually owned and cultivated in communal style: the actual land was the property of the village, and the fruits of the harvest belonged more or less equitably to all members of the community. Perhaps most important, there was stability and consistency in the lives of traditional people. The continuity of their traditions sustained them in times of trouble and taught them in times of plenty not to expect much improvement in the future.[2]

Whether or not the traditional way of life is seen as good and positive appears to depend as much on the observer as on the historical reality itself. One political scientist, John Kautsky, has described pre-modern social orders in terms that avoid judgments about the values of the traditional life style.[3]

First, Kautsky notes that the societies of traditional countries were highly decentralized. That is, they consisted of numerous small villages spread throughout remote valleys or along winding rivers, with little central control or direction of their lives. Since communications were restricted to face-to-face conversation, and transportation was limited to that powered by humans and animals, remote villages enjoyed the luxury (or suffered the disadvantages) of being fairly free from control by central government authorities, despite what the theoretical powers of that political authority might have been.

The economic basis of traditional society was overwhelmingly agricultural. As much as 80 to 90 percent of a traditional society's labor force would be employed in tilling the land and in related activities (the comparable statistic for a modern, industrial society such as the United States is 5 to 7 percent). Since land was the basis for the society's economic structure, ownership of the land was the basis of power. Power, in turn, was very unequally distributed between a landed aristocracy, who owned the land and who received most of the benefits from its use, and a massive, poor, peasant class. Government for the aristocrats was little more than a device to manage the subordinate classes, to extract what surplus there was from agricultural pursuits, and to spend that surplus in the time-honored aims of the aristocratic classes: making war, amusing themselves, and fighting with other aristocrats for the privilege of maintaining their position. They did not envision any societal change, but they surely would have opposed such change if they could have imagined it. They opposed the spread of capitalism to their jurisdictions, and they sought to keep the lower rural classes bound to them in every way.

The peasant class generally accepted this arrangement, because they, too, benefited from the system. They did not benefit in a material sense, as we in the modern world would understand it. Their lives were poor or, better yet, impoverished, and they lacked even a semblance of the advantages of a wealthier society: health care, housing, and entertainment, for instance. But, in their complex relationships with the upper classes, the peasants enjoyed a security that emerged from a stable place in the constellation of social units within which they lived. To change this would have implied movement, from a village to a larger town, as well as social movement to another kind of unit. Societal modernization would have meant submitting oneself to the impersonal control of the economic work unit. All of these changes would have been unfavorable and unlikely to the peasant, but threatening and frightening as well. As long as the society remained traditional, neither peasants nor aristocracy had anything to fear, since the fatalism and apathy of rural pre-modern life prevented the lower classes from even imagining an improvement to their lives.

Matters stayed this way for centuries, as Europe awakened from its own Dark Ages and began to look about for worlds to conquer.

[2] Robert E. Gamer, *The Developing Nations: A Comparative Perspective* (Boston: Allyn and Bacon, 1976), Chapter 2.
[3] John H. Kautsky, *The Political Consequences of Modernization* (New York: Wiley, 1972), Chapter 1.

Europeans first encountered the traditional world in the Western Hemisphere or, to be more specific, in the island chains that cross the Caribbean Sea and in the littoral washed by its waters. Spreading inland through Mexico, Central America, and south through Peru and Chile, the Spanish *conquistadores* carried the power of Spain abroad in the name of the King and of the Roman Catholic Church. On the eastern side of the South American continent, separated from the Spanish colonies by a line confirmed by the pope in 1506, Portuguese explorers emulated their fellow Iberians and established their hold over what would become Brazil. (In addition, during the sixteenth century, the Portuguese established their rule over Angola and Mozambique, in Africa, and the Spice Islands and the East Indies.)

Spanish rule in Latin America (and, to a great extent, in the Philippine Islands) was characterized above all by its legalist basis, its centralist allocation of powers, and its authoritarian treatment of dissent. Despite the distances separating Madrid from its colonial holdings and the time required to transverse them, Spain insisted on maintaining tight control over its various political dependencies. At the same time, Spain's insistence on the rigid fulfillment of the law to its exact letter encouraged local *de facto* autonomy, accompanied by a good deal of cynicism about the need to obey the laws issued from Madrid. Finally, there were no opportunities for dissent to be lodged from the colonies, despite the early growth of local settler colonies in several major cities, including Buenos Aires, Caracas, Lima, and Mexico City. Local political participation was regarded as radical and upsetting by the Spanish monarchy. Thus, in 1810, when the Spanish colonies began to cut away from Spain in the aftermath of the Napoleonic wars, there was little heritage of local self-government and practically no indigenous business or political élite interested in pursuing the objective of enhancing human dignity; instead, there was the still-rigid cultural artifacts of traditional society.[4]

After the decolonization process was completed in Latin America in the early 1820s (with the exception of the Caribbean countries of Cuba, Haiti, and Santo Domingo, which would come to independence later), the former Spanish-Portuguese colonial domination was replaced by a neocolonial (or quasicolonial) relationship between Latin America and Great Britain and, later, between Latin America and the United States. In these relationships, the important currency of power was not law or constitutional prerogative, but money and its material products: trade, commerce, raw material extraction, manufacturing, and the attendant social changes. As a consequence of differential rates of industrialization, Latin American countries became the suppliers to Great Britain and the United States of industrial raw materials and exotic consumer goods while serving as a market for the manufactured products exported from the two industrializing countries.

Other European countries began their process of expansion somewhat later; and other parts of the world were exposed to European influence only at the beginning of the eighteenth century, or later. During the seventeenth and eighteenth centuries, the principal expansionist countries were Great Britain, France, Belgium, and Holland. Their efforts at expansion were turned first toward South and Southeast Asia and, later, toward sub-Saharan Africa.

The entry of England and Holland into the colonial arena differed greatly from the entry of Spain and Portugal. The Iberian influence had been spread first by soldiers and, subsequently, by agents of the Church; in the case of the British and Dutch, trade and political and strategic advantage were the foremost concerns. Accordingly, the two governments formed joint public-private companies to trade with newly discovered areas. In 1600, the British East Indies Company was founded, followed 2 years later by the Dutch East

[4] Claudio Veliz, "Centralism and Nationalism in Latin America," *Foreign Affairs 47* (1) (October 1968), pp. 69 83.

Indies Company. Other European powers followed suit and, throughout Asia in the eighteenth century and throughout Africa later, trading posts and economic enclaves sprang up, injecting Western currencies, influence, and thought into traditional societies.[5]

Through the first three-quarters of the nineteenth century, colonial influences spread primarily by informal means and in accord with economic, political, and strategic impulses. That is, the colonial powers sought to penetrate the traditional regions of Asia and Africa by means of trade, and they negotiated commercial agreements or "treaties" with tribal chieftains or village heads. Western control was strong, but still informal. The system of informal trade penetration had an inherent bias toward expansion of control and toward more formal dominance of the remote areas. As each trading area was secured, the local commercial official in charge became responsible for the maintenance of order in the region, including the frontier regions that marked the area off from neighboring, still "uncivilized" zones, where traditional societies lay untouched by the colonial system. At the first sign of disturbance on the border, the colonial power seized the opportunity to expand its influence and to establish new boundaries around its zone of influence. In this act, however, the authorities unwittingly lengthened the boundary to be secured and magnified the possibilities for additional disturbances in the future, which would necessitate even further encroachment into previously unsettled lands. The expansionist imperative of colonial trading arrangements was unmistakable.

By 1870, the pressures for formal political control over colonial preserves had mounted to such a degree that the European powers launched a series of expansionist moves that effectively divided up almost all of the remaining "unclaimed" land area of the globe. From 1870 to 1900, the European colonial

states added to their direct political control abroad more than 10 million square miles of territory and about 150 million people (about 20 percent of the earth's land area and about 10 percent of the world's population). Britain was the largest beneficiary of this expansion: nearly half of the land area and nearly 60 percent of the people brought under colonial rule became subjects of the British government. The British Empire stretched from the Indian subcontinent westward to Egypt, Sudan, Uganda, Kenya, and other areas of Africa, to British Guiana in South America, and to Malaya and Burma in Southeast Asia. The French were second in the scramble for colonies, claiming 3.5 million square miles and about 26 million persons, mostly inhabitants of Africa and Southeast Asia. Germany, Italy, and Belgium also acquired significant colonies in Africa; in the Pacific, Japan and the United States joined in the expansion drive. The hardest-hit region was Africa. In 1870, only about 10 percent of the continent was under alien control; by 1900, only 10 percent remained independent.

Traditional societies in the Middle East remained isolated from European colonization efforts until after World War I. The war brought about the destruction of the Ottoman Empire, and the Versailles Peace Conference of 1919 was the scene of unscrupulous bargaining and division of the spoils of war in the area. Under the League of Nations Mandate system, Britain and France established control over most of the Middle East, excluding Turkey, Iran, and Saudi Arabia. Syria, Iraq, and Lebanon were designated as mandates, and Palestine was established as the special responsibility of Britain, despite the protestations of the Palestinian Arabs.

One of the supreme ironies of the entire colonial experience involves the role of the great wars in extending the system and in bringing it to a close. World War I was fought by the United States as a struggle for the right of self-determination of all peoples, but it resulted in the expansion of colonial empires into areas

[5] Benjamin J. Cohen, *The Question of Imperialism: The Political Economy of Dominance and Dependence* (New York: Basic Books, 1973), Chapter 2.

previously saved from colonialism. In contrast, World War II had little to do with self-determination as a cause, yet it left in its wake the conditions that led directly to the dissolution of nearly all the formal colonial possessions around the world. In 1945, the Japanese had been driven out of all of their colonial holdings, as had Italy. Germany had been denied expansion once again. In addition, Great Britain, France, Belgium, and Holland had all been so weakened by the war that they were unable to maintain control over their possessions for more than a decade or two. The year 1945 would mark the definitive beginning of the end of Europe's 500-year-long domination of the world. As European power receded, it left behind the emerging political systems of the Third World, as well, many would say, as a lingering system of informal, "neocolonial" influence and control.

AN ASSESSMENT OF COLONIAL RULE

What do we mean by a "colonial relationship?" A typical dictionary definition of "colonial" is "a relationship between two groups of people characterized by a highly unequal distribution of power." A colonial relationship is one between a very strong group and a very weak group, in which the weak are dependent and the strong dominant. To apply that idea to this discussion, let us further assume that (at least) the strong group is formally organized into a national state; the weak, dependent group may or may not be so organized.

The exact nature of the colonial relationship derives from the various ways in which each side may perceive its links with and its privileges and obligations toward the other. The powerful, dominant nation may wish to absorb the weak nation and make them citizens in their own society, with full privileges and responsibilities; or, conversely, the strong nation may wish to keep the weak group at arm's length, extracting the benefits from the relationship without incurring any of the costs. The former case can be exemplified by the United States with regard to the American Indians, former black slaves, Mexicans living in California, or Hawaiians. The French also tried to assimilate colonial peoples into their society, as in the case of the Algerians or the Vietnamese; they even granted them seats in the national legislature and positions in the national cabinets. The Portuguese did likewise in their colonies in Africa, Angola, and Mozambique. On the other hand, the Dutch in Indonesia practiced the rule of cultural relativism, allowed native rulers to continue in power more or less undisturbed, and made no effort to transform Indonesians into citizens of the Dutch nation. The British fell somewhere in between. They were interested primarily in the maintenance of order; where native rulers could accomplish this task, they were left alone; where native rule faltered, the British substituted their own bureaucracy. In each case, the British objective was to implant the rule of law and government by representative institutions, without necessarily intending for all colonial peoples to become Britons or even loyal British subjects.

From the point of view of the weaker side, however, the colonial bond was inherently an unstable one. If the weak found the relationship to their liking, they moved closer to the mother country and eventually were absorbed into it; this happened with Alaska and Hawaii. At times, this took place even if the weak peoples were not particularly fond of the colonial regime, if they thought they had no choice, or if they perceived long-run benefits to be derived from closer association with their powerful benefactor. For many years, the quasicolonial relationship between Panama and the United States has been of this type, although that is no doubt changing. In most cases, however, the weaker peoples were unhappy with their subordinate relationship, and they became more so as the waves of modernization and nationalism swept through the Third World. The obvious outcome in these cases has been guerrilla insurgency, terrorism, and wars of national liberation. Such violence marked the passage to national independence of virtually all of Latin America, Algeria, Israel, Angola, Bangladesh, Indonesia, Vietnam, Malaya, Kenya, and other states. The success of these movements can be traced partially to the distance between the insurgent colony and the metropole, as well as to the diminishing value of the colony to the economic and political goals of the mother country. In instances where the colonial peoples live on the same territory with the dominant peoples, separation may be much more difficult and violent, since the central authority will fight much harder to retain control over the separatists.

An accurate assessment of the colonial experience should weigh all of the things the Europeans brought to their colonies, both the good things and the bad, both the benefits of colonialism and the costs.[6]

The most obvious contribution of the Europeans to traditional countries has been modern technology. This does not imply that all technologies are either good or bad, or that Western technology introduced into traditional societies always has had either a good or bad impact. Instead, technology for the Third World has been a mixed blessing, just as it has been for the areas where it originated, Western Europe and North America.

Some specific examples of technology as introduced into traditional countries will help to clarify the costs and benefits of such a contribution. Transportation technology, including railroads, highways, and small airports, has obviously contributed greatly to the opening up of remote, interior portions of many Third World countries. An analysis of the spatial spread of modernization within a newly independent country would reveal that the impact of modernization is heavily in-

fluenced by the transportation infrastructure built by the colonial power and left behind after its departure.[7] The control of the new government over its jurisdiction is shaped strongly by the existing rail, air, and road facilities constructed by the mother country. Frequently, however, the metropolitan country constructed its transportation network to serve some existing economic necessity that had little to do with the over-all development of the country. Since Third World areas usually served the industrialized world as sources of raw materials and exotic tropical food products, the transportation facilities were built primarily to facilitate the exportation of these commodities. The remaining needs of the country, for internal lines of communication and transportation, for instance, were ignored. In some Central America countries today, for example, the only railroads in existence were those constructed by the banana companies to move their produce to the seaports and, from there, to markets in North America and Europe. Any relationship to the internal needs of the host country was purely coincidental. The same kind of conclusions can be drawn about communication facilities, including telephone, telegraph, radio, television, and print media (newspapers, magazines, and postal services).

A second important kind of technological contribution made by European colonizers to the Third World lies in the area of hygiene and health care. Through the introduction of mass innoculations, public health clinics, pre- and post-natal care, food shipments under programs such as "Food for Peace," and other advances, the Western world has succeeded in altering the death rates of many Third World countries. No doubt this is to be applauded. Yet, as we will learn in Chapter 2, the combination of falling death rates as a consequence of Western health care techniques, and of stable birth rates, as a consequence of rigid

[6] For a detailed discussion of the same theme, see Rupert Emerson, *From Empire to Nation: The Rise to Self-Assertion of Asian and African Peoples* (Cambridge, Mass.: Harvard, 1960).

[7] Peter R. Gould, "Tanzania 1920–63: The Spatial Impress of the Modernization Process," *World Politics XXII* (2) (January 1970), pp. 149–170.

social structures, attitudes, and mores, has produced a frightening population explosion in the Third World.

Still another area of Western technology that has had mixed blessings for Third World countries has been in manufacturing and agriculture. With little thought for its total inpact, Western business representatives have pressed backward areas to adopt Western techniques in manufacturing (mass production, assembly-line techniques) and in farming (heavy use of equipment, pesticides, fertilizers); this has had a variety of effects. These technologies have improved the individual worker productivity in many traditional countries and thereby have made more products available on the market, perhaps even at a reduced price. But there have been costs to these innovations. Modern manufacturing techniques have reduced the need for labor and have thrown many potential workers out of a job, thereby reducing the aggregate purchasing power of the society. The same thing has happened on the farm. Fewer workers are needed to produce more food, so aggregate demand falls, and more and more heads of families are out of work. Furthermore, the Third World countries are discovering that the adoption of Western manufacturing technologies makes them *more* vulnerable to external pressures instead of less vulnerable. The use of modern industrial facilities makes the economy more dependent on foreign sources of raw materials and energy, especially petroleum. In the agricultural area, the use of petroleum-based fertilizers has cost many Third World countries a great deal, since the cost of crude oil has risen.

A fourth kind of technology introduced by the European states was in the form of weapons and other military equipment. Western domination over traditional societies was facilitated greatly, if not actually made possible, by their use of firearms and other lethal technologies to force the more backward peoples to submit to their rule. Later, as the natives learned to turn this new technology against their former masters, and as the number of weapons available in the develop-

ing world increased enormously, modern weapons technology helped to accelerate the destruction of the European colonial empire. Yet, after helping emerging nations to gain their independence, modern weapons technology is certainly making political life in the Third World more difficult. These weapons, of radically increased lethality, make local disputes much more costly in terms of human life and property, as the evidence from the Lebanese civil war of 1975 to 1976 will attest. The Western powers left behind not only the military equipment of a modern army, but the military organization needed to use it. After a while, these new military leaders frequently came to power in these nations, determined to impose on them the order and discipline of the barracks. As we note in Chapter 5, military intervention in politics has been one of the most serious problems Third World states have had to deal with since 1945. In addition, the adoption of military technology from the Great Powers, or from other industrialized states, tends to make the recipient countries dependent on the countries of origin for training, ammunition, and replacement parts; this perpetuates the dominant-dependent relationship even after it has formally ended.

Perhaps the most significant aspect of the introduction of Western technology through the colonial system has been in the attitudes of Third World citizens with regard to nature. We will discuss more extensively in Chapter 3 the question of the prevalent personality structures and attitudes in both traditional and modern countries. Traditional persons usually possess what behavioral scientists call a fatalistic view of life, which means that they usually do not believe that human beings can change nature but, instead must adjust to its vagaries. Modern persons, however, feel that they *can* change nature through technology. Generally the technology brought to traditional societies by colonists may have wrought its most important change in the *minds* of heretofore traditional peoples.

A second important European contribution

to the traditional lands of the Third World has been education.[8] Education here means a formal, school-based transmission of knowledge and more informal socialization techniques based on family, kin groups and, in many instances, the mass media. All of these educational media will be considered at length in Chapter 3.

In most instances, when Europeans arrived in the traditional societies of Latin America, Africa, or Asia, they found no native educational systems. Traditional communities utilized the family, and other village-based organs of communication, to transmit certain essential lessons to their growing young; beyond that, these cultures were simply not organized to make education a formal, institutionalized endeavor.

It was not until after World War II that most colonial administrations began to take any measures at all to improve public-supported education in their territories. Prior to the 1940s, the support of the colonial government for public education had been very scanty and had depended more on local funds than on any allocations from the wealthy mother country. Thus, for example, in 1942, Indonesia, with a population of more than 70 million, could count fewer than 1000 natives who had completed a college education. During British control of Egyptian education, which came nominally to an end in 1922, illiteracy remained constant, at more than 90 percent of the total population. In Tunisia in 1945, under the French Protectorate, less than 10 percent of the eligible children were attending primary schools. Even in nations that had shaken off colonial rule earlier, such as Latin America nations, the remnants of an underfinanced and mismanaged educational system left 80 percent of the population illiterate at the close of World War II.

If the over-all quantity of European-supported education can be severely criticized, it is still true that in certain very specific quali-tative terms, the impact of European education has been enormous throughout the Third World. Western education, especially higher education in Paris or London, eventually created the articulate, activist, nationalist leaders of the native middle class, the intelligentsia of the local societies, and these people provided the leadership and the ideas for the dissolution of colonial ties.

Beyond the leadership élites of Third World nationalist movements, Western education had an equally important impact on the masses of Africa and Asia, primarily by heightening their awareness of their own ethnic and national identities. Citizens of established Western nations often forget just how modern the notions of nationalism, national identity, and ethnic self-determination are. Only since the end of the eighteenth century have people started to think of themselves as members of a national group, a set of citizens whose boundaries were larger than, and transcended, those more narrow enclosures of language, ethnic heritage, village grouping, clan, or something else altogether different. Western-introduced education, with civics training directed from the mother country, aided by text books with Western-style "national" maps and other symbols, helped to divert young attentions away from traditional indentifications and toward the broader self-image. Many traditional areas acquired their present national, territorial label only as a result of the decisions of their colonial rulers. In the Western Hemisphere, ancient kingdoms, such as that of the Incas, were destroyed; in their place stood entities such as the Vice-Royalty of Lima, to be replaced still again by the nation of Peru. In West Africa, the British grouped together tribes that had literally nothing in common, and they called their creation "Nigeria." The same process was repeated in the Indian subcontinent; after termination of the British rule, the nation of Pakistan was created to shelter the religious freedoms of millions of Muslims, who felt that if they were included in a larger unit with predominantly Hindu

[8] A useful compendium of articles on this subject is James S. Coleman, ed., *Education and Political Development* (Princeton, N.J.: Princeton, 1965).

India, their rights to worship would be suppressed. The label "Indochina" is itself of European origin, as were the various subregional identities forced on the Vietnamese people by the French. Despite the artificial character of these national identities, nationalist leaders in the Third World have discovered that the symbols of nationhood are powerful weapons to wield against their former European masters. The typical citizen of, say, Nigeria, might not have known what Nigeria stood *for* in the late 1950s, he or she at least knew that it stood *against* continued British rule, and therefore merited support and allegiance. Once independence is achieved, the uniting force of nationalism becomes thin and fragile; and separatist movements have frequently aggravated what is at best a very difficult process of nation-building. But, with all its weaknesses, the idea of the nation as the core of one's identity has proven to be one of the most powerful motivating forces in modern world politics.

Another major European colonial contribution to the Third world is the modern system of commerce and trade; this includes the ways in which this system disrupted traditional methods of relating individuals to one another and to some broader social unit.[9]

Whatever else might be said about traditional societies as they were on the eve of European intrusion, they at least fed themselves relatively satisfactorily. As noted, traditional society was agricultural in character; the overwhelming majority of its workers were employed in growing food for the community. The land was generally owned by some sort of communal arrangement, although the exact nature of the land tenure system obviously varied widely across the Southern Hemisphere. Private ownership constituted the exception and not the rule. Land was dedicated to the cultivation of one of the three kinds of crops from which traditional peoples could maintain a more than subsistence diet: cereal

grains (wheat, maize, and rice); tubers (sweet potatoes, potatoes, and yams); and legumes (beans, lentils, and peas). These were the only foods that satisfied the nutritional and commercial requirements of traditional peoples before colonialization; the evidence shows that they were all grown and cultivated extensively throughout the area now known as the Third World. Obviously, virtually all of a community's food needs were self-met; there was little need for or interest in trading and little surplus available to be traded.

With the arrival of the Europeans and their ideas of trade and commerce, the traditional techniques of farming, the traditional forms of land tenure, and the traditional crops were all cast aside in favor of more modern ways to employ the obviously great agricultural riches of the Third World. First, the intruding colonial powers altered traditional forms of landownership and allowed private citizens to purchase large plots of land, to enclose this land, and to plant on it whatever they wished. In Latin America, the Spanish government went one step further and rewarded the adventurers and *conquistadores* with huge grants of land; the grants included ownership of the native Indians who happened to reside in the villages on this land. In Asia and Africa, the colonial countries first confiscated the land from village or communal ownership, then sold it to private companies or individual citizens, who were supposed to use the land "productively." This usually meant that the land was not to be used to grow crops for local consumption, but for trade to the colonial countries. Since Europe was already rich in cereal grains, tubers, and legumes, the lands of the Third World were turned to the production of crops that had little nutritional value, but that commanded high prices in the developed markets of Europe and North America. Thus was born the agricultural system of the colonial world, the dedication of rich farmland to the cultivation of coffee, cocoa, sugar cane, pepper, hemp, bananas, rubber, peanuts, and tobacco. In other instances, if land contained rich mineral de-

[9] Celso Furtado, *Economic Development of Latin America: A Survey from Colonial Times to the Cuban Revolution* (London: Cambridge, 1970).

posits, it was exploited not for what it could grow, but for what lay under it; the flow of minerals also began to mark trade patterns between the industrializing countries and their colonies to the south. During the nineteenth century, copper, tin, and iron, nitrates, and coal were all shipped from the colonial empires to the industrial center. In the twentieth century, these flows have been joined by perhaps the most important raw material for an industrial society, petroleum.

Most of these linkages have mattered little economically to the industrialized countries, but they have been catastrophic to the Third World. Instead of land being used to grow food to feed the communities that till the soil, we see land used to grow exotic, tropical crops for shipment abroad to grace the tables of Europeans or Americans. Instead of communal ownership of the land, with an equitable distribution of its fruits, we see the concentration of the land in the hands of a few favored entrepreneurs, and resultant impoverishment of the remainder. Instead of the steady and secure working of the soil for what it gives to the community, we see the extension of the cash nexus to the workers, linking them precariously to the whims of a market system not only beyond their control, but literally beyond their comprehension.[10]

Clearly, modernization of the techniques for owning and exploiting the soil is not, in itself, destructive of the ways in which people live. Every modern state of Europe experienced the same transformations in their drive to modernity. The rural, agrarian classes had to be pushed in the direction of capitalist exploitation of the soil; property had to be enclosed and private ownership adopted in order for the incentives of the market to compel full and efficient use of the land; and the rural working class had to be forced off the land and into the cities in order for an urban industrial class to come into existence to support modernization. The way in which these transformations took place in a country like England was beneficial and helpful for the overall development of the society.

In the colonized areas, however, the intrusion of modern trade and commerce has destroyed traditional lifestyles without substituting, or aiding in the development of, alternatives. Agricultural and mining products did not remain in the community or even in the nation but, instead, were sent abroad. The modern commercial sectors of the traditional countries constituted economic enclaves, separate and isolated communities; they were cut off from the host nation or colony and had their own set of laws and social services. The benefits of these enclaves rarely were extended to the larger community. The proceeds from the sale of these products were usually kept in the financial system of the mother country or, at best, were returned to the enclave to improve its standard of living, but without touching the lives of the great majority of native citizens. Rural workers *were* forced from their communal lands and were made to labor for European owners and managers at highly unstable wages; they worked at jobs that depended not on natural forces like the weather, which could be seen and felt, but on distant forces like the international market economy, which were neither experienced firsthand or understood. Bert Adams writes that in Africa, colonists used both political coercion, conscription, slavery, and economic coercion, the "head" or "hut" tax, to force natives to leave the land and provide the human raw material for Western economic ventures in mines and factories.[11] Local industry did not grow, because the enclaves imported what they needed for their own use. Worker productivity did not rise, because the enclaves were not faced with local competition and therefore did not need to lower production costs. Social services were not provided, and wages were not stabilized or improved, because native workers had not mastered the skills of labor organization and

[10] This idea is explored extensively in Jeffrey M. Paige, "Inequality and Insurgency in Vietnam: A Reanalysis," *World Politics XXIII* (1) (October 1970), pp. 24-37.

[11] Bert N. Adams, "Kinship Systems and Adaptation to Modernization," *Studies in Comparative International Development IV* (3) (1968-1969), p. 50.

collective bargaining. The colonial system created many economic inequities by needlessly disrupting traditional modes of economic cooperation without replacing them with more stable, more productive arrangements that would spread the benefits of modernization evenly throughout the world.

The final result of European domination of the Southern Hemisphere can be termed as cultural "inferiority complex," or a belief inculcated in the colonial peoples that Europeans were superior to them in economic and political relationships and, therefore, deserved to rule them. When the Europeans began their conquest and colonization of the traditional peoples of the Third World, they regarded their new charges as little children, too primitive to be trusted with their own fate. Since, the conquerors reasoned, it was obvious which group was the more powerful, it was obvious which group should rule and which should submit. The dominant colonial administration managed to justify its own arrogance by reference either to religious superiority (as in American President William McKinley's agonizing decision to assume responsibility to bring Christianity to the Philippines) to race (as in Rudyard Kipling's reference to "the white man's burden"), or to a general cultural superiority (as in the French insistence on their "civilizing mission"). The British held only the utmost contempt and disregard for the abilities of the Indians. Lord Cornwallis is quoted as saying, "every native of Hindustan is corrupt," and Lord Wellesly described Indians as "vulgar, ignorant, rude, familiar and stupid." As late as 1934, Indians were considered genetically inferior and therefore not qualified to hold jobs on a par with the British.[12] Whatever the origin, this feeling of religious, racial, or cultural superiority naturally conveyed itself to the natives, both in the formal sense (through the colonial education system) and

in the countless informal tensions that characterized the prevailing master-servant relationship.

Ironically, it was also the European introduction of the psychological attributes of modernity, particularly their emphasis on self-rule and self-determination, that eventually led to the creation of a class of nationalist intellectuals who manifestly rejected the idea of European superiority and who determined to expel the light-skinned invaders from their country. Psychologists have learned that a culturally modern person accepts ultimate responsible for the successes and failures of life, and that external powers or forces cannot assume this intensely personal duty. Consequently, the more modern people become in attitudinal terms, the more they are inclined to reject external attempts to rule them and to assert their own responsibility for self-governance. Apparently, within the group of Western-educated nationalists who have led the struggle against European domination in the Third World, this assertion of personal responsibility has assumed great importance. This has resulted in the demand of colonial states that they be permitted to rule themselves, even if the outcome is not necessarily comfortable or fruitful. As they often state, "We would rather be governed like hell by ourselves than well by someone else."

After centuries of seeing their country governed from abroad, aided many times by members of their own group who were willing to cooperate with the foreigners, ardent nationalists like Juan Bosch of the Dominican Republic can only agonize over the desire for independence and self-control of his nation's destiny. Bosch's cry of anguish must stand for similar expressions heard through the Third World since World War II.

> [For the American Ambassador], dealing with me was no easy matter. . . . I was sensitive to anything that might affect Dominican sovereignty. My poor country had had, from the first breath of its life as a republic, a string of political leaders who had dedicated all their skills and resources

---

[12] Saleem Qureshi, "Political Violence in the South Asian Subcontinent," in Yonah Alexander, ed., *International Terrorism: National, Regional and Global Perspectives* (New York: Praeger, 1976), p. 160.

to looking for any foreign power on which to unload our independence. . . .

I felt wounded, as if it were a personal affront, at the spectacle of so many men without faith in the destiny of their own country. In my childhood, I had seen the Dominican flag coming down from the public buildings to give way to the U.S. banner. No one will ever know what my seven-year-old soul suffered at the sight. . . .

Perhaps I love my little Antilles country so passionately because when I became aware of it as a nation, I realized that it was not that at all, but a dominion. This caused me indescribable pain, and often kept me awake a long time after I had been sent to bed. . . . By the time I was ten, I was ashamed that Santana, who annexed the country to Spain in 1863, and Baez, who wanted to turn Samana [Bay] over to the United States, were Dominicans. As the years passed, that pain and that shame became transformed into passionate patriotism.[13]

As a consequence of these dramatic attitudinal changes in developing countries, one discovers that the leaders of the nationalist movements in the Third World look toward modern industrial society with a complex mixture of love and hate, fear and admiration. On the one hand, they ardently desire to liberate their countries and their people from the suppression of foreign domination; but they realize that to accomplish this feat, they must modernize their societies and industrialize their economic structures. In short, they must turn their backs on the traditional ways of doing things and embrace modernity, with all of its pitfalls and shortcomings. The symbols of industrial society, such as steel mills and modern capital cities, become more than that: they were transformed into the very expression of national independence. On the other hand, these nationalist intellectuals try desperately to retain the essence of their traditional ways and to avoid the flaws of modern

industrial society. They laud the "golden age" of their peoples, before the arrival of the Europeans, and they seek ways to preserve the fragile and intricate social structures of the traditional village-based communal life, which is under constant assault from modernization. Not surprisingly, these attempts to blend modern and pre-modern ways of life generate substantial tensions in political ideology and everyday life among many Third World peoples.[14] We will consider the psychological and cultural implications of this phenomenon in Chapter 3.

THE DECOLONIZATION PROCESS SINCE 1945

As observed earlier, 1945, and the end of World War II, signaled the end of Europe's formal domination of its far-flung empires. The devastation of the war left the major colonial powers battered and exhausted; they had little interest in renewed struggle over their fringe territories. The early victories of Japan, on the other hand, had shown the world's nonwhite races that a non-European power could defeat a predominantly white nation in combat; this restored a great deal of self-confidence in the Third World's peoples. Finally, the principles of self-determination, as taught in the Western schools and as enunciated in the United Nations Charter, began to have an effect on the nationalist élites of Africa and Asia. The result was a swelling surge of antiimperialist sentiment that rocked the European colonial powers and forced them to reconsider the very essence of their imperial pretensions.

In 1945, the largest empire in the world was Great Britain. More than one-fourth of the world's population, about 600 million people, were governed from London. By 1948, about two-thirds of this total were living in independence. In these years, the nations of South Asia—India, Pakistan, and Ceylon (now Sri

[13] Juan Bosch, *The Unfinished Experiment* (New York: Praeger, 1965), pp. 162-163.

[14] Mary Matossian, "Ideologies of Delayed Industrialization: Some Tensions and Ambiguities," *Economic Development and Cultural Change VI* (3) (April 1958), pp. 217-228.

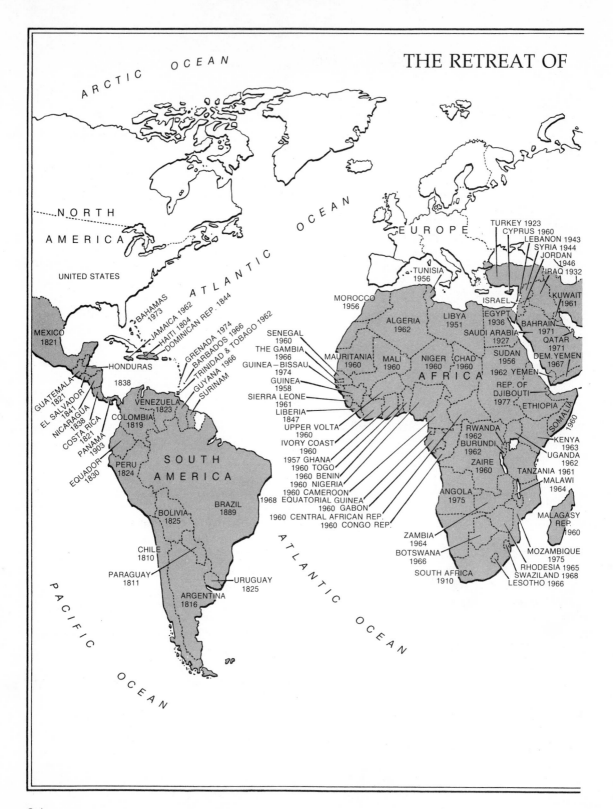

THE RETREAT OF

COLONIALISM: 1800 to 1976

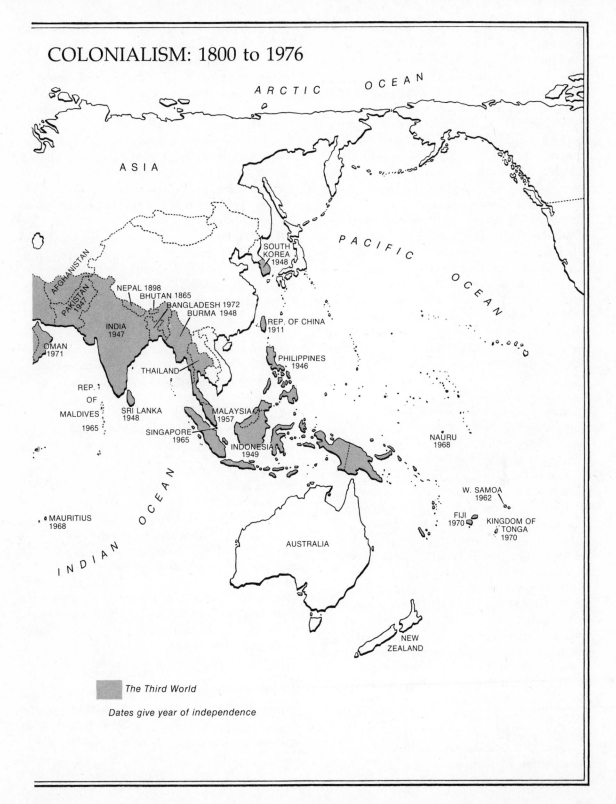

ARCTIC OCEAN

ASIA

PACIFIC OCEAN

AFGHANISTAN

NEPAL 1898
BHUTAN 1865
BANGLADESH 1972
BURMA 1948

PAKISTAN 1947

SOUTH KOREA 1948

REP. OF CHINA 1911

INDIA 1947

OMAN 1971

THAILAND

PHILIPPINES 1946

REP. OF MALDIVES 1965

SRI LANKA 1948

MALAYSIA 1957

SINGAPORE 1965

INDONESIA 1949

NAURU 1968

MAURITIUS 1968

INDIAN OCEAN

W. SAMOA 1962

FIJI 1970

KINGDOM OF TONGA 1970

AUSTRALIA

NEW ZEALAND

The Third World

Dates give year of independence

Lanka)—were created, and Burma, Egypt, and Iraq also successfully asserted their independence, followed soon after by Jordan. Following the partition of Palestine, Israel claimed its independence and, by the early 1950s, informed British opinion recognized the inevitability of the disintegration of its empire. In 1956 and 1957, the granting of independence to the Sudan, Malaya, and Ghana initiated the process of emancipation in large scale. Today, the once-fabled British Empire consists of a few scattered islands in the Western Hemisphere (such as Bermuda) and in the Pacific (Gilbert and Ellice Islands), and a handful of strategic points that England is loath to give up (Gibraltar and Hong Kong are the most important). The second largest empire in 1945 was France and, although France fought much harder than England to retain its colonial holdings, the outcome was the same. Soon after the war, Syria and Lebanon were given their independence and, in 1954, after the disastrous French-Indochina War, Laos, Cambodia, and the two halves of Vietnam left the French sphere. In 1956, Tunisia and Morocco were freed after agitation and guerrilla war and, in 1958, after Charles de Gaulle's return to power, France's African holdings were gradually reduced; first Guinea (1958) and later (1960) the remainder of French Equatorial and West African possessions and Malagasy (Madagascar) were liberated. Algeria was the possession that France was most reluctant to release, probably because of its proximity to the mother country and because of the many French citizens living in Algeria; but, by 1962, the violence and destruction of the Algerian war had so weakened French resolve that the nation's possessions there were terminated as well. As of the middle of the 1970s, French possessions include some scattered holdings in the Western Hemisphere (French Guiana, Guadeloupe, and Martinique) and some islands in the Pacific (New Caledonia and New Hebrides).

The same story applies to the smaller colonial systems still in existence in 1945. The Japanese empire was divided among the vic-

tors of the war: the United States, Russia, and China. Korea was partitioned and granted its dual independence. Italy's overseas possessions—Ethiopia, Libya, and Somalia—were quickly freed. In 1946, the United States granted independence to the Philippines, and statehood was granted to two other possessions—Alaska and Hawaii. Okinawa was returned to Japan in 1971. The Dutch lost Indonesia almost immediately after the war; and Belgium gradually loosened its hold on its African possessions—the Belgian Congo (now Zaire), Burundi, and Rwanda.

The Third World empires that lasted the longest were those that belonged to countries that lived under dictatorial rule at home: Spain and Portugal. However, even in these cases, inevitable changes in the mother country (the deaths of Franco and Salazar) have brought new governments to power; the result has been a rapid decolonization of the Spanish Sahara and of Portugal's possessions: Angola, Guinea, and Mozambique.

CONCLUSIONS: ETHNONATIONALISM AND HUMAN DIGNITY

Formal, legal control of the Third World from Europe and North America seems to be definitively coming to a close.

However, this does not indicate a lessening of the tensions of ethnonationalism, the belief that people should be governed only by others of their same ethnic group.[15] When we consider that dozens of self-aware ethnic groups are compressed into the boundaries of about 150 distinct national entities, we see immediately the revolutionary potential of ethnic pride and self-defense.

In the Third World, the phenomenon of decolonization, with all its ramifications, has yet to run its course. Two special problems emerge. First, the trend toward ethnic self-consciousness in newly created nations has a momentum of its own, a momentum that has

[15] Walker Connor, "The Politics of Ethnonationalism," *Journal of International Affairs* 27 (1) (1973), pp. 1–21.

Guerrilla fighters of the Eritrean Liberation Front raise their weapons in celebration of a victory in the struggle against the Government of Ethiopia. The ELF is one of the many ethnic and regional separatist movements given impetus by the spread of decolonization around the world since World War II. Note that the fighters are holding both AK-47 rifles, manufactured in the Soviet Union, and American-made M-14's, thus indicating their ability to receive aid from both of the superpowers.

led to the fragmentation of several of the nations left behind by the former European colonial powers and to unsuccessful threats to the stability of several others. At the beginning of the decolonization period in Africa, secession attempts such as those of Katanga (in the Congo) and Biafra (in Nigeria) failed; many other African states may feel that they have successfully weathered the storm. In South Asia, on the other hand, Bangladesh (formerly East Pakistan) has successfully separated itself from Pakistan (itself a separation from India); and the potential in Southeast Asia for fragmentation continues to be severe. We should expect more such upheavals in the future, as previously submerged peoples attempt to build a political order that is more rational and more responsive to ethnic feeling than that imposed by foreign rulers. We will return to this theme in Chapter 2.

The second residual problem is the continued struggle against economic and other forms of domination still exercised by the industrialized nations over Third World peoples. As we will discuss in greater detail in Chapter 2, the poor nations can be expected to take more and more forceful steps to redress the balance of resources and wealth distribution around the world. The abortive efforts of Chile's late President Salvador Allende to bring his nation's resources under its control and the oil embargo of 1973 are only the opening shots in this new phase of the decolonization struggle.

Indeed, many of the policy decisions made by the governments of Third World countries can best be understood as part of the very long process of undoing what was done to them by the colonial experience. You may find it easier to understand politics in the Third World in the 1970s by remembering that these events and policies owe their origins to hundreds of years of foreign rule, will all of its benefits and imperfections.

Suggestions for Further Reading

Black, Cyril E., *The Dynamics of Modernization* (New York: Harper and Row, 1966).

Cohen, Benjamin J., *The Question of Imperialism: The Political Economy of Dominance and Dependence* (New York: Basic Books, 1973).

Deutsch, Karl W., and William J. Foltz, eds., *Nation-Building* (New York: Atherton, 1963).

Easton, Stewart C., *The Rise and Fall of Western Colonialism* (New York: Praeger, 1964).

Emerson, Rupert, *From Empire to Nation: The Rise to Self-Assertion of Asian and African Peoples* (Cambridge, Mass.: Harvard, 1960).

Foster, George M., *Traditional Cultures, and the Impact of Technological Change* (New York: Harper & Bros., 1962).

Furnivall, J. S., *Colonial Policy and Practice* (Cambridge, England: Cambridge, 1948).

Furtado, Celso, *Economic Development of Latin America: A Survey from Colonial Times to the Cuban Revolution* (London: Cambridge, 1970).

Hodgkin, Thomas, *Nationalism in Colonial Africa* (London: Muller, 1956).

Hunter, Guy, *Modernizing Peasant Societies: A Comparative Study in Asia and Africa* (New York: Oxford, 1969).

Kautsky, John H., *The Political Consequences of Modernization* (New York: Wiley, 1972).

Mannoni, Dominique O., *Prospero and Caliban: The Psychology of Colonization,* trans. by Pamela Powerland (New York: Praeger, 1956).

Wallerstein, Immanuel, ed., *Social Change: The Colonial Situation* (New York: Wiley, 1966).

Wolf, Eric R., *Peasants* (Englewood-Cliffs, N.J.: Prentice-Hall, 1966).

CHAPTER TWO

Social and Economic Problems in the Third World

From the vantage point of the political leaders of the Third World, the question of how to enhance human dignity through public policies quickly focuses on one central issue: inequality. Third World leaders who desire to raise the level of human dignity of their citizens must face the fact that the desirable goods, services, and values of life are distributed in a grossly unequal way among the earth's inhabitants. Public policies aimed at enhancing human dignity must deal with this inequality and find ways to redistribute the world's wealth and power more nearly equitably, both across national boundaries and within their nations. If this could be accomplished, they believe, other indicators of human dignity would be improved accordingly.

Throughout this textbook, we will deal with the concept of the Third World and, at times, if we are not careful, it may appear as if all of the states of the Third World formed one homogeneous whole. For our purposes, the nations of the Third World are all of the independent nation-states of Central and South America and the Caribbean, the Middle East and North Africa, sub-Saharan Africa, and Asia and the Pacific. We exclude from our definition all the nations in these regions that have adopted clearly and unequivocally the development pattern of either the industrial Westernized democracies or the centrally directed authoritarian regimes inspired by Marxist-Leninist philosophy. Thus, we will eliminate not only the communist states of the regions listed, such as North Korea, Vietnam, Cambodia, Laos, and Cuba, but those that are clearly in the camp of the Western democracies: Israel and Japan. Some states are apparently inclined strongly in one direction or another; a similar listing made a decade from now might not even include them in the Third World at all. These states might include radical Marxist-oriented countries such as Angola and Libya, as well as those firmly established as Western democracies, such as Mexico and Venezuela. It is still too early to locate these latter countries without question outside the Third World boundaries; so we continue the customary practice of including them in the Third World region until the outlines of their political style become somewhat clearer. Organized and defined in this way, the Third World consists of 112 nations: 26 in Latin America, 23 in Asia and the Pacific, 19 in the Middle East and North Africa, and 44 in Africa, south of the Sahara.

The Third World category is a "residual" category, made up of nations whose only com-

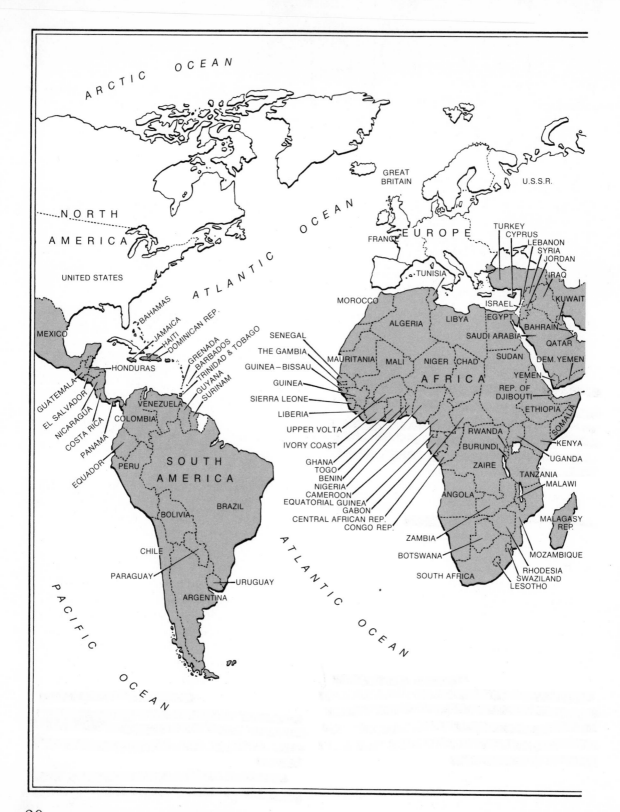

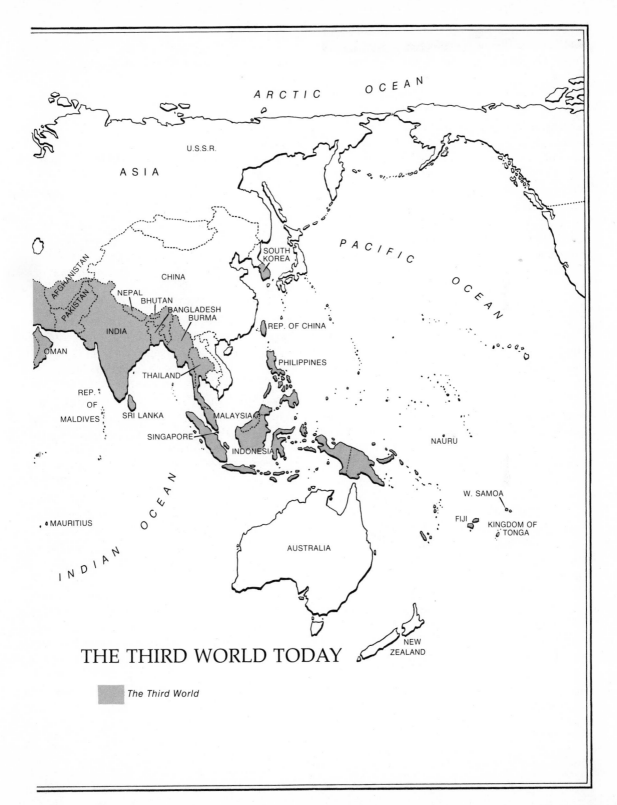

THE THIRD WORLD TODAY

The Third World

mon link is that they do not fit cleanly into either of the other two categories of nations. Third World nations are neither Western industrialized democracies nor authoritarian Marxist regimes. But exactly what are these nations? The Third World category contains a very wide variety of social, historical, economic, political, and ethnic dimensions; only some of them can be indicated here.[1] Take the question of size, for example. In the Third World, we find huge states, such as Brazil (more than 3 million square miles, larger than the United States, excluding Alaska), and Argentina and India (more than 1 million square miles each); and we also find some very tiny nations that are only isolated islands (like Barbados, 166 square miles, or about the size of Columbus, Ohio), or cities that have separated themselves from their surrounding country (like Singapore, 224 square miles). Third World states differ widely in population, too, all the way from mammoth India, whose 620 million people make her the second most populous nation in the world, down to some of the tiny oil-rich states in the Arabian peninsula such as Qatar, with a population of only about 180,000. The Third World has landlocked countries, like Bolivia, and long island chains, like Indonesia. There are nations that are rich agricultural areas, like the rice areas of Southeast Asia; and there are regions where the wealth is derived from the minerals drawn from beneath the ground, such as the oil areas of the Middle East. The Third World has nations that have been independent and active members of the international system for more than 150 years, like Argentina; and it has nations that have existed for barely a few months and are almost completely ignored by the rest of the international community; an example is Papua New Guinea, formerly a member of the British Commonwealth administered by Australia. And, as we will note shortly, the states of the Third World do not even share their condition of poverty; a few nations in the region possess at least statistically some of the highest per capita incomes in the world.

DIMENSIONS OF ECONOMIC INEQUALITY

Consider Tables 2.1 and 2.2, which contain data on all of the nations in the world for 1965 and 1974; the information is available and reliable for these years. You will notice that the world's population in 1965 amounted to slightly more than 3.3 billion persons, who lived in 123 separate and independent nations. The area that we call the Third World contained 84 of these nations, and slightly more than 1½ billion persons, or about 46 percent of the world's total population. We have divided the nations not only into the First, Second and Third Worlds but, in addition, have divided them according to per capita gross national product (GNP) for the respective years. You will see that the Third World's nations are divided as follows: more than 1.4 billion people live in 66 nations that show a per capita GNP of less than $500; a little less than 100 million live in 14 nations that have a per capita GNP of between $501 and $1000 annually; and only 33 million people from the Third World live in four nations that show a per capita GNP of more than $1001 per year. In addition, in the poorest 66 nations, the mean per capita GNP amounts to no more than $209 per year. Of the four nations in the "rich" category, three (Kuwait, Libya, and Venezuela) are oil-exporting nations that have been particularly fortunate to possess a raw material for which world demand is especially high and inelastic. Although the statistics from these countries tend to skew the overall income and wealth data from the Third World, they do not generally reflect self-sustaining economic and political development, with the possible exception of Venezuela.

When we turn to Table 2.2, we see that global inequalities of wealth are becoming

[1] A good source of factual information about all the world's political systems is Arthur S. Banks, ed., *Political Handbook of the World: 1976* (New York: McGraw-Hill, 1976).

TABLE 2.1
Distribution of GNP Among the First, Second, and Third Worlds, 1965

Per Capita GNP	First World	Second World	Third World	Total
Poor nations <$500	None	4 nations $258 mean GNP/capita 780.6 million population	66 nations $209 mean GNP/capita 1405.3 million population	70 nations $226 mean GNP/capita 2185.9 million population
Middle-income nations $501–$1000	2 nations $684 mean 9.3 million population	3 nations $695 mean GNP/capita 28.4 million population	14 nations $709 mean GNP/capita 98.6 million population	19 nations $704 mean GNP/capita 136.3 million population
Rich nations $1001<	23 nations $3142 mean GNP/capita 642.8 million population	7 nations $1636 mean GNP/capita 330.7 million population	4 nations $3090 mean GNP/capita 33.7 million population	34 nations $2646 mean GNP/capita 1007.2 million population
Total	25 nations $3107 mean GNP/capita 652.1 million population	14 nations $669 mean GNP/capita 1,139.7 million population	84 nations $304 mean GNP/capita 1537.6 million population	123 nations $978 mean GNP/capita 3329.4 million population

Source: U.S. Arms Control and Disarmament Agency, *World Military Expenditures and Arms Transfers 1965–1974* (Washington: USGPO, 1976). Table includes only those countries for which data are available.

Note: First World = Western industrial countries; Second World = authoritarian Marxist countries; Third World = all Latin American, Middle Eastern, Asian, and African countries not in above categories.

sharper. Now, the 4.3 billion people of the world are divided into 136 nations, of which 95 are located in the Third World. The Third World's population has passed 2.2 billion, or about 52 percent of the world's total. Of the total Third World population, about 80 percent live in poor nations, about 15 percent live in middle-income nations (per capita GNP between $501 and $1000 annually), and the remaining 5 percent live in relatively wealthy countries. Again, of the 12 nations from the Third World with higher GNP per capita, seven are major exporters of either crude oil or other valuable minerals (Gabon, Kuwait, Libya, Qatar, the United Arab Emirates, Venezuela, and Saudi Arabia). This record compares favorably with the data from 1965, when the Third World's population was divided roughly as follows: 90 percent in poor nations, 6 percent in middle-income nations, and 4 percent in rich nations.

However, even this modest progress achieved over a 10-year period fades into insignificance when one looks at the growing disparity between Third World and First World nations. While the GNP per capita of the poorest 65 nations barely increased at all, showing a rise from $209 to $223, the wealthiest 25 nations of the industrialized West showed an increase from $3107 to $4035, a rise of nearly $1000 per person annually, almost 30 percent in 10 years, or an average

TABLE 2.2

Distribution of GNP Among the First, Second, and Third Worlds, 1974

Per Capita GNP	First World	Second World	Third World	Total
Poor nations <$500	None	4 nations $209 mean GNP/ capita 962.1 million population	65 nations $223 mean GNP/ capita 1840.8 million population	69 nations $218 mean GNP/ capita 2802.9 million population
Middle-income nations $501–$1000	None	2 nations $561 mean GNP/ capita 10.5 million population	20 nations $730 mean GNP/ capita 341.9 million population	22 nations $725 mean GNP/ capita 352.4 million population
Rich nations $1001<	25 nations $4035 mean GNP/capita 707 million population	8 nations $2274 mean GNP/capita 379 million population	12 nations $3004 mean GNP/capita 76.6 million population	45 nations $3393 mean GNP/capita 1162.6 million population
Total	25 nations $4035 mean GNP/capita 707 million population	16 nations $791 mean GNP/capita 1351.6 million population	95 nations $394 mean GNP/capita 2259.3 million population	136 nations $1114 mean GNP/capita 4317.9 million population

Source: U.S. Arms Control and Disarmament Agency, *World Military Expenditures and Arms Transfers 1965–1974* (Washington: USGPO, 1976). Table includes only those countries for which data are available.

Note: First World = Western industrial countries; Second World = authoritarian Marxist countries; Third World = all Latin American, Middle Eastern, Asian, and African countries not in above categories.

gain of 3 percent per year. Economic progress in the Third World was not spread evenly throughout the region but, instead, was concentrated in a small cluster of countries, some of which appear to have their development policies well under control (Algeria, Brazil, Taiwan, the Dominican Republic, and Malaysia, for example) and a few that are riding the crest of high oil prices. The total number of satisfactory cases would probably not exceed a dozen. An equally small number of national economies slipped backward during the period, either because of a collapse in world prices for a particular raw material or because of an unusual degree of political turmoil. The great majority of states, however, have neither improved nor declined during the decade from 1965 to 1974. Their GNP per capita status, their indices of agricultural and industrial production, and other indicators of economic development are just about where they were 10 years ago. If the entire global economy were stagnated, such a performance would not stand out as peculiar. But, as we have already noted, while the poor nations remain poor, the rich nations are surging ahead, notwithstanding the temporary setback of the recession in the industrial countries from 1973 to 1975.

The combination of a much higher rate of expansion and a much higher beginning base number for the industrialized countries means that the gap between rich and poor nations is widening rapidly. At present rates of growth, the 25 rich nations of the industrial area will double their GNP per capita from about $4000 to about $8000 by the end of this century, while the poor nations of the Third World will be fortunate to have increased their GNP per capita from $223 to $350 during the same period.

In terms of stark statistics, this is the dilemma of the Third World today. Behind these dry statistics, however, are real human beings, most of whom live in constant anxiety about the stability of their job and income. A recent world wide Gallup Poll found, for example, that two-thirds of all respondents in Latin America, Africa, and Asia say that they worry "all" or "most of the time" about meeting family expenses. Half of them report insufficient money to provide their families with food, and an even higher percentage say there are times when they cannot afford to buy them clothes. About half are unable to pay for the simplest medical care. As a consequence of such material poverty, only 28 percent of the Latin Americans, 8 percent of the Africans, and 6 percent of the Indians interviewed considered themselves fully satisfied with their lives.[2]

THE CAUSES OF INEQUALITY: SOME POPULAR THEORIES

Because global economic inequality is such an obstacle to human dignity in the Third World, it has received a great deal of attention from political leaders and scholars who have attempted to find the causes of the problem and, thereby, to discover a solution to it as well.

Many different theories have been proposed to explain the causes of poverty in the Third World. Some theories place the causes outside the Third World as, for example, in the nature

[2] George H. Gallup, "What Mankind Thinks About Itself," *Reader's Digest* (October 1976), pp. 132–136. For a good discussion of poverty in the Third World from the vantage point of specific country case studies, see Charles Elliott, *Patterns of Poverty in the Third World* (New York: Praeger, 1975).

of the international system. Other theories locate the cause of poverty within the national political systems of Third World countries. If the theory focuses primarily on the world outside of the Third World nations, it may emphasize either the purposive thwarting of legitimate Third World desires by profit-hungry capitalism in league with imperialistic Great Powers, or it may concentrate instead on the impersonal, relatively automatic workings of an international system composed of industrial and raw material exporting countries. If the theory deals instead with conditions inside the nations of the Third World, then it may deal with some of these themes: resource deficiencies; rigidities in social structures (with special emphasis on the population explosion, on education, or on urbanization); ethnic, linguistic, or racial characteristics; psychological factors; or political structures and processes. Since this textbook is about politics, Chapters 4, 5, and 6 examine these latter factors and take up in detail assertions that Third World nations generally lack the kind of political order necessary to bring about badly needed socioeconomic reforms. In Chapter 3, we will discuss the political culture and socialization processes of Third World countries in general, and we will examine psychological factors, included in the preceding list. In this chapter, we summarize the remaining theories concerning the causes of poverty in the Third World.

International Sources of Third World Poverty

One of the most prominent theories used to explain the poverty of backward peoples has been the one that states that the rich nations exploit and suppress the poor nations. The motivation of the wealthy nations varies. In some theories, the villains are big corporations that manipulate politics behind the scenes in the wealthy countries; they employ the great power of these nations to secure markets for their products and sources for their raw materials in the poor nations. In other theories, the true mischief makers are not business leaders but, instead, the government élites themselves, who establish Great Power influence throughout the poorer nations in order to play the game of international power politics on the territory of states that cannot defend themselves from being used in this manner.

The best known of the economic theories are those associated with Karl Marx and V. I. Lenin. Their work has been interpreted and updated in our times by three prominent American economists, Paul Baran, Paul Sweezy, and Harry Magdoff.[3]

The imperialistic imperative of modern capitalist society, say these writers, derives from the inevitable tendency of monopoly capitalism to generate insufficient demand at home to absorb its surplus production. Lenin wrote of this as a problem of underconsumption, stemming from the growing discrepancy between what workers produce (increasing worker productivity) and what they are allowed to consume (decreasing share of output to workers in the form of wages). Critics of traditional Leninist theorizing respond to this assertion by pointing to the vigor of the trade union movement in the industrialized countries, and the consequent capacity of the workers to gain an increasing share of what they produce. In an effort to modernize Lenin's theory and bring it into line with twentieth-century, politicoeconomic realities in the capitalist states, Baran and Sweezy have altered conventional Marxist-Leninist theory to read as follows: the tendency toward excess surplus derives from the expansion or growth imperative of monopoly capitalism. That is, modern business philosophy in capitalist society condemns to extinction any firm or corporation that does not try to maximize its share of the market and, thereby, grow in the process. Hence, the trend toward mergers and oligopolies within

the industrialized states and the counterpart trend toward the spread of multinational firms abroad develop. Despite the growing proportion of industrial output diverted into the hands of labor, profits (the equivalent of surplus in the Baran-Sweezy formulation) rise even faster, and the investing class (the capitalist entrepreneurs) are at a loss to find ways to dispose of, or to absorb, these profits. The answer, say the Marxists, lie in the poorly developed markets of the Third World.

According to this reasoning, the capitalist monopolies and multi-national firms of the industrial economies have spread abroad in an effort to use the purchasing power of the Third World consumers to drain off, or absorb, the excess production of the industrialized West. In order to do this, the multi-national firms must maintain significant control over the economic and political fortunes and directions of the weak states of the Third World. The overseas outlets of the Western firms must be permitted to bring their products into the developing countries free of import restrictions such as duties and licenses. Local Third World firms that might compete with Western products are to be discouraged from operating and should be denied the working capital they need to become established. The consumption tastes of Third World consumers must be manipulated through Western-dominated mass media, particularly motion pictures, radio, and television, to induce them to purchase exotic items from the United States and Western Europe, even if they do cost more. Labor unions in Third World states are discouraged from putting undue pressure on the local factories and manufacturing installations of the Western firms, in order that the multi-nationals can take advantage of cheap labor costs abroad. Finally, the governments of the host nations in the Third World must not regulate the Western-based firms, tax their local profits, or interfere otherwise in their operations. In order to achieve such a docile operating environment abroad, it is argued, large Western corporations have cooperated with and used the governments of

[3] Paul Baran and Paul Sweezy, *Monopoly Capital* (New York: Monthly Review Press, 1966). Harry Magdoff, *The Age of Imperialism* (New York: Monthly Review Press, 1969).

the Western powers, particularly that of the United States, to suppress local reform movements in Third World states that appeared to stand a chance of altering the privileged status of the foreign corporations. Proponents of the Marxist-Leninist theory of imperialism would use this argument to explain Western intervention against a number of radical Third World leaders, including Allende of Chile (1973), Arbenz in Guatemala (1954), Mossadegh in Iran (1953), Castro in Cuba (1961), and Nasser in Egypt (1958).

Although the Marxist-Leninist theory of imperialism has received a great deal of attention and support from Western intellectuals and Third World political leaders, its principal flaw lies in its assertion that all of the above things will inevitably happen, regardless of what Western leaders desire, simply because of the inherent flaws in the capitalist system. Benjamin Cohen, in *The Question of Imperialism,*[4] has called into question not the possibility of such outcomes, but the inevitability of them. Is it not possible, asks Cohen, to find other ways of accounting for the dominance-dependence relationship between the powerful and the weak states in international relations? First, Cohen argues, monopoly capitalism does not necessarily lead to the production of an unabsorbable excess surplus, or profit. Even in pluralist democracies in the larger Western states, labor unions have represented the working class sufficiently well so that profits as a percent of GNP have actually been declining gradually since the 1930s. Even if we admit the tendency toward the generation of excess profits, Cohen says, there are other ways in which these profits can be absorbed besides exploiting the Third World consumers. For one thing, businesses in the capitalist system may be induced to lower prices to increase consumption, especially if their sector of the economy is reasonably competitive, as many are. Second, the government can intervene in the economy to drain off these prof-

its through transfer payments to the poor and middle-income citizens, thereby redistributing income, and increasing consumption at home. Finally, the government may come to the rescue of the capitalists by absorbing these profits itself, primarily through expenditures on military equipment. Thus, says Cohen, imperial exploitation of the Third World markets is only one possible outcome of monopoly capitalism; there are others, depending on the shape of domestic politics in the First World.

This variation on the Marxist-Leninist theme leads us to still another explanation of Third World poverty and weakness, one derived not from the economic imperatives of monopoly capitalism, but from the military imperatives of the game of Great Power politics.[5] According to this version of imperialism, Third World states are kept in a state of weakness, poverty, and dependence by the Western powers because of the way in which Great Power struggles are carried out. As a result of nearly 100 years of bloody struggle in Europe, the major world powers have learned an important lesson: when possible, Great Power confrontation should be carried out on the soil of an intermediate state, one that cannot prevent its own territory from being used as a battleground for foreign struggles. If anything, the shift to nuclear weapons and the exponential growth in the lethality of Great Power arsenals have reinforced this belief. In the late nineteenth and early twentieth centuries, Great Powers confronted one another directly and worked out the prevailing "rules of the game" of international politics through a direct testing process. Today, the rules of the game emerge from a testing process carried out between proxies of the Great Powers on the soil of poor, weak states that have no stake in the larger struggle, but whose leaders cannot defend their territory from these external interventions.

A brief review of the major confrontations of the Cold War reveals a recurring pattern. Korea, Vietnam, the Philippines, Malaya, the

[4] Benjamin J. Cohen, *The Question of Imperialism: The Political Economy of Dominance and Dependence* (New York: Basic Books, 1973).

[5] Melvin Gurtov, *The United States Against the Third World* (New York: Praeger, 1974).

Middle East, Lebanon, the Suez Canal, the Congo, Nigeria, Angola, Rhodesia, Chile, Cuba, Guatemala, and the Dominican Republic have three things in common. They are (or were) Third World countries with little if any stake in the global struggle between the capitalist and Marxist versions of historical destiny. Next, they are usually in the "seams" between the shifting monolithic worlds ruled from Washington and Moscow. Finally, they constitute what geopoliticians call "shatter zones," regions that are unable to govern their own political directions and to control their own internal political processes. These shatter zones are usually prone to internal disturbances and violence, as first one force and then another struggles for, and gains, power. This disorder frequently offers the excuse for the Great Powers to intervene to restore order, if only to forestall counterintervention by the adversary. The tendency of expanding economies to produce economic surplus, which is siphoned off into military expenditures, completes the theoretical circle by leading to the creation of large, standing military establishments, which then look for ways to be used.

Still another way of looking at the problem of global inequalities of wealth and power states that the poverty and dependence of the Third World stem not from any intentional policy decisions made in Washington, London, or Moscow but, instead, simply from the impersonal and automatic workings of an international system that is constructed so as to condemn raw materials exporting nations to lose their share of the benefits of production. This theory is usually called the Prebisch thesis, after its first exponent, Argentine economist Raul Prebisch. Prebisch, as Secretary General of the United Nations Economic Commission for Latin America (UN-ECLA), wrote in 1949 the seminal essay in this field, *The Economic Development of Latin America and its Principal Problems.*[6]

[6] United Nations Economic Commission for Latin America, *The Economic Development of Latin America and Its Principal Problems,* UN Department of Economic Affairs, Lake Success, N.Y., 1950.

Although originally intended as an explanation of the causes of underdevelopment in Latin America, the Prebisch thesis has now been adopted by many radical but non-Marxist regimes throughout the Third World as the best way to explain their economic relations with the industrialized world.

For many years (centuries, in fact), classical economists have followed the laissez-faire position first articulated by Adam Smith in 1776, that the economic interests of all nations were best served under a system of free trade and economic specialization, wherein each trading party performed the economic functions for which it enjoyed a *relative* (not an absolute) advantage. Smith and others of the free trade school were able to demonstrate that each trading partner benefited most from such specialization because the sum total of the economic "pie" grew most rapidly under such a system. Even though some states obviously benefited more than others, economic specialization and free trade made each partner better off than he would be under any other kind of arrangement, by providing for the most rational allocation of resources around the system. In other words, states that manufactured things best exported manufactured items; states that possessed rich deposits of raw materials should export those. Governments should refrain from intervening in the process through devices such as tariffs, subsidies, and taxes; intervention would distort the natural workings of the system. This system has been called the "doctrine of national harmony" by British historian E. H. Carr, because it asserts that all economic interests, worldwide, are in natural harmony, and government interference can only make them worse.[7] Adam Smith, of course, referred to the system as the "invisible hand," meaning that the sum total of all individual private economic decisions was equivalent to raising the general welfare for all the parties to the system.

Prebisch's theory departs significantly from

[7] Edward H. Carr, *The Twenty Years' Crisis, 1919–1939,* 2nd ed. (New York: St. Martin's, 1958).

the classical, laissez-faire approach. According to Prebisch, the free trade system works against the interests of the nations that export raw materials (the "periphery" nations), and in favor of the interests of the industrialized, wealthy nations that export manufactured goods (the "center" nations). The reason for this stems not from any evil intent on the part of the center countries, but from the very structure of the international economic system.

Simply, the prevailing distribution of economic functions around the globe allocates the benefits of economic interchange in an unequal fashion, with the industrialized countries retaining more than their fair share of the benefits of trade. The center is able to retain a greater than fair share because of the impact of technology and social structure on economic productivity. In the center countries, their relatively greater access to manufacturing technology means that worker productivity can be linked to laborsaving devices instead of to increased employment. In addition, the organization of the workers into powerful unions means that the fruits of this increase in productivity are passed back to the workers in the form of increased wages; this leads, in turn, to increased savings, investment, and government revenues. Increases in productivity in the periphery, on the other hand, are lost through unnecessary consumption or through remittances back to the industrialized countries. We have already seen in other contexts some of the reasons for the inability of Third World countries to retain the benefits of increased productivity: the low state of development of labor unions means that the workers have little leverage to apply against the foreign companies; the few manufacturing installations that do exist are not tightly linked to the host economy (the enclave theory), so there is little "spillover" into the local technological environment; and, finally, the host government is too weak to extract from the enclave industry any resources to devote to domestic development.

In addition to the problem of retention of the fruits of improved productivity, the raw materials exporting countries also are hurt by the prevailing price structure in the international economy. Prices for manufactured goods are relatively rigid, both at home and abroad, because of the strength of labor unions and because of the powerful position of multinational corporations and their ability to administer price levels or control overall price structures for their products. The prices of raw materials and agricultural products, on the other hand, are very elastic, and fluctuate wildly, creating alternate years of bonanza and depression. Thus, raw materials exporting nations cannot plan adequately for the future without knowing more definitely the levels of financial resources they will have to draw on. Finally, the link between income levels and demand also works against the prices of raw materials. In general, as one's income rises, the percentage of income devoted to manufactured products rises at a faster rate than does the percent of income devoted to the purchase of raw materials and food. Since incomes are rising in both the center and the periphery countries, the demand for manufactured goods must rise more than the demand for unprocessed raw materials. In both instances, the outcome works against the countries that export raw materials.

There are other, less important aspects of Prebisch's theory that help to explain the causes of Third World poverty. Investment capital, for example, helps to perpetuate industrial control over the factors of production in the periphery nations by insuring that all local production installations are geared to the export trade. Local savings and, therefore, local investment remain small because of the workers' inability to raise their share of the surplus and because of the government's inability to tax the sectors where the excess in located: foreign businesses and local traditional economic groups, such as landowners and traders. Inflation is a persistent structural problem, not because of an excess of demand, but because of the rigidities of supply: rigidities in agricultural production; rigidities in transportation infrastructure; inadequacies in labor; and persistent pressure on the balance of payments because of the unpredictable changes in raw materials prices on the world market.

Prebisch, unlike the Marxists, finds the solution to the problem of Third World poverty not only in the international system, but also at home. Internationally, Prebisch has recommended that the center countries give special treatment to the raw material exports of the Third World and devote increased financial resources to aid Third World governments that are trying to reform their domestic economies, but lack the funds to do so. But, asserts Prebisch, Third World governments must assume a major burden in reforming their internal economic structures, to make them more responsive to demand pressures, to retain a greater share of the earnings of production within the country, to increase the taxation of possible sources of revenue to increase government revenues and, perhaps most important, to build up domestic industry to the point where the nation consumes its own locally produced manufactured products, no matter what the cost. Only through such import substitution, claims Prebisch, can the Third World emerge from its "peripheral" status in the foreseeable future.[8]

National Sources of Third World Poverty

Population. Before 1700, world population grew very slowly, probably at the average rate of about 0.2 percent per year. As far as demographers can tell, the population of the world in 1750 was about ½ billion. World population began to grow more rapidly at about the time of the Industrial Revolution and, although it has declined in certain areas and during certain historical periods, the overall pattern has been one of exponential growth rates. By 1850, world population stood at about 1.3 billion; by 1900, it was 1.6 billion; by 1970, it was 3.6 billion; and, in the middle of the 1970s, world population exceeded 4 billion. Demographers now estimate that the world's population will continue to grow, although at a declining rate of increase, until sometime near the end of the next century, when a stable population will be achieved at somewhere between 8 and 15 billion persons.[9]

The social phenomenon that we call the population "explosion" is caused by the demographic transition that occurs in countries that are experiencing modernization. During stage 1 of the demographic transition, characteristic of traditional countries with a low standard of living, population levels are kept low and stable through a combination of high birth and death rates. In traditional countries, the birth rate tends to be about 40 to 50 per 1000, the death rate is about 30 to 40 per 1000, and the resultant population growth rate is about 1 percent annually, meaning that the population will double in about 70 years. As a country begins to make the transition from traditional to modern status, however, advanced technology and increasing standards of living have a differential impact on birth and death rates. The introduction of advanced medical and hygiene technologies from the wealthy nations, as well as an improved diet, all combine to reduce the death rate (particularly among infants) to perhaps 20 to 30 per 1000, but birth rates remain at their traditional level (because of the resistance of customs and mores concerning desired family size), so population now grows at the rate of 2 to 3 percent per year. Under these conditions, population will double every 25 to 35 years. Stage 3 of the demographic transition appears in countries that are more or less completely modernized and industrialized. While death rates remain at about 20 to 30 per 1000, birth rates also drop to about the same level. Eventually, if this happens for enough years in succession (about

[8] James D. Cockcroft, Andre Gunder Frank, and Dale L. Johnson, *Dependence and Underdevelopment: Latin America's Political Economy* (Garden City, N.Y.: Doubleday, 1972).

[9] Tomas Frejka, "The Prospects for a Stationary World Population," *Scientific American* **228,**(3) (March 1973), pp. 15–23.

This traffic jam in central Bombay, India, illustrates the effect of the uneven spread of industrialization to the large cities of the Third World. Rapid population growth and the increasing availability of automobiles even in poor countries have combined to overwhelm the road network of major cities, such as Bombay.

two generations are required), population levels off.

Most Third World countries are in stage 2 of the demographic transition. Developed countries experienced population growth rates of less than 1 percent during the 1970s, but the underdeveloped countries showed rates ranging much higher, usually between 2.25 and 2.5 percent annually. The overall rate in Latin America was, and continues to be, the highest regional rate in the world: 2.9 percent. Taiwan's rate was about 3 percent during the early 1960s, but has dropped in recent years to nearer to 2 percent. In Thailand, the rate has exceeded 3 percent consistently since 1946. In Sri Lanka, the rate during the 1960s was about 2.5 percent, but it, too, has been dropping. At the beginning of the 1970s, the world's population was divided roughly 30:70 between the developed and less developed countries (both communist and Third World). By 2000, if current rates of population growth hold steady, the ratio will change to 20:80. Asia will contain 40 percent of the world's

population, Latin America and Africa, 10 to 12 percent. Europe, on the other hand, will decline to 6 percent of the total, the Soviet Union, to 4 percent; and North America, to 4.5 percent.

High rates of population growth affect Third World poverty levels in several important ways. The addition of so many new people to the population absorbs much of the new productivity that the developing states manage to squeeze out of an inadequate industrial base, an inadequate agricultural sector, and an inadequate social infrastructure (schools, hospitals, housing, and so on). Although the rates of population growth seem small, the bulk totals of new population every year are staggering. At present rates of growth, 75 million new persons are added to the world's population every year. To feed the yearly increment requires nearly 20 million tons of additional grain each year, more than the entire Canadian wheat crop. The resources of Sri Lanka are presently inadequate to support its 13 million people yet, in 80 years, by a con-

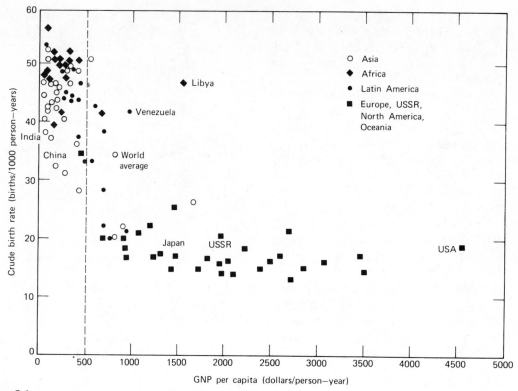

Figure 2.1
Crude Birth Rates versus GNP per Capita, 1971. (*Source*: Donella H. Meadows, et al., *The Limits to Growth*, New York: Universe, 1972, p. 112.)

servative estimate, its population will exceed 30 million. To cope with its population increase, Egypt must build and equip a city the size of Washington, D.C., each year. India must build *ten* such cities per year.

Population growth in developing countries occurs in a way that burdens economically productive sectors with new persons who are not immediately productive. Age distribution in a rapidly growing population shifts downward, since the young segments of the population grow more rapidly than do the older ones. Thus, the proportion of the working age population steadily declines. In Africa as a whole in 1965, the working-age population (ages 15 to 65) amounted to only 54 percent of the total; in some countries, such as Algeria, Niger, and Chad, the percentage was even lower. Since not all working-age persons are actually economically productive, the proportion of the

labor force to the total population in Africa declined to about 40 percent in 1970, and is expected to drop even lower through the decade.

The other way in which rapid population growth increases the burden on the economically productive sectors is through the phenomenon of rapid urbanization. In every region of the Third World, cities are growing more rapidly than the general population. In Africa as a whole, from 1965 to 1970, the urban population grew at an annual rate of more than 6 percent, about twice the rate of population growth in general. At that rate, urban areas in Africa will double in size in less than 12 years. In Latin America, the same is true. From 1960 to 1970, Rio de Janeiro grew at the annual rate of 4.1 percent; Santiago, 4.1 percent; Mexico City, 4.5 percent; Lima, 5.8 percent, and Caracas, 4.7 percent. The sudden and dramatic rise in urban populations is presenting the Third World's countries with insurmountable problems in housing, food, medical care, sanitation, transportation, and public security.[10]

A third impact is derived from the relationship between lowered birth rates and per capita income, and between these two factors and resource consumption. Although demographers are not certain about this, it appears that out of all the possible factors that *could* cause birth rates to decline, the only factor that is predictable consistently is per capita income. That is, as a nation's per capita income rises, desired family size declines, probably because the cost/benefit balance of each additional child tends to discourage having large families. Figure 2.1 portrays this relationship. Therefore, while government programs encouraging birth control (as in Sri Lanka) or encouraging male sterilization (as in India) may have some local impact, in the long run, and in general, the world's population will stabilize only when and if per capita wealth increases beyond subsistence levels.

The principal drawback to this solution lies in the third variable, resource consumption. As an individual's income increases, his or her burden on the earth resources and pollution absorption capacity also increase. Of the total increase in energy consumption in the United States from 1947 to 1973, nearly 60 percent was due to increased affluence, and only 40 percent was due to increased population. Thus, each wealthy person places a burden on the earth's resources about five times as great as his or her poor counterpart. Figure 2.2 illustrates this phenomenon on a worldwide basis.

From the vantage point of the Third World, the implications of these findings should be sobering. If birth rates can be reduced only by means of increasing per capita wealth, but if increased affluence spells a greater burden on already scarce resources, the prospects for eco-

Primitive farming techniques are still used in many parts of the Third World. This particular scene is from the Nile Delta region of Egypt. Since the construction of the Aswan Dam, the Nile doesn't flood this region, and irrigation is difficult without tools and technical assistance. Again, the uneven spread of industrialization creates imbalance that make life more difficult for poor inhabitants of the Third World.

nomic progress by the world's poor nations appear dim indeed.[11]

Agricultural Production and Land Tenure. A rapidly growing population would not be an undue cause for alarm if the society in question could somehow mobilize the resources to feed, house, and clothe its newly arrived members; this requirement places heavy demands on the agricultural sector to grow the needed food, fibers, and lumber to meet this demand. Unfortunately, the record shows that agriculture in the Third World is, at best, holding even with population growth; in many instances, it is actually falling behind badly. From a base index number of 100, representing per capita agricultural production prior to World War II, per capita production levels from 1965 to 1966 had declined to 94 in mainland Asia (excluding China) and to 92 in Latin America, increased slightly to 101 in maritime Asia and to 102 in Africa, and showed appreciable gains to 114 in the Middle East. Since Third World countries remain overwhelmingly agrarian in their labor force, with

[10] Robert W. Fox, *Urban Population Growth Trends in Latin America*, (Washington D.C.: Interamerican Development Bank, 1975).

[11] Nathan Keyfitz, "World Resources and the World Middle Class," *Scientific American* **235** (1) (July 1976), pp. 28-35.

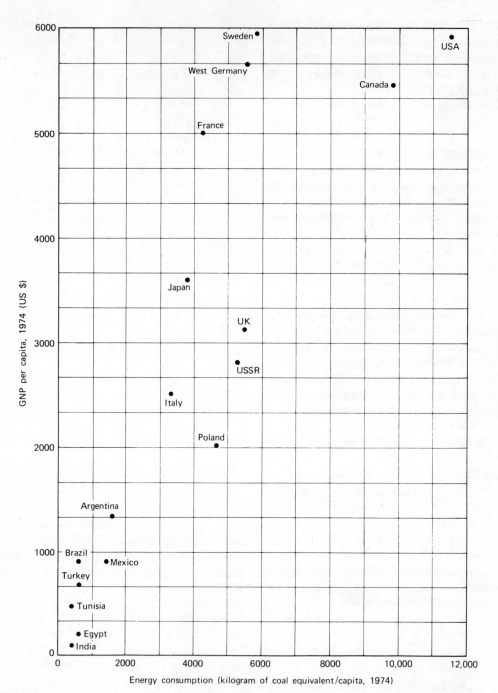

Figure 2.2
Energy Consumption and GNP/Capita, 1974. (*Sources.* GNP/capita—US ACDA, *World Military Expenditures and Arms Transfers, 1965–1974*, US GPO, Washington, 1976. Energy consumption—UN *Statistical Yearbook, 1974.*)

50 to 70 percent of the economically active population still employed in tilling the land, these countries must look to this sector for major gains in worker productivity. Their failure to register major gains in agricultural production remains a major cause of Third World poverty and structural weakness.

The causes of underproduction in agriculture in the Third World are both technological and socioeconomic.[12] On the one hand, per acre crop yields remain low because of the poor nations' inability to devote high levels of agricultural technology to their farming effort. Technologies such as improved seeds, pesticides, herbicides, fertilizer, irrigation, animal husbandry, marketing, transportation, and storage of crops all remain substantially beyond the reach of the average small farmer in virtually all of the Third World. The ability of the industrialized world to apply modern technology to farming means that the gap between rich and poor nations has been widening in agriculture just as it has been in manufacturing. From 1948 to 1965, while North America and Europe registered annual rates of improvement in yield of major crops (cereals, tubers, oil seeds, cotton) of between 2.5 and 7.0 percent, Africa, Asia, and Latin America were able to achieve improvement rates of no more than 1.5 to 2.0 percent in most areas. This achievement by the industrialized countries explains how we in the West can consume between 3000 and 4000 calories per day and still dedicate only about 5 to 7 percent of our work force to agriculture, while people in the developing nations, with ten times as great a proportion of their work force in agriculture, still can consume only about 2000 calories per day (the minimum to maintain reasonably good health, according to many nutritionists).

The second major reason behind the low agricultural productivity of the Third World lies in the land tenure system, or the way in which land is owned and exploited. In most Third World nations, the rural sector remains that part of the nation most strongly wedded to traditional, antimodern ways of living, and this is reflected particularly sharply in the way in which landownership is determined. The exact system differs across the Third World, but the effects are usually the same: little incentive to maximize production, unstable land title, uneconomic size and distribution of parcels, and a highly unequal distribution of social power in rural areas based on landownership.

In Latin America, one of the areas with the greatest agricultural problems, the land tenure problem is one of highly unequal distribution of land combined with uneconomical size of parcels.[13] This is the familiar phenomenon of the *minifundia*, the many extremely small parcels, existing along side the *latifundia*, the few extremely large holdings. In Peru in 1961, for example, 88 percent of the parcels accounted for about 7 percent of the land, while 1 percent of the holdings accounted for over 80 percent of the land. In Chile, 37 percent of the farms contained only 0.2 percent of the land, while 6.9 percent of the parcels contained 81.3 percent of the land. Other nations outside Latin America also suffer from this problem. Even in Egypt after nearly 10 years of vigorous land reform activity by a progressive regime, in 1961, 5.6 percent of the farm owners held 45.2 percent of the land, 59 percent of the owners held 8 percent of the land, and more than three-quarters of a million families, about 23 percent of the total, possessed no land at all.

In sub-Saharan Africa and in much of Asia, the problems of land tenure follow a somewhat different pattern. In Africa, much rural land is still owned communally, which means that individuals do not own the land, but work it for the benefit of the entire village. Each villager is assigned a parcel to work, and the proceeds are shared by the general population. There is little emphasis on production for commercial purposes, and most of the food and fiber are consumed within the village.

[12] Gunnar Myrdal, *The Challenge of World Poverty* (New York: Vintage, 1970), Chapter 4.

[13] Celso Furtado, *Economic Development of Latin America* (Cambridge, England: Cambridge, 1970).

Much of this land is now being encroached on by commercial plantations, which grow food crops such as cocoa and peanuts for export. Young men leave their villages to join the flood of migrant farm laborers who move from plantation to plantation, trying to save enough money to return to their village; but their savings are quickly dissipated in uneconomic consumption, and they return to their village to form a part of the growing rural *lumpenproletariat,* underemployed, landless, and mired in poverty.[14] The few individuals who manage to obtain a small parcel of private property find themselves almost completely at the mercy of the swarms of intermediaries who control the farmers' access to the far-off markets: the brokers, the owners of the means of transport, the money-changers, the mill and silo managers, and so forth. This latter problem, the undue control of the farmers by intermediaries, has also aggravated rural poverty in South and Southeast Asia. In Thailand, for example, government plans to establish new groups of prosperous small farmers in the rich rice lands upcountry from Bangkok failed to break the hold of the absentee landlords in the north and of the parasitic intermediaries in the other rice-growing areas.[15] As a consequence, although nonfarm GNP per capita has risen nearly 60 percent from 1960 to 1970, from $739 to $1156, the farm share of the same economic pie has grown only slightly, from $103 to $139 in the same period.

Social Class Structure and Income Distribution. Still another severe social problem affecting levels of human dignity in the Third World is that of highly unequal social class structures and the way in which these structures affect political power, wealth, and economic development. French scholar R. Gendarme has outlined a typical social class structure of the sort frequently found in underdeveloped countries.[16] The following is based on Gendarme's formulation.

At the bottom of the social scale are what Gendarme calls the "urban sub-proletariat," or urban dwellers who are only occasionally employed, rural folk only recently arrived in the city and not yet accustomed to city life, illicit street vendors, and people with minor service trades such as shoeshine boys, porters, and rickshaw drivers. In addition, the urban lower class includes servants of the rich, who may account for as much as 10 percent of the urban population, according to Gendarme. Rounding out the bottom of the social ladder are the masses of rural poor, landless farmers who work on an erratic basis and who live at a subsistence level. In Egypt, the landless rural population may amount to as many as 3.8 million persons, about 20 percent of the country's total rural population. In Iran, writes Gendarme, 60 percent of the country's rural families own no land; in Ecuador, out of a total (rural and urban) population of about 3 million, 500,000 people receive no money income at all, and about 1 million receive only between $30 and $40 per year.

At the next level up the social ladder, we find the urban artisan and working-class groups. The artisans, still a powerful force in traditional societies, work as tailors, shoemakers, potters, blacksmiths, and weavers. The urban wage earners, on the other hand, work in factories, are accustomed to assembly-line discipline and regular employment, and are settled into an urban routine that means they are more or less modernized. Factory employees may account for no more than 30 percent of the total economically active population of an underdeveloped country, as opposed to 60 percent or more in an industrialized one.

The closest resemblance to a typical Western middle class one finds in the Third

---

[14] P. C. Lloyd, *Africa in Social Change* (Baltimore: Penguin, 1975).

[15] Brewster Grace, *Population Growth in Thailand, Part I: Population and Social Structure,* American Universities Field Staff *Reports* (Asia), **XXII** (1) (1974), p. 7.

[16] R. Gendarme, "Reflections on the Approaches to the Problems of Distribution in Underdeveloped Countries," in Jean Marchal and Bernard Ducros, eds., *The Distribution of National Income* (London: Macmillan, 1968), pp. 361–388.

World consists primarily of civil servants, government bureaucrats, and army officers. Because the state is frequently the most progressive employer in a developing economy, large percentages of high school and college graduates can find work no other place and become absorbed into a very large bureaucracy. In Ghana, P. C. Lloyd reports, 40 percent of the workers are employed by the government; in other West African states, the figure is likely to be as high as half. The armies of developing states, although very small by Western standards, have come to play an extremely important role in the development of their societies, partly because of their more modern outlook, partly because of their superior social discipline, and partly because of their monopoly of the armed forces in the country. We will examine the military's role in Third World politics in greater detail in Chapter 5.

At the top of the social scale come the bourgeois and aristocratic classes. Despite their high social standing and their high income levels, this is actually a very heterogeneous social grouping; some of the upper classes are decidedly modern in their attitudes, while others are staunchly committed to retaining the country's traditional way of life. Within the upper class, we are likely to find landlords, a tiny fraction of the total rural population, who enjoy ownership of the vast majority of rural property; the old aristocracy, which can trace its origins back to pre-colonial days, and frequently asserts some sort of royal lineage; the educated, nationalist élite found mostly in the liberal professions, such as law, medicine, engineering and architecture; and traders, business leaders, bankers, and other economic forces.

The data presented in Table 2-3 portray the distribution of income in selected Third World

TABLE 2.3
Income Distribution in Selected Third World Countries
(Percent of Total to Each Quintile)

	Bottom Quintile	Second Quintile	Third Quintile	Fourth Quintile	Top Quantile
Mexico (1963 1964)	3.6	6.9	10.9	20.1	58.5
Brazil (1966)	6.0	8.4	11.8	17.5	56.3
Argentina (1966)	7.0	10.3	13.2	17.6	52.0
Lebanon (1960)	———25.0———			15.0	60.0
India (1956)	——18.7——		14.8	19.7	46.8
Thailand (urban, 1970)	6.5	10.5	15.0	22.5	45.5
Thailand (rural, 1970)	5.5	8.5	14.0	21.0	51.0

Sources: Celso Furtado, *Economic Development of Latin America* (Cambridge, England: Cambridge University Press, 1970), p. 61.

Elias Gannage, "The Distribution of Income in Underdeveloped Countries," in Jean Marchal and Bernard Ducros, eds., *The Distribution of National Income* (London: Macmillan, 1968), p. 330.

Brewster Grace, *Population Growth in Thailand, Park I: Population and Social Structure.* American Universities Field Staff *Reports* (Asia), *XXII, 1* (1974), p. 8.

countries in recent years. Income is distributed in a highly unequal fashion in virtually every country for which we have reliable data. The top 20 percent of the population in each country earns as much as half of the country's income each year, and in at least one case—Lebanon—the percentage rises to 60 percent. The percentages decline sharply thereafter, so that the bottom 20 percent in a typical Third World country earns from 3 to 5 percent of the total national income.

Moral considerations aside, in purely economic terms, unequal income distribution does not necessarily mean that the country is not progressive or developing. Income is distributed unequally in all of the industrialized democracies, including the United States, where the top 20 percent of the population earns about 40 percent of the national income. Income inequalities in developing countries appear to be much more of a social and political problem for at least three reasons. The low-income sectors of the population are so poverty stricken that the gap between rich and poor is greater than in the industrialized countries, the affluence of the upper-income groups becomes much more visible, and the issue becomes politically much more volatile. Furthermore, because of the close links among income, education, and social power, the great disparities in income levels in the Third World also mean great disparities in power. One often hears radical regimes assert the need for land tenure reform, not for economic purposes, but to break the political power of the landed gentry. Also, much of the income, wealth, and social power in Third World countries is concentrated in the hands of traditional groups whose members, as we saw earlier, are not only not interested in modernization and industrialization, but are determined to fight their introduction through public policies whenever and wherever they can.

Cultural Schisms in the Mosaic Societies. Third World countries have been characterized aptly as "mosaic societies," be-cause they are made up of many separate pieces, each of which adds to the whole picture without being absorbed or assimilated into any other segment.[17] This is not a problem unique to the Third World, as the recent agonies in Ulster, Quebec, and Detroit attest. One recent survey of the question of ethnonationalism, the belief that people should be governed only by others of their same ethnic group, tells us that there are only 14 nations in the world substantially free of at least one significant minority, that Japan is the only one of these that has a substantial population, and that only 4 percent of the world's population lives in a nation state that corresponds closely to a single ethnic group. This same survey went on to assert that, as of 1973, 58 nations were "currently or recently troubled by internal discord predicated upon ethnic diversity."[18]

It is obviously difficult to generalize about such a problem, but it still seems that ethnic discord is a much more serious obstacle to national development in the Third World than it is in most of the industrial countries. There are several reasons for this. Many Third World countries, particularly in Africa and Asia, are enclosed by "artificial" boundaries that were imposed on the country by the departing colonial power and do not reflect true tribal or ethnic divisions. In addition, the struggle against the colonial power led many of the nationalist leaders to emphasize each person's inherent right to self-determination, an ideology that turns out to be a two-edged sword that can be wielded by an ethnic minority against a newly created regime, just as that regime used it against the colonial mother country. Also, the general trend of modernization seems to exacerbate tribal, ethnic, or linguistic feelings. Sharp increases in mass media expose countless thousands of people to new cultural symbols, awakening in

[17] W. Howard Wriggins, *The Ruler's Imperative: Stategies for Political Survival in Asia and Africa* (New York: Columbia, 1969), p. 22.
[18] Walker Connor, "The Politics of Ethnonationalism," *Journal of International Affairs,* **27** (1) (1973), pp. 1–21.

them a cultural consciousness that leads to new ideas about the "them" and "us" of their world. Rapid social change frequently drives bewildered traditional peoples back into the comparative safety of mystical religions and tribal cults, which tend to emphasize the dividing lines in human society. Rapid economic change can produce sharp inequalities in the distribution of the gains of industrialization; not infrequently, these economic inequities correspond to some kind of ethnic division. Finally, we must note the comparative fragility of many of the Third World's nations, whose people have not yet become committed to the nation as a symbol of a going concern, one that deserves their loyalty and dedication. In such instances, ethnic divisions loom large as the cause of conflict, violence, and even the breakup of the state.

Third World nations are divided by the customary social fault lines seen elsewhere. Language is one such source of division. Ghana, with a population of 10 million, has five major languages; India has eight major languages and over 800 dialects. In the Philippines, no one language can be understood by as many as one-third of the people. Nigerians speak four major languages; in Zaire, four languages are used for communication between Europeans and natives, four others are used in primary education, and three more are used only in certain localities.[19] Even in Latin America, where the nations have had much time to resolve these problems, Indian languages such as Quechua and Guarani present obstacles to communication in the Andean countries.

Religious ties and beliefs are also sources of conflict in the Third World. In the middle of the 1970s, the gravest instance of this is found in Lebanon, where the population is divided into six principal socioreligious groupings: the Christian Maronites (about 23 percent of the total population), the Greek Orthodox (7 percent), the Armenians (5 percent), the Sunni Moslems (26 percent), the Shiite Moslems (27 percent), and the Druze (7

percent). The chief division in Sri Lanka is between the 2.5 million people of the Tamil Hindu minority, and the 9 million of the Sinhalese Buddhist majority. In the former South Vietnam, conflict among the syncretic Christian faith, the Cao Dai, the Catholics, and the Buddhist sect, the Hoa Hao, further weakened the already shaky political order and contributed to the downfall of the U.S.-sponsored regime.

Racial differences and tribal allegiances compound the problem of national unity, especially in Africa and Asia. Nigeria and Zaire (at the time called the Congo) both experienced severe challenges from separatist movements soon after gaining their independence, in both cases the source of conflict was tribal loyalties and feelings of persecution (often aggravated by outside intervention). The presence of many racially different overseas minorities has sparked conflicts, as in the case of the Indians in several East African countries or of the Chinese in Maylasia and Singapore. Even though many Latin Americans may proclaim that their countries are more tolerant of racial differences, persons of European origins seem to enjoy greater advantages economically, socially, and politically than persons of mixed racial ancestry.

CONCLUSIONS: ECONOMIC AND SOCIAL BARRIERS TO HUMAN DIGNITY

As the preceding brief review makes clear, Third World governments desirous of raising the levels of human dignity in their societies must first come to grips with a number of severe social and economic problems. The international economic system within which the Third World must live is one obvious source of difficulty. Multi-national corporations and Great Powers use developing countries to further their own goals and ambitions; only infrequently does this treatment redound to the benefit of the poor nations themselves.

Within each Third World nation, however,

[19] Rupert Emerson, *From Empire to Nation* (Cambridge, Mass.: Harvard, 1960).

lies a set of social and economic problems that will be just as intractable as those of the international arena. Explosive population growth absorbs increased industrial and agricultural production, meaning that even the most prosperous Third World economies must run harder and harder just to stay in place. Social class structure and inequalities in income distribution create political conflict, economic waste, and the misallocation of scarce resources. Ethnic, tribal, linguistic, and racial differences complete the list of the noneconomic obstacles to human progress.

The list is a formidable one. Even the most stable and creative of political systems would have difficulty in managing any of these problems in isolation, much less the entire set together. In the following chapters, we will examine governments in the Third World as they attempt to cope with problems that seem at times to be overwhelming in scope and intensity.

Suggestions for Further Reading

Agarwal, Amar Narayan, and S. P. Singh, eds., *The Economics of Underdevelopment* (New York: Oxford, 1963).

Angelopoulos, Angelos, *The Third World and the Rich Countries: Prospects for the Year 2000* (New York: Praeger, 1972).

Baran, Paul, and Paul Sweezy, *Monopoly Capital* (New York: Monthly Review Press, 1966).

Bauer, P. T., and Basil S. Yamey, *The Economics of Under-Developed Countries* (Chicago: Chicago, 1957).

Connor, Walker, "The Politics of Ethnonationalism", *Journal of International Affairs 27* (1) (1973), pp. 1–21.

Elliott, Charles, *Patterns of Poverty in the Third World* (New York: Praeger, 1975).

Holt, R. J., and J. E. Turner, *The Political Basis of Economic Development* (New York: Van Nostrand, 1966).

Hoselitz, Bert F., *Sociological Aspects of Economic Growth* (New York: Free Press, 1960).

Johnson, Harry G., ed., *Economic Nationalism in Old and New States* (Chicago: Chicago, 1967).

Kerr, Clark, et al., *Industrialism and Industrial Man,* (Cambridge, Mass.: Harvard, 1960).

Lloyd, P.C., *Africa in Social Change* (Baltimore: Penguin, 1967).

Myrdal, Gunnar, *Asian Drama: An Inquiry Into the Poverty of Nations* (New York: Pantheon, 1968).

————, *The Challenge of World Poverty* (New York: Vintage, 1970).

CHAPTER THREE

Psychological Aspects of Modernization

In Chapter 2, we outlined a number of major economic and social obstacles to raising the level of human dignity in the Third World. Much of what goes on in politics in developing countries is aimed at removing these obstacles by reforming the social, economic, and political structures. Despite the determined and, at times, heroic efforts of political leaders, few countries in the Third World seem to be making significant progress toward this goal. One reason for this difficulty may lie in the psychological features of the societies in question. If the attitudes, modes of thinking, and forms of interpersonal relationships are not supportive of political and economic reform, the changes will not endure, no matter how well designed or financed they may be.

For this reason, many Third World regimes now spend significant resources on policies intended to alter or influence the traditional psychological characteristics of their people. They do this out of a conviction that traditional cultures impede the implementation of policies to raise the level of human dignity. In this chapter, we examine some of the principal features of traditional and modern ways of thinking[1] and discuss the links between these different modes of thought and the enactment of public policy. All policies have their costs, however, and we must also consider the costs of government programs aimed at changing the way in which people think.

Some people in every society wish to preserve the old, the tried, and the tested ways of thinking and doing. They perceive, with justification, that modern ways of thinking have disadvantages as well as advantages. Perhaps, after reading this chapter, you will also decide that traditional values and habits should be conserved and that modernization of one's mental processes is too costly to be worth it. Nevertheless, most Third World leaders who are trying to reform their societies believe that such reform must include psychological changes. Whether or not this is wise, or even feasible, are questions you should be better prepared to contend with at the end of this chapter.

FROM TRADITION TO MODERNITY: THE DIMENSIONS OF CHANGE

Psychological modernization is a multi-dimensional phenomenon, meaning that it is a

[1] As we use the terms "traditional" and "modern" here, they stand for ideal types, or mental constructs, that we use to illustrate our argument. They do not exist in the real world. All of us are mixtures of traditional and modern ways of thinking and acting. All cultures form a continuum from traditional to modern, and none can be regarded as entirely of one type.

process that affects many, if not most, of the mental structures of an individual. Human beings do not become modern only in certain parts of their personality, but apparently must make the transition along a wide range of mental activities. In fact, if the changes do not take place across this wide range, the chances are greater that modernity will not become established within the individual's personality, and a return to traditional modes of thinking, feeling, and acting will occur. More frequently what happens is that an attempt to reconcile traditional and modern mental structures within a single individual produces psychological strain or tension, leading to forms of behavior that are unstable or unhealthy for the broader society.

The changes involved in psychological modernization affect four areas of one's mental functioning: ego structures, attitudes, cognition (or the handling of information), and behavior.[2]

Changes in Ego Structure

At the very core of one's mental structures lie the devices that the ego uses to guide and direct the personality in its encounters with the environment, as well as the protective techniques (defense mechanisms) that are brought into play to shield the personality from threat and attack. These structures are deeply embedded in the personality and are the outcome of very early childhood experiences, especially within the family setting. Until recently, many psychologists regarded these structures as being virtually unchangeable after adolescense, except under traumatic conditions. Thanks to the work of Erik

Erikson, ideas about this are beginning to change.[3] The dimensions of the ego that appear most relevant to psychological modernity are those that have to do with one's openness to change; with feelings of efficacy and optimism; with an ability to empathize with others; and with an inclination toward moderate risk taking.

A traditional person is inclined to be skeptical toward change. In fact, the very definition of "traditional" would probably include reverence for the old and the tested, and suspicion toward the new and the untried. A modern person, on the other hand, is not only open and receptive to change, but looks about for it, even at the cost of uprooting self and family, and moving to a different location. A modern person's readiness for change extends to more than just job, home, or customs; he or she is also inclined to be receptive to new modes of production or of cultivation and to new political forms. Change, even when it comes rapidly, is usually not threatening or unmanageable for the modern person.

Next, a traditional person relates to the natural environment with a feeling of resignation and with a sensation that he or she must accept what nature imposes without trying to alter the inevitable. This characteristic of the traditional person, which we call "fatalism," is indicative of the degree to which the tradition-bound individual feels that life is controlled by external forces, beyond control. Typical of this sort of mentality would be the farmer who refuses to take resolute action to rid a crop of pests out of the belief that the pests are an act of God, against which the farmer cannot struggle. A modern person, on the other hand, acts decisively to overcome nature, and its obstacles. He or she believes that destiny is in his or her own control, and that he or she can influence events that have a bearing on his or her life. A modern person feels efficacious and capable of resolving many of the problems that confront daily life, without having to resort to spiritual or external assistance.

[2] This analysis is based on the following works: Alex Inkeles and David H. Smith, *Becoming Modern: Individual Change in Six Developing Countries* (Cambridge, Mass.: Harvard, 1974). Daniel Lerner, *The Passing of Traditional Society* (Glencoe, Ill.: Free Press, 1958). David McClelland, *The Achieving Society* (New York: Free Press, 1967). Joseph A. Kahl, *The Measurement of Modernism: A Study of Values in Brazil and Mexico* (Austin: Texas, 1968), Latin American Monographs No. 12. Kenneth S. Sherrill, "The Attitudes of Modernity," *Comparative Politics 1* (2) (January 1969), pp. 184-210.

[3] Erik Erikson, *Childhood and Society,* 2nd ed. (New York: Norton, 1963).

A third dimension of ego structure affected by modernization involves a person's dealings with others. A traditional person does not trust others, especially if they come from beyond the immediate circle of friends or kin groups; strangers are to be suspected, not dealt with openly. Relations going in the opposite direction are also difficult, because a traditional person lacks the ability to empathize with others, to put himself or herself in their position, and to imagine how the world looks from their vantage point. A modern person, however, possesses the opposite of both of these characteristics. Modernity communicates to an individual to trust in others, especially if he or she has some sort of rule or legal document to insure that the impersonal other can be expected to behave in a certain manner. Bureaucracies, that great social invention of the modern world, could not work if it were not for the tendency of modern people to trust others to conform to a written set of rules. A modern person also has the ability to empathize with others, to imagine what sorts of problems they may be suffering from, and to adjust personal behavior to the feelings of others. Some social psychologists even assert that a modern person has greater respect for the dignity and worth of weak and poor people, of women and aged people, and of other groups that have been discriminated against until recent times.

Finally, a traditional person has a tendency to avoid taking risks in daily life. This fatalism, low sense of efficacy, and unwillingness to accept change combine to make a traditional person a "low-risk" person, who tries to reduce all life choices to those guaranteed to come out successfully. New agricultural techniques, for example, are avoided unless they offer complete certainty of working to yield a larger crop. Movement to the city, likewise, is avoided; to do so creates uncertainty and risk. A traditional person is not so much interested in achieving success as is in avoiding failure; the best way to avoid failure is to attempt nothing unless success is guaranteed. In the real world, this is usually the equivalent of doing nothing. A modern person accepts a moderate amount of risk in life. He or she understands that certain tasks offer only a medium chance for success; but he or she also feels that the outcome of the task can be influenced by throwing skill and intelligence into the balance. A modern person wishes to achieve positive things; merely avoiding failure is not sufficient. Modern psychology leads to the creation of an entrepreneurial class, as well as to highly motivated and well-trained workers. In many ways, this dimension is the key to the economic development of a society.

Changes in Attitudes

Moving away from the core of a person's mental activities, we come across the wide-ranging variety of social, economic, and political attitudes that mark an individual's day-to-day relationships with the world. As these attitudes and opinions are acquired somewhat later in life than the ego structures mentioned earlier, they are, in theory, more easily changed or discarded as new information about the real world becomes available. This is particularly true for individuals who are more modern and, therefore relatively more open to change and new experiences.

There appear to be six major sets of attitudes that undergo change as a person makes the transition from tradition to modernity. First, the very propensity to form and hold opinions begins to broaden, thereby making it easier for a modernizing person to develop a wide and rich set of beliefs and feelings about new and unusual phenomena. A traditional person would be less likely to have numerous opinions about things far removed from daily life and more likely to answer "I don't know" to an interviewer's questions about such issues. A modern person, in contrast, forms, changes, and discards opinions at a rapid pace in reflection of the rapidly changing world.

Second, modern and traditional people differ in their attitude about time. Traditional persons, reared in primarily agricultural settings, gear their lives to much broader and vaguer notions of time requirements. Time for a rural dweller in a traditional country is linked to the seasons instead of to clocks or watches. Modern persons, however, are much more attuned to the formal requirements of clocks and watches. Schools, factories, businesses, and other complex institutions depend on their members arriving and departing more or less together; and the modern institution teaches its participants the importance of time if they have not already learned it prior to entering.

Closely related to the attitudes they have on time are the feelings modern people have about planning. Modernity implies an ability to bring order out of chaos, to impose a rigorous framework of analytical thought over the otherwise unorganized data of our surroundings. A traditional person resists planning, since what is going to happen will happen anyway, without human intervention. A modern person, on the other hand, intervenes in the flow of events to plan, to develop preferred sequences of events, and to impose his or her own sense of order on the environment.

A modern person believes in the efficacy of science and the scientific method as a means for people to get nature under control. Some tradition-bound persons hold that the world is completely random, with no structure and, thus, no predictability. Others hold that whatever structure that may exist is unknowable to ordinary mortals and can only be reached through spiritual appeals to some divine power. Efforts to apply rationality and science to real problems are doomed to failure. A modern person, in contrast, believes in the inherent rationality of the universe, and so holds that science can be used to rid humanity of some of its worst problems. One interesting illustration of this dimension is in the area of birth control. A traditional person argues against artificial attempts to control or alter the conception of children; a modern person accepts not only the possibility of achieving this goal, but the desirability, if not the necessity, of doing so.

Modern and traditional people differ in their attitudes about how society should reward its members. Modern persons, who are more achievement oriented, assert that society should distribute its rewards according to only one criterion: how well individuals perform their societally assigned task. Traditional people are more ascriptive, which means that they believe that society should reward its members according to some criterion (or criteria) other than role performance. Such criteria might include one's religion, race, language, ethnic group, gender, and age. Obviously, as society generally moves toward a more achievement-oriented means of rewarding its members, individual persons must abandon ascriptive modes of interacting with their fellow citizens.

Finally, we should mention the shift from particularism to universalism as an example of attitudinal change in a modernizing society. Particularism is the belief that a particular group has the right to promote its own specific interests without reference to the interests of any larger or more inclusive entity. Universalism implies a belief that one's ultimate loyalty should be directed toward a social or political entity larger than one's own narrow parochial grouping. When applied at the concrete level in a traditional society, particularism means the supremacy of one's clan, kin group, family, tribe, language group, religious order, or ethnic grouping. The explicit political application of universalism in a modern context means the granting of ultimate supremacy to the nation. Although some citizens in the industrialized West may have begun to shift their loyalty to transnational entities, or even to some global entity (such as all of humanity), those residents of the Third World who are emerging into psychological modernity focus primarily on the nation as the political unit to which they attach their commitments.

Changes in Information and Behavior

From attitudes, let us move to the outer mental structures, where we find the cognitive dimension of the personality. The cognitive mental processes deal with what we know about the outside world, as opposed to how we feel about it. In a political context, the cognitive dimension is closely related to the conative aspect of personality, or the behavioral side of mental functioning. For this reason, we will consider knowledge and behavior simultaneously, with special emphasis on their political ramifications.

The single most important cognitive-behavioral aspect of psychological modernization is that having to do with information, and how a person goes about getting it. A traditional person lives in a world largely lacking in simple bits of information. Furthermore, he or she has few resources that would permit seeking out needed information. Literacy rates are apt to be quite low in poor and developing countries, indicating that many people are effectively cut off from a flow of information through the printed media that most of us in the industrialized countries take for granted. In addition, electronic forms of the mass media, telephones, motion pictures, radio, and television, are only crudely developed in most emerging countries, with the likely exception of the country's capital city. Figure 3.1 indi-

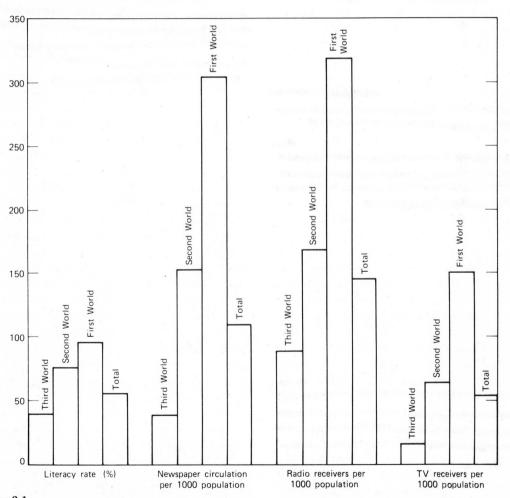

Figure 3.1
Distribution of Communications Resources to First, Second and Third Worlds, Circa 1967. (*Source.* Charles Taylor and Michael Hudson, *World Handbook of Political and Social Indicators*, Yale, New Haven, 1972, 2nd. ed.)

Psychological Aspects of Modernization 55

cates the relative poverty of information within which Third World citizens live. Modern people, in contrast, not only possess large amounts of information, but devote significant resources to the search for more data that they can use to order their lives.

We see this transformation from traditional to modern most clearly when we consider the political behavior of the two types of individuals. Traditional persons typically do not have many political opinions, and they lack the necessary information that would enable them to form opinions about an issue. Modern individuals, on the other hand, possess ample attitudes and opinions about political issues; they know where and how to go about getting the information they need to form an opinion about any new issues that might arise in their surroundings. The same generalization applies to the exchange of political opinions, or what is essentially a social act. Traditional people do not share opinions with others, since conversation about things they cannot change (the regime in the far-off capital, for instance) is a waste of time. Modern persons, however, appear quite ready to exchange opinions about political issues with each other, especially if the environment is supportive. There are, of course, many social settings within which it would be inappropriate or inadvisable for the holder of a minority opinion to engage the dominant majority in debate over some political issue; but, these exceptions aside, the exchange of political ideas in a modern society is much more frequent than in traditional surroundings.

As we move on to consider what modern and traditional persons actually do in politics, the contrast stands out even more starkly.[4] On the input side of politics, where citizens are supposed to bring their demands, grievances, and support to the attention of policy makers, we find traditional people almost totally inactive. Their fatalism, their lack of faith in their own efficacy, and their inability to join with others in common enterprise makes them unable to mount an effective campaign to influence the political system; and their lack of information about politics makes them ignorant of how, where, and by what means to exert their pressure, even if they were so inclined. Modern persons, on the other hand, possess not only the motivation, the activist spirit, and the interpersonal and organizational skills to advance their interests through the political input process, but they know how best to make their influence felt to achieve their goals. The gap between traditional and modern is somewhat less on the output side of the policy process, where people (and groups) are less concerned with influencing policy before it is made and more concerned with protecting themselves from its adverse effects during the implementation stages. People in traditional societies are apt to have a fairly well-developed set of skills that they can put to use to protect themselves from the impact of a given policy; and there are always the ubiquitous intermediaries around whose main job it is to obtain special treatment from the state bureaucracy for their clients. We will meet these intermediaries again as we move on in subsequent chapters to consider the governmental structures of Third World countries. In modern societies, however, the task of protecting a citizen or a group from the adverse impact of public policy falls more into the realm of legitimate interest group activities and less into the jurisdiction of informal intermediaries or back-alley "wheeler-dealers." All of this helps explain why, in modern political settings, we are more apt to find formal associations, interest groups, and political parties operating on both ends of the political process to influence policy before it is made, and to protect their members or clients afterward, when it is being implemented. Although such an arrangement appears to be largely institutional, it could not survive for long if the basic personality and political culture of modernity did not strongly support it.

[4] Gabriel Almond and Sidney Verba, *The Civic Culture* (Princeton, N.J.: Princeton, 1963).

PSYCHOLOGICAL CONSEQUENCES OF RAPID CHANGE

If you consider the changes we have discussed as a complete set, or "package," of mental transformations that a person must undergo as he or she makes the change from traditional to modern, it is obvious that we are talking about massive personality alterations. These alterations do not ordinarily come about easily or painlessly; in fact, there is usually considerable turmoil involved in psychological modernization. This problem begins to take on political ramifications whenever the personal turmoil suffered by modernizing men and women erupts into societal disturbances that cannot be contained within the prevailing social and political institutions. Nevertheless, governments and modernizing élites in Third World countries cannot afford to ignore the problem of psychological change or to treat it as a "given" in their human resources environment; if the basic personality[5] of a developing nation is not brought along in tune with the demands of a modern society, the process of political change may founder and slip backward.

The psychological effects of rapid modernization are a particular version of what Alvin Toffler calls "future shock," or change at such a rapid pace that one's mental and physical resources are overwhelmed.[6] Toffler was writing about the impact of high-speed change in modern, industrial society, but his observations also apply to persons caught in the dizzying whirl of psychocultural modernization.

Making the change from tradition to modernity requires unlearning or discarding inappropriate behavioral tendencies, information, attitudes, and ego structures and replacing

[5] The term "basic personality" means, according to Ralph Linton, "that personality configuration which is shared by the bulk of the society's members as a result of the early experiences which they have in common." From the introduction to Abram Kardiner, et al., *The Psychological Frontiers of Society* (New York: Columbia, 1945), p. viii.
[6] Alvin Toffler, *Future Shock* (New York: Bantam, 1971).

them with their modern counterparts. Modernizing people must reassess their repertoire of mental structures, determine which of these are inappropriate for a modern society, and cast them off in favor of others more attuned to the needs of modernity.

Human beings learn in one of four ways. First, our environment conditions our behavior in the correct directions by the granting or withholding rewards, or by the application and withdrawal of punishments. Through repeated encounters with sets of such rewards and punishments, humans learn by the process of adding rewarded behavioral choices and discarding nonrewarded or punished ones. For more complex social activities, we rely on modeling, or social learning, a process that enables us to learn entire packages of behaviors at once by observing others engaged in a particular action and then emulating them. In addition, we may transfer lessons learned in one sphere of activity to another area of our lives through the learning process known as generalization. And, finally, the process of exemplification allows us to internalize a rule or guideline of an institution and make it our own as a lesson for personal behavior. An example of this latter process would be seen in an individual who, after working in a factory run according to a set schedule of events, learned the value of scheduling personal events, also. We can assume, then, that the process of psychocultural modernization within an individual will be less disruptive, and will endure longer, if (1) the person is rewarded substantially for having made the shift; (2) the environment provides ample models in the form of other modern persons who can be emulated; (3) the person has an opportunity to transfer the lessons of modernity from one sphere of life (school, for instance) to another (business); and (4) if the person is placed in institutions or organizations that are run along modern lines and that provide ample opportunity to copy their behavioral principles.

Under the best of circumstances,

psychocultural changes of this magnitude involve what some psychologists call "object loss," a condition marked by a person's perception that he or she has been deprived of, or must do without, some object (another person, an aspect of one's own self-concept, a tangible resource, or a cultural abstraction) that is invested with emotion and that is culturally defined as valuable.[7] In this particular case, the "object" that is "lost" is the set of mental structures that were appropriate in a traditional setting, but that are out of step in a modern surrounding. Some degree of object loss is inescapable: we all lose loved ones and valued objects as part of the normal process of living. Many such losses are well within the normal range of predictability, however, and society generally provides us with institutions, rituals, and compensation to cushion us against the shock. Occasionally, however, entire social aggregates, such as ethnic groups or social classes, may experience object loss together as the result of the sudden change of some important group characteristic. When this happens, social "buffer" institutions are less effective, since society itself had a stake in maintaining the *status quo ante*. Rapid psychocultural modernization of a developing country is one such instance.

As a very general term, "object loss" embraces two somewhat more narrow kinds of psychological disturbances that can affect the stability of developing countries. One of these is relative deprivation; this is a person's perception that there is a significant gap between the objects (goods, conditions of life, opportunities, symbols, and the like) to which he or she feels legitimately entitled (expectations) and the objects that he or she can reasonably hope to attain and keep (capabilities). The awareness of this gap is often called frustration, and the frequent outcome of a frustrating condition is the direction of aggression against a convenient and symbolic target.[8] A second

kind of object loss disturbance is called cognitive dissonance. Psychologist Leon Festinger asserts that one of the most important human drives is that which impels us to desire internal consistency of opinions, perceptions, expectations, and the whole general range of mental structures. A human being in possession of contradictory mental structures feels uncomfortable, and this discomfort energizes the person to seek to correct the condition. The awareness of internal inconsistencies or contradictions in one's mental makeup is called cognitive dissonance, and actions taken to soften or eliminate these contradictions are called dissonance reduction.[9]

Up to now, we have dealt with object loss at a fairly abstract level. Let us now consider some problems of developing countries to see actual conditions of relative deprivation and cognitive dissonance at work. Consider, for example, the plight of the Indian intellectual caught between the traditional demands of the family and kin group, on the one hand, and the modern requirements of adult experiences, education, and profession, on the other. I. R. Sinai writes of the agony of this individual.

> ... people like me are heirs to two sets of customs, are shaped in our daily lives by dual codes of behavior. For example: my generation on the one hand declared its agnosticism and on the other tamely succumbed to the old rituals; we yearned for romantic love but were reconciled to marriage by the well-established method of matching horoscopes to a girl selected for us by our parents; outside our homes we smoked, consumed alcohol, and ate meat, when available, but at home we were rigidly puritan and vegetarian; we glibly talked about individual salvation although we belonged to a very closely knit joint-family system.[10]

Sinai is writing of cognitive dissonance; yet relative deprivation can also produce dis-

[7] Fred Weinstein and Gerlad M. Platt, *Psychoanalytic Sociology* (Baltimore: Johns Hopkins, 1973).
[8] Ted Robert Gurr, *Why Men Rebel* (Princeton, N.J.: Princeton, 1970).

[9] Leon Festinger, *A Theory of Cognitive Dissonance* (Evanston, Ill.: Row, Peterson, 1957).
[10] I. R. Sinai, *The Challenge of Modernization* (New York: Norton, 1964), p. 64.

turbances in rapidly modernizing societies. In some cases, stable, tradition-bound groups try to hold fast to unchanging expectations, but find their resources eroding away under the pressure of modernization. In the East African countries of Kenya and Tanzania, for example, small farming villages are caught between the unrelenting increase in population and the finite amount of land available for cultivation. Since the traditional methods of passing land from one generation to another are not adequate to resolve this problem, the inhabitants of these small villages see the average size of the agricultural parcel dwindle away to the point of not being economically viable. In other instances, more modernized groups, such as urban, middle-class political leaders, see a gap develop between their high (and rising) expectations of what can be accomplished under an independent, democratic, national reform government, and their perceptions of what actually does happen: not reform, but corruption; not economic progress, but decay; not self-denying leadership, but self-indulgent abuse of power. The result in numerous instances has been for the most powerful modernizing élite, the armed forces, to intervene to restore order and begin anew the drive to development. We will return to this phenomenon again in detail in Chapter 5, when we consider government structures.

For the individual in Latin America, Asia, Africa, or the Middle East, caught in the midst of the turmoil of modernization, several broad kinds of mechanisms are available to help cope with the tensions of rapid change. Withdrawal, either partially through drugs or totally through suicide, offers one low-risk escape from modern life; indeed, we often find that developing countries are experiencing increases in drug use and in suicide rates, as they try to transform their cultures. For many individuals who look to the supernatural for aid, mysticism, witchcraft, and magic play an important role. In many countries of the Third World, in Mexico, in other areas of the Caribbean, in West Africa, and in Southeast Asia, the transformation of society from tradi-

tional to modern has been accompanied by an increase in popular belief in sorcery, voodoo, witches, spirits, and other agents of supernatural power. Some of the frustration of psychocultural change is expressed in social pathology. Homicides, divorces, crimes of passion, theft and burglary, and other forms of socially disruptive aggression are on the increase, as a frustrated and discontent individual, caught in the grip of forces he or she cannot understand, strikes out against symbolic targets, usually in the family and the immediate circle of friends and kin groups. And, finally, mental illness may rise along with levels of modernization, as many individuals succumb to the stress and tension of rapid change.

What we have described are the negative effects of psychological change, the consequences that disrupt society and one's personal life and divert a reform government's attention away from larger, more institutional problems. That these individual level responses to modernization can mean the undoing of the national development efforts seems obvious. Governments in the Third World have found that they cannot simply leave the traditional political culture alone and expect it to change as the nation's institutions change. Neither can a modernizing regime ignore the danger signals contained in the rising rate of social pathology in its country: suicides, homicides, drug addiction, alcoholism, and the rest. Thus, whether they want to or not, modernizing governments have found themselves confronted with the need to intervene in the very subtle and elusive process of psychocultural change, to smooth its adverse effects, and to speed it up if they can.

PSYCHOCULTURAL MODERNIZATION: SOCIAL AGENTS, PUBLIC POLICIES

As Figure 3.2 indicates, the various agents of psychological modernization can be arranged across a wide spectrum, according to the type of mental activity they are designed to alter.

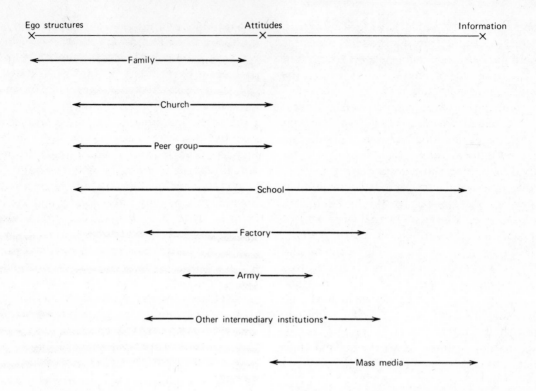

Ego structures   Attitudes   Information

Family

Church

Peer group

School

Factory

Army

Other intermediary institutions*

Mass media

*Labor union, agricultural cooperative, neighborhood associations.

Figure 3.2
Impact of Various Modernizing Agents on Three Levels of Mental Activity (Length of Arrow Indicates Approximate Range of Impact of Each Agent).

At the far left of the spectrum we find the mental activities located at the core of one's personality; we have labeled then "ego structures." In the center of the line fall the mental activities midway between the personality's core and its periphery; we refer to these as "attitudes." At the far right of the scale we encounter the mental activities that are most superficial; we refer to them to as "cognitive," or having to do with information.

Arrayed in similar fashion below the spectrum are the social institutions, or agents of modernization, that have special impact on certain specified areas of one's psychological functioning. The family, for example, being the first socializing agent encountered by the young child, has most of its impact on the core of mental activity, the ego; but many family-taught lessons also pertain to attitudes, values,

and preferences. Churches and peer groups, such as youth gangs or Scout troops, primarily affect attitudes, but they also have considerable impact on ego structures. The school probably affects a wider range of mental activities, because it conveys information, influences attitudes and value choices, and also has some ability to transform ego structures. Several intermediary institutions, such as the factory, military service, labor unions, and agricultural cooperatives, are of obvious importance to the modernization process. Most of the work of these institutions is performed in the changing of attitudes, while relatively less of their activity has to do with the transmission of information. Finally, the mass communications media, such as radio, television, motion pictures, and newspapers, have a great deal of influence in the transmission of raw and distilled information, and they may alter individual attitudes, although their ability to change deep-seated ego structures is relatively small, unless they are supported by other institutional arrangements.

Public policies designed to shape and direct the modernization process must take into account the nature of the political culture in most Third World countries, the interplay between levels of mental activity, and the character of the social change agents, as depicted in Figure 3.2

Let us begin at the lowest level of mental functioning. Traditional family practices, child-rearing practices, and peer group pressures have been investigated in great detail by visiting Western social scientists; the results of these investigations generally point to real and major problems for any government seeking to modernize the ego structures of its country's basic personality. In brief, the evidence is that traditional child-rearing practices and other early childhood socialization techniques found in the Third World do not prepare the growing child to take an active and constructive role in modern politics. Although we cannot survey all of the many details of such widely varying techniques, let us focus on just a few typical characteristics to illustrate these conclusions. We will divide our survey into three periods of early socialization: child-rearing, social pressures of the extended family, and sexual role performance.

In many traditional cultures, such as those of Southeast Asia, child-rearing typically begins with much permissiveness, indulgence, and affection. Young children are allowed virtual autonomy within their tiny universe; their every demand is granted; and all of their siblings and older relatives (aunts, uncles) take great pains to respond to the crying infant or toddler. Suddenly, however, without warning or preparation, the young child or adolescent is plunged into the world of the adult, both socially and sexually. There is much pressure placed on the child at this point to perform at very high standards, and there is severe punishment for failure. Child-rearing prac-

tices that have been indulgent and affectionate to this point now turn sullen and teasing; the child begins to lose the confidence that had been his or hers as a 2- or 3-year old. This pattern of child-rearing practices has been called the "betrayal syndrome" because of its clear-cut tendency to teach the small child that he or she cannot trust anyone in a position of authority, not even mother, and that the world is an unpredictable and malevolent place, to be endured, but not to be changed.[11]

Antimodern lessons continue to be learned through peer group pressures in many Third World areas, as exemplified by the social forces of the Arab world. The Arab child is not a free agent in his or her society, but is bound and constrained by numerous social commitments, duties, and obligations. Many different social groupings of which he or she is a member take deep interest in the behavior of the member, and regularly pronounce on this behavior. Many areas of social contacts must be consulted before acting, and many different individuals must be placated in the act. Social punishment is turned against wayward, non-conformist members of the group, and takes the form of scolding, ridicule, face-to-face insults, shaming, and other forms of intimidation. The consequence of this form of social pressure is a basic personality that takes its cues for behavior from external sources instead of measuring its behavior against inner standards of excellence. Persons who grow up in this sort of environment frequently exhibit tradition-bound behavior patterns as adults: scapegoating; distrust of foreigners; belief in conspiracies; and blaming of unseen forces for failure. Clearly these do not contribute to psychological modernization, any more than did the more deeply rooted family child-rearing practices examined earlier.[12]

We conclude this brief inquiry into traditional early socialization practices by men-

[11] Lucian W. Pye, *Politics, Personality and Nation Building: Burma's Search for Identity* (New Haven, Conn.: Yale, 1968).
[12] Sania Hamady, *Temperament and Character of the Arabs* (New York: Twayne, 1960).

This rural elementary school in El Salvador must hold classes outside because of a lack of available building space. Literacy rates in Third World countries generally range between 50 and 75 percent. One important reason is the scarcity of school facilities in rural areas.

tioning the pressure on extreme sexual role performance under which young males grow to maturity in many Latin American countries. The drive to dominate others through the proving of one's masculinity is almost the cultural imperative of many Latin American societies, including Mexico, Venezuela, and countries further south, such as Argentina. This cultural phenomenon is labeled *"machismo,"* after the Spanish word *macho,* or male. From an early age, a young boy's attention is directed to the size of his genitals and the aggressiveness of his sexual exploits. The boy's father emphasizes rapid sexual maturation and encourages the boy to explore his own sensuality, in most cases before the boy is physiologically or psychologically ready. This pressure leads to the establishment of goals of sexual performance far beyond the reach of most mature males and to sexual failure or inadequacy. The disappointment of Latin American males felt in this area is reflected in their defensiveness and aggressiveness in other social spheres, as well as in their manifest need to dominate others. A social order built on this kind of "lesson" will be one in which compromise and adjustment of interests will

be seen not as moderation, but as weakness, and even as homosexuality.[13]

Although we have detailed several major ways in which traditional socialization practices leave antimodern residues in ego structures across the Third World, the fact is that most modernizing regimes in Latin America, Africa, and Asia simply cannot muster the kind of political power necessary to intervene actively into these intimate and very personal practices. Only in a few countries have governments sought to change the ways in which families shape the personality of their young; however, in most instances, these policies consist of removing children from the family environment before traditional lessons have been learned, and placing them in state-run institutions, such as day care facilities, nurseries, or kindergartens. In this way, radical governments, such as those in Cuba or China, have succeeded in breaking the grip of the family on future generations. But only the most revolutionary governments (those of the Second World) have been able to bring to bear

[13] Carl E. Batt, "Mexican Character: An Adlerian Interpretation," *Journal of Individual Psychology* 25 (2) (November 1969), pp. 183–201.

enough political power and public will to throw off the dead hand of tradition, as it is exemplified in antimodern child-rearing techniques. This is not to say that changes in child-rearing will not occur, through the natural workings of economic, educational, and social modernization. Peter Lloyd reports that élite families in West African countries such as Nigeria are already applying modern child-rearing techniques in order to bring their offspring into the modern world as positive, activist, change-oriented, and achieving adults.[14] But, significantly, these changes are occuring in spite of government policy, not because of it. As far as public policy is concerned, family and peer group socialization practices are beyond the reach of most Third World governments.

We turn now to the intermediate socializing institutions: the school, the army, the factory, and other linkages, such as labor unions and agricultural cooperatives. In later chapters, we will return to an examination of the role these intermediate institutions play in channeling population participation into the political arena and in providing much-needed information for policy makers concerning the effects of their decisions. In this section, however, we are most interested in the ways in which these institutions can be used to alter the basic personality of traditional groups.

Generally, modern institutions help to modernize the people in them by means of the learning principle we discussed earlier: exemplification. Modern institutions, of the sort we have just listed, are organized, maintained, and operated according to a set of principles that are based, in turn, on a modern outlook on life. They are bureaucratic in nature, emphasizing the impersonal and predictable meeting of responsibilities. They are regular and routinized, again stressing the ability of people to predict the behavior of their superiors, subordinates, and peers. The emphasis on rules and on the fair application of these rules leads people to become more trustful of

their environment and of impersonal, unknown others. Modern institutions are achievement oriented, rewarding the people in them more for their performance of societally assigned roles than for some ascriptive characteristic, such as race or religion. In addition, many of these institutions, such as the armed forces, the factory, and the agricultural cooperative, offer to their members clear examples of people dominating nature. Members of these groups are taught to operate and maintain heavy equipment and machinery, to manipulate the natural world to bend it to human needs, and to work productively with large amounts of energy and raw materials.

Completely traditional societies are, on the whole, institutionally impoverished, meaning that they have none, or few of these institutional arrangements within which people can learn to apply the rules of modernity to their daily lives. Thus, in many developing Third World countries, the first decisions regarding social change are frequently aimed at establishing or encouraging such institutions. Schools are usually first on the list, not only because of their impact on traditional modes of thought, but also because of their teaching of literacy to an illiterate populace.[15] In Turkey, after the modernizing revolution of Mustafa Kemal (Ataturk) in 1919, not only were local schools and universities made the recipients of rapidly increased investments, but certain important philosophical changes in education were introduced, as well. Village institutes were established to receive a select cadre of children who were removed from their family and village environment at the age of 14 years, and sent to special boarding schools for future teachers. Religious instruction in schools was terminated, as was the teaching of Arabic and Persian, so the contacts that had linked the traditional Islamic groups with the nation's youth were severed. From 1923 to 1941, the number of students in Turkish elementary schools grew

[14] Peter Lloyd, *Africa in Social Change* (Baltimore: Penguin, 1975), pp. 181–190.

[15] James S. Coleman, ed., *Education and Political Development* (Princeton, N.J.: Princeton, 1965).

from about one-third of a million to nearly 1 million, while college-level enrollment increased nearly fourfold.

The army is another intermediary institution that reform governments in the Third World have depended on, not only to educate large numbers of young recruits drawn from rural, traditional villages and low-income slums in big cities, but also to provide the officer corps its training in modernity, which frequently leads to the creation of new, forward-looking officers. In Ghana, under now-deposed leader Kwame Nkrumah, the government sponsored the creation of the paramilitary Workers' Brigade, a uniformed organization that absorbed unemployed and ill-educated youths who had been cut loose from family and tribal ties and turned them into a loosely disciplined construction unit, used particularly in public works building. In addition to serving their country and supplying symbolic evidence of the government's existence and activity, the Brigade also provided its members with rudimentary education, health care, social coordination, discipline, and a sense of responsibility.

Still a third kind of intermediary institution designed to aid in the psychological modernization of traditional peoples is the government-sponsored agricultural cooperative, as exemplified by the Comilla experiment in Bangladesh (formerly East Pakistan). In 1959 and 1960, the Pakistan Academy for Rural Development was launched in Comilla District as an effort to eliminate rural backwardness in the region by means of a coordinated, comprehensive attack on many aspects of rural traditional agrarian society. Through the Academy, villagers and small farmers were first collected into cooperatives, which were linked together with each other and with the Academy as the central coordinating force.

Indira Gandhi, at the time (February 1977) Prime Minister of India, is seen addressing a huge crowd in the city of Benares. India was then experiencing a campaign to vote on the restoration of constitutional government, temporarily suspended by Mrs. Gandhi's administration. The vote was in favor of a restoration of the constitutional regime, and Mrs. Gandhi was forced to leave office. She was subsequently imprisoned by her successors. Note the measures to keep the crowd from coming too close to the speaker.

The cooperatives were shown the benefits of mutual cooperation in joint solving of problems, and the Academy provided them with substantial assistance in water development, operation and maintenance of tractors, marketing, and a number of important social services, such as midwife training and local elementary schools. But the key to the success of the Comilla experiment was the Academy's insistence on mass participation in the project. Each cooperative decided jointly on the communal need for resources, and each cooperative jointly guaranteed each individual loan made to its members. Instead of simply being the recipient of technical help by a group of élite bureaucrats from the capital city, the Comilla cooperatives were genuine schools of modernity for their members.

The previous examples are important reflections of public policy in Third World countries, where governments have tried to construct the intermediate institutions so badly needed to bring the mental structures of modernity to their still traditional peoples. Although these examples are impressive, they are still characteristic of only a minority of reform regimes. Governments throughout the Third World are discovering tremendous obstacles to the building of institutional linkages between the modern and traditional sectors of the country. Since this is a problem affecting mass popular participation in politics, we will postpone until Chapter 4 any further discussion of the institutional aspects of political change.

The inability of nearly all governments to influence the formation of ego structures through family and peer socialization, and of most governments to shape attitudes through intermediary institutions, has led many regimes in the Third World to concentrate their efforts on the informational end of the spectrum: the creation and transmission of symbols, usually through the mass communications media.[16] The fact that the mass communication of patriotic and modern mobilizing symbols has little impact on the more deeply rooted mental structures of traditional people apparently matters only slightly, if at all, to Third World leaders. What these leaders seek is, first, to dominate the media of communication with the symbols of their regime and, frequently, of their person; and, second, to prevent the mass media in their country from being used to criticize, or dissent from, governmental policies.

Many observers of politics in the Third World have commented on the tendency of leadership in these countries to be based on the personal appeal of a particularly charismatic figure, such as Juan Peron of Argentina, Nasser of Egypt, Sukarno of Indonesia, or Nkrumah of Ghana. In a country where the institutional forms of modern government were lacking or in disrepair, leaders such as these could offer to their people the symbol of action, of power, of the solutions to the many problems that assaulted them in their daily lives. No government in the world is fortunate enough to have tangible resources sufficient to distribute to each citizen to meet his or her needs; so, each government is thrown back onto its symbolic resources. That is, each government must distribute psychic benefits to those people who do not receive material benefits from a given policy decision. Where tangible or material resources are in especially short supply, however, as is the case in any poor country, and where loyalty to the national goverment is fading or nonexistent, symbolic resources must fill the gap to buy time while the government tries to solve the countless material problems confronting it. This is the real meaning of symbolic or personalistic politics in the Third World.

Far more serious for anyone concerned about the state of civil liberties in the Third World today is the increasing use of press censorship by governments in developing countries to prevent criticism of their policies and decisions. Reports reaching the West from various countries throughout the Third World indicate that the free press of these countries

[16] Lucian W. Pye, ed., *Communications and Political Development* (Princeton, N.J.: Princeton, 1963).

is under such an assault that it may not survive intact. A survey of the state of freedom of reporting and of operations of the mass communications media in the 112 nations of the Third World in 1976 reveals the following.[17]

In five nations, the private news media enjoy virtually complete freedom, and there is no official news agency or government-controlled medium to give a "sanitized" version of the news.

In 40 nations, the private news media enjoy substantial freedom to investigate and report the news, but there is an official news agency, combined with government control of at least one medium of communication, to insure that the regime's position is presented to the people.

In 43 nations, the private news media exist along side the official, government-sponsored media; but the controls—both official and unofficial—placed on the private media are so strong that they constitute censorship. The style and degree of press censorship vary greatly within this group. In India, for example, news magazines and newspapers are required to submit all copy to government censors prior to publication. In Iran, government advertising is such a critical source of revenue for all newspapers that they hew to the official line without having to be coerced. In Mexico and Peru, government control over the source of scarce newsprint is sufficient to quiet potential criticism of government policies. In Tanzania, a 1968 law allows the president to ban any newspaper if he considers such action to be in the "national interest." The constitution of Libya guarantees press freedom as long as it does not interfere with the principles of the Libyan revolution. In the Philippines, since the imposition of marital law in 1972, newspaper activity has been under the jurisdiction of the government's Mass Media Council. In Turkey, a nominally free press censors itself through a Press Council Court of Honor, aided by of-

ficial favoritism in the placement of advertising. At the extreme, in Uganda, President Idi Amin has ordered the jailing and torture of journalists who insisted on reporting their criticism of the Ugandan government.

In 19 countries, there is no private communications sector. All media of communication belong to the government.

Data are not available on five countries; but it is assumed that the media of mass communications are so little developed that control and use of them do not constitute major political issues in these countries.

In addition to controlling the news media in their own countries, many Third World governments are now seeking to restrict the news reporting agencies in their countries to purely indigenous organizations, and to exclude the Western-based international news agencies, such as Reuters, United Press International, and the BBC. These Western agencies, say Third World leaders, are an embarrassment to developing countries because they print only the bad news about local conditions, never bringing out the good aspects of Third World politics. Furthermore, and probably much more serious a problem, some international news agencies have been reported to be the "fronts" for the Central Intelligence Agency and other organizations run by Western governments. For example, prior to the fall of the government of Marxist Salvador Allende, the CIA sent scores of foreign reporters to Chile to bring back unfavorable material on the Allende regime in order to affect the opinion of influential political and business leaders in the United States regarding the Allende government. Whether or not these plans will come to fruition will depend greatly on the ability of Third World governments to develop their own international news agency to replace the Western, biased journalists. In view of their inability to develop such news agencies on a purely national basis, one is inclined to doubt their capacity to mount a more sophisticated transnational effort in the foreseeable future.

Beyond policies designed to control the

[17] Arthur S. Banks, ed., *Political Handbook of the World: 1976* (New York, McGraw-Hill, 1976).

private news media, however, Third World governments have done little, if anything, to stimulate the spread of mass communications into the traditional regions of their countries. In contrast with communist regimes, such as that of Cuba, where television and radio are relied on heavily to exhort the public to be supportive of the government and of the revolution, Third World governments seem little inclined to exploit the great symbolic potential of broadcasting and telecasting. The case of India is instructive. In 1966, there were 11 radio receivers for each 1000 people in India, and television was virtually nonexistent. Yet, in the country's First Five-Year Plan, only 0.2 percent of total expenditures were allocated to develop broadcasting, while education expenditures were 60 times as great. The same allocation characterized the Second Plan, while in the Third Plan, broadcasting expenditures slipped to 0.1 percent of the total. And, of course, actual expenditures ran considerably below those planned. In the area of mass communications, Third World policies to ease the strain of psychological modernization seem to be too little and too late to accomplish their goals.

CONCLUSIONS: PSYCHOLOGICAL MODERNIZATION AND HUMAN DIGNITY

Human dignity begins in the minds of human beings. If a person is at peace with his or her surroundings and social order, outside observers should respect this peace. If a person believes that he or she enjoys a dignified existence, then we must accord that view our respect, even though the person's outward appearance may contradict it.

It is important to avoid equating "tradition" with "bad" and "modern" with "good." Many aspects of traditional life, such as the conservation of natural resources or the solidity of the family circle, are of great value and should be preserved. Likewise, there are some features of modern value structures that degrade human dignity, such as the social disintegration of big city slums and the widespread destruction and waste of natural resources.

But this is a textbook about politics, and specifically about politics in the Third World. Regardless of what we may think of their decision, most reform-minded Third World political leaders believe that traditional modes of thought and behavior stand in their way, and they are determined to correct this problem. As far as we know, no society has ever set out on the journey to modernity and then subsequently decided to return to their traditional origins voluntarily; it is unlikely that any large group of individuals have ever done so either. In recognition of that fact, this textbook has adopted a working definition of human dignity that owes much to Western, modern ways of thinking. In making this choice, we seek not to pass judgment on the wisdom of Third World leaders who have directed their societies toward modernity but, instead, to evelute their methods of reaching that goal and to measure their success, or failure. Given the nature of the goal (that is, modernity), certain aspects of traditional thought can certainly be regarded as obstacles or barriers. However, the costs of removing them will inevitably be high; and, since thinking is the most personal of all acts, each of us must decide whether the price is too high for the benefits to be derived.

Suggestions for Further Reading

Almond, Gabriel, and Sidney Verba, *The Civic Culture* (Princeton, N.J.: Princeton, 1963).

Brokensha, David, *Social Change at Larteh, Ghana* (Oxford: Clarendon, 1966).

Coleman, James C., ed., *Education and Political Development* (Princeton, N.J.: Princeton, 1965).

Doob, Leonard, W., *Becoming More Civilized: A Psychological Explanation* (New Haven, Conn.: Yale, 1960).

Gurr, Ted Robert, *Why Men Rebel* (Princeton, N.J.: Princeton, 1970).

Inkeles, Alex, and David H. Smith, *Becoming Modern: Individual Change in Six Developing Countries* (Cambridge, Mass.: Harvard, 1974).

Kahl, Joseph A., *The Measurement of Modernism: A Study of Values in Brazil and Mexico* (Austin: Texas, 1968).

Lerner, Daniel, *The Passing of Traditional Society* (Glencoe, Ill.: Free Press, 1958).

McClelland, David, *The Achieving Society* (New York: Free Press, 1967).

Nash, Manning, *The Golden Road to Modernity: Village Life in Contemporary Burma* (Chicago: Chicago, 1965).

Pye, Lucian W., ed., *Communications and Political Development* (Princeton, N.J.: Princeton, 1963).

———, *Politics, Personality and Nation Building: Burma's Search for Identity* (New Haven, Conn.: Yale, 1962).

———, **and Sidney Verba,** eds., *Political Culture and Political Development* (Princeton, N.J.: Princeton, 1963).

Redfield, Robert, *A Village that Chose Progress: Cham Kom Revisited* (Chicago: Chicago, 1950).

CHAPTER FOUR

Political Participation in the Third World

It is customarily assumed by the proponents of liberal democracy that there is a direct and causal relationship between the spread of mass participation in politics, on the one hand, and levels of human dignity, on the other. In other words, public policies designed to raise the level of human dignity in a society are the direct outgrowth of an increase in mass participation in the political process, primarily through voting in elections and exposure to mass communications.

In this chapter, we will examine this idea as it is applied to politics in the Third World. We are interested specifically in uncovering the connections between mass participation in politics and public policies in Third World countries. If an increase in mass political participation has not brought about an increase in the level of human dignity in many developing countries, the fundamental theoretical cornerstone of liberal democracy would certainly be of dubious validity in typical Third World settings. Furthermore, if we discover this to be the case, we must ask why the link between mass participation and human dignity seems to have been broken, at least in the case of many Third World polities. Let us consider, then, how in the Third World the individual citizen who is not a political professional relates to the government and how those relationships affect public policies.

DIMENSIONS OF POLITICAL PARTICIPATION

The words "political participation" mean many different things to different people, depending on the political culture in which they live. We will use the meaning developed by political scientists Samuel Huntington and Joan Nelson: "activity by private citizens designed to influence governmental decision-making."[1] Political participation has to do specifically with overt, observable behavior or activity. In Chapter 3, we considered the more elusive, inner states of political actors, the attitudes of tradition and modernity. In this chapter, we move one step closer to the actual performance of political systems by examining the actions taken by these citizens to influence their government's decisions. We are concerned with the behavior of private citizens, the individuals who do not make politics a profession, but who engage in political behavior as an avocation, or intermittently. We

[1] Samuel P. Huntington and Joan M. Nelson, *No Easy Choice: Political Participation in Developing Countries* (Cambridge, Mass.: Harvard, 1976).

69

will be examining only the activities intended to influence or alter some action or decision forthcoming from a government agency. Many events have political ramifications, even if they are unintended. These may range from a natural disaster such as an earthquake to an act designed to influence some other area of human society (a strike or boycott, for example), but that spills over into the political sphere unintentionally. We will limit our inquiry here only to the activities expressly intended by the actor to influence governmental policy. This aspect of the definition includes all forms of activity intended to alter public policy, including violent and nonviolent behavior, legal and illegal action.

Finally, we will discuss both autonomous and mobilized behavior in the political arena. This distinction has relatively little significance for Americans, but it is of major importance for citizens of the Third World. In brief, the distinction is this: political participation is autonomous when the actor intends his or her behavior to influence governmental decisions; it is mobilized when the action is intended by someone other than the actor to influence policy. In many traditional settings in the Third World, individual citizens engage in politically relevant behavior (such as voting or attending rallies) not because they believe that their actions will influence government policy, but because some influential or powerful figure in their community (such as a village chief or a union boss) has instructed or otherwise encouraged them to undertake such activities. When we reach our discussion of the patron-client system in Third World politics, we will be referring extensively to the idea of mobilized political participation.

Many observers of traditional politics believe that we should not include mobilized participation in our study, since it is not really participation inspired by an individual citizen's belief in his or her own efficacy. We believe, however, that a complete understanding of politics in the Third World cannot be gained without including this kind of participation. Mobilized participation may blend im-

perceptibly into autonomous action, either because the actor internalizes (that is, learns, the action and incorporates it into the repertoire of political choices), or because what starts out as mobilized participation from the vantage point of the actor may end up being regarded as autonomous by the policy-makers who are on the receiving end of the participants' messages. Many Third World governments actively reach out to mobilize their own citizens through mass mobilization parties or other institutional linkages. These official mobilization efforts arise from a government's desire to show to potential opponents the popular support they enjoy, either generally or for a particular policy or decision. Since this aspect of politics is so profoundly important in the transitional societies of the Third World, we cannot ignore the behavior or its implications.

We have so far been using the term political participation as if it were a phrase that stood for or represented only one single kind of behavior. Actually, the concept of political participation covers a variety of behavioral patterns, including: (1) electoral activity, including voting, working in campaigns, seeking to persuade others to vote for a given candidate or party, or otherwise trying to alter the outcome of an election; (2) lobbying, which means contracting government officials in order to influence their attitudes and behavior on issues that affect significant numbers of people; (3) organizational activity other than lobbying, designed to influence the general "climate" within which policy-making takes place (such as efforts to influence public opinion on a given issue); (4) individual contacting of public officials to express grievances on a matter relating to a single individual; and (5) violence, meaning efforts to influence government decisions by doing physical damage to persons or property.

Even though most studies of political participation focus on voting behavior and other forms of electoral activity, we must understand that the other categories are widely used throughout all political systems. However, in any given political system, the precise mixture of forms of participation may vary considerably. A government that has outlawed elections and parties obviously is not encouraging much electoral activity; but that simply means that we must look deeper to discover the ways its citizens *are* expressing their demands, their needs, and their opinions to the government.

Let us consider some data on relative levels of political participation in different political systems. Examine Tables 4.1 to 4.4. Levels of political participation vary widely; no single political system may be characterized as having a higher level of participation than another. Voting levels tend to be quite high among the communist states and somewhat less so in the Western democracies, but these levels fluctuate greatly in the Third World. Similarly, in the area of protest demonstra-

TABLE 4.1
Selected Percentages of Adult Population Voting in National Elections, middle 1960's

Soviet Union	97.7
Gabon	97.3
East Germany	92.1
Cameroon	83.3
Belgium	79.4
Venezuela	78.8
Sri Lanka	75.0
Turkey	72.3
Gambia	70.2
United States	56.8
India	55.8
Mexico	49.8
Malaysia	48.0
Brazil	44.2

Source: Charles Taylor and Michael Hudson, *World Handbook of Political and Social Indicators,* 2nd ed. (New Haven, Conn.: Yale, 1972), pp. 54–56.

TABLE 4.2
Number of Political Protest Demonstrations Recorded in Selected Countries, 1948–1967

United States	1200
India	201
Belgium	67
Turkey	49
East Germany	46
Venezuela	40
Mexico	32
Brazil	28
Soviet Union	25
Sri Lanka	22
Malaysia	22
Gabon	7
Gambia	0
Cameroon	0

Source: Charles Taylor and Michael Hudson, *World Handbook of Political and Social Indicators,* 2nd ed (New Haven, Conn.: Yale, 1972), pp. 88–93.

tions, a few Third World countries have experienced high levels of mass public protest (although none reaches the level of the United States), while other traditional societies have virtually no public protest activity at all. Electoral competitiveness and honesty are also qualities that are distributed unevenly across the Third World. According to Table 4.3, 26 percent of the Third World states had competitive and reasonably free elections during the middle 1960s, slightly more than 35 percent had elections that deviated significantly from the competitive and free norm, nearly 17 percent held elections that deviated greatly from the competitive and free norm, and 5 percent held no elections at all (15 percent lacked sufficient data for categorization). Finally, in examining Table 4.4, we discover that behavior beyond voting occurs most

TABLE 4.3
Electoral Irregularities, middle 1960s

	First World	Second World	Third World	Total
Elections competitive and reasonably free	23	0	25	48
Elections deviated significantly from competitive and free norm	0	1	34	35
Elections deviated to extreme degree from competitive and free norm	1	10	16	27
Insufficient data to make judgment	0	1	15	16
Countries with no known elections during period	1	1	5	7

Source: Charles Taylor and Michael Hudson, *World Handbook of Political and Social Indicators* 2nd ed (New Haven, Conn.: Yale, 1972), pp. 57–58.

TABLE 4.4
Percentage of the Population Engaging in One or More Political Acts Beyond Voting, 1966–1969

	Number of political acts beyond voting					
	1	2	3	4	5	6
United States	64	40	26	16	9	5
Japan	62	35	19	11	5	2
Nigeria	56	30	13	2	1	—
Austria	52	41	17	8	4	2
India	36	18	10	6	4	2

Source: Norman H. Nie and Sidney Verba, "Political Participation," in Fred Greenstein and Nelson Polsby, eds., *Handbook of Political Science* (Reading, Mass.: Addison-Wesley, 1975), Vol. III, p. 29.

often in the industrial Western states, but that significant élites in countries like India carry on much political activity beyond the casting of their single vote. Obviously, simply on quantitative grounds, the Third World cannot be characterized as lacking political participation, inert, or apathetic. Nonetheless, it is also obvious that, in general, political participation levels (other than voting) in the Third World do not match those recorded in the Western democracies.

INCREASED PARTICIPATION: THE INSTITUTIONAL DIMENSION

Political participation is something that individual persons engage in; political institutions exist merely as the psychological and cultural context within which individuals interact, in politics as well as in any other area of society. When we say, for example, that a certain political party supports a specific candidate or demands a certain kind of policy, we are actually engaging in a sort of "shorthand" to describe these events. The party as an institution can support or demand nothing; these activities are undertaken by specific individuals who act and speak *in the name of* the party, a privilege given to them by other members of the party and conferred on them symbolically by granting to them a certain role (party chairperson, for example). Thus, although only individuals act, the institutional context within which they act is all-important, because it determines how others will react to their behavior.

Political leaders of the Third World are confronted with a major problem in their efforts to mobilize previously traditional groups and to weld them tightly into the modernizing political system. In Chapter 3, we saw some of the difficulties they encountered in designing institutions that would convert traditional personalities into modern ones with a minimum of disruption. In this chapter, we see the same kind of difficulties experienced in a somewhat

different context; that is, how to mobilize previously inert citizens and make them active citizens, without disruption or "political decay."[2]

Many Third World nations suffer from what anthropoligist Manning Nash has called "multiple societies."[3] The multiple society is a divided social order consisting of two separate social systems that are bound together by a single set of economic, political, and legal bonds. One segment of this divided society is national in scope, lives in an urban area (usually the capital), identifies with the nation as an abstract concept, maintains relations with other nations, and is in touch with the trends of modernity around the world. The national segment of the multiple society supplies the nation with its political, economic, and intellectual élites. It has access to resources of economic and political power and is the arena within which the contests over the use of these resources is focused. The other segment (or segments) of the multiple society is region- or village-based. It lives in the countryside, in small towns or villages, or in big-city slums, and rarely identifies itself as a part of the nation. It is traditional in attitude, but may be undergoing certain aspects of the transition to modernity, particularly in the economic sphere. Its only resources are regional in nature, and even these are tiny when compared with the resources of the national élite.

The tension of political modernization arises from the difficulties encountered in attempting to link together these two halves of the multiple society. The two halves are poorly connected. The national segment is the planner, the organizer, the decision-maker for the nation; the rural, village segment is rarely more than the raw material for political purposes. Communications rarely pass freely between the two segments.

Three devices, or social forms, have been

[2] Samuel P. Huntington, *Political Order in Changing Societies* (New Haven, Conn.: Yale, 1968).
[3] Manning Nash, *The Golden Road to Modernity: Village Life in Contemporary Burma* (Chicago: Chicago, 1965).

used to link together the two segments of the multiple society: (1) the mass communications media, (2) modernizing political institutions, such as the political party and the interest group, and (3) the patron-client system.

We have already discussed in another context the governmental use of the mass communications media (see Chapter 3).[4] We found, as you may recall, that the mass media had little lasting effect on the more substantial dimensions of attitudinal change. In the same way, we find that the mass media are of little value in providing the linkages needed to mobilize the village-based segment of the multiple society and to give it a vigorous role in policy making at the national level. There are several reasons why the mass media are inefficient instruments for mobilizing mass participation. Use of the mass media requires an investment of something of value, such as money, time, energy, or attention span. In the rural and low-income areas of the Third World, all of these things are in extremely short supply, and there is rarely little surplus left to expend on an activity for which there is so little demonstrable reward. The mass media are of value only in communicating information and in providing people with an intellectual framework that they can use to make sense of their surroundings. We have been stressing here the *institutional* context of participation because, among other reasons, the institutions of participation act as a sort of school of modernization by making traditional peoples aware of the countless demands of interpersonal exchanges and dealings. In providing traditional peoples with only information, the mass media offer only one dimension (and by far the least important one) of political participation. Without the institutional surroundings of the political group or party, the new participants will not learn the valuable lessons of how to get things accomplished by working with others in politics.

Perhaps the most significant reason why the mass media cannot mobilize rural folk is that they tend to be channeled through the single source of power and authority in each village or neighborhood. In a moment, we will encounter the patron-client system so prevalent in Third World local politics, and we will begin to get some idea of how politics is carried on in the day-to-day life of traditional peoples. For now, let us just observe that the political "boss," or patron, of each village, tribe, or neighborhood effectively controls the mass media, just as he or she controls everything else of value. What the people know of the mass media is usually what the patron wants them to know. In the remote Mexican village of Chan Kom, for example, anthropologist Robert Redfield found that only two or three men regularly read a city newspaper; among them was the village patron, Don Eus. "The knowledge that other people in Chan Kom have of the matters reported or urged in these papers comes to them largely as Don Eus, having read the paper, explains the contents as the men sit together in the plaza in the evening."[5] Manning Nash found much the same sort of situation in small villages in Burma where, at least in one case, the village patron received a copy of the city newspaper and left it in a special place outside his home for others in the village to peruse at their convenience. No one else in the village received the publication, leaving the village chief in virtually complete control over the mass media exposure of the people of the village. Since traditional culture states that the validity of an item of information is determined by its source, and not by the degree to which it conforms to some abstract standard of scientific correctness, traditional society cannot use the mass communications media as a tool to transform its people into active, mobilized citizens.

This, brings us to the set of modernizing in-

[4] Lucian W. Pye, ed., *Communications and Political Development* (Princeton, N.J.: Princeton, 1963).

[5] Robert Redfield, *A Village that Chose Progress: Cham Kom Revisited* (Chicago: Chicago, 1950), p. 144.

stitutions considered so important by Western scholars: the political party and the associational interest group, the agricultural cooperative and the labor union, the neighborhood civic association, and the ethnic interest group.

Historically, political parties have appeared in political systems under one or more of three conditions.[6] First, in the older parliamentary systems of Western Europe and North America, parties were preceded by the emergence within parliament of factions that organized themselves internally and then turned their attention to the winning of electoral support from within the broader populace. Clearly, the development of parties under these circumstances had to be accompanied by the growth of the electorate which, in turn, was linked to reforms in the electoral law. In the Third World, the only area where this development had a chance to occur was in the more advanced regions of Latin America, particularly Argentina and Chile, where Liberal and Conservative parties came into being during the midnineteenth century. However, where these groupings did emerge, they failed to enlist popular support and became stunted in their growth, either because they were unable to relate to the needs of the masses or because their unprincipled exploitation and manipulation of the electoral laws caused a wholesale degeneration of public morality, which led eventually to military rule, as in Argentina.

Parties can also emerge during a specific developmental crisis that has to do either with the legitimacy of the regime, with the establishment of an integrated national society, or with the channeling of large numbers of newly mobilized persons into political activity. In the new nations of Africa and Asia, the struggle against the colonial rulers provided the setting for the creation of nationalist parties; their main function was to mobilize popular support for the battle against the metropolitan country and to convince everyone concerned (including themselves) that their nation had the right to exist as a separate social and political entity. Where large unassimilated ethnic groups declined to pay homage to the new national entity, it was expected that the nationalist mobilization party would provide them with the new identification they needed. There are several classic examples of such a party: the Congress Party of India, the Convention People's Party in Ghana, and the Tanganyika African National Union of Tanganyika (now Tanzania). In other cases, parties like Malaysia's Alliance Party or the PDCI of the Ivory Coast have been particularly effective in over-riding ethnic and regional loyalties and in mobilizing disparate peoples into a single, embracing national system.[7] In those instances where a single nationalist party was not formed prior to independence, such as in Nigeria, much greater latitude was given to the unassimilated ethnic and tribal minorities; consequences for national unity here have been quite negative.

A third condition accompanying the formation of political parties has to do with the social modernization of the country and the need to harness the unleashed social forces and turn them to some political benefit. In this case, political parties emerge from a society that is being assaulted by the forces of modernization—communications, economic development, mass education, the disruption of traditional social forms and attitudes—and that lacks the organizational framework to discipline itself. The alternative appears to be chaos; men and women are uprooted psychologically and lack social and political reference points. The modernizing nationalist

[6] Joseph LaPalombara and Myron Weiner, "The Origin and Development of Political Parties," in Joseph LaPalombara and Myron Weiner, eds., *Political Parties and Political Development* (Princeton, N.J.: Princeton, 1966), pp. 3–42.

[7] Richard E. Stryker, "A Local Perspective on Developmental Strategy in the Ivory Coast," in Michael F. Lofchie, ed., *The State of Nations: Constraints on Development in Independent Africa* (Berkeley: California, 1971), pp. 134–135.

reform party then is created, not to lead the nation to independence (that has already been accomplished), but to help establish order in a disorderly world. There are a few clear-cut examples of such a party, particularly in Latin America: Accion Democratica in Venezuela, the Institutional Revolutionary Party in Mexico, and the National Liberation Party of Costa Rica. In other areas of the Third World, modernizing parties would include the Republican People's Party of Turkey and the Destourian Socialist Party of Tunisia.

Regardless of the social or political origins of parties in the Third World, they seldom perform exactly the same kind of functions that are carried out by their counterpart organizations in Western democracies. In the United States we are accustomed to thinking of political parties as possessing four characteristics (at least in theory): (1) organizational continuity, a life span that outlasts the life of its current leadership; (2) an organizational structure that is permanent and that extends down to the local level; (3) a leadership determined to capture and hold decision-making power, not simply to influence the exercise of such power; and (4) an effort to persuade voters to vote for their candidates.

Political parties in the Third World are, at the same time, both more and less than this formulation. The more successful parties are well organized down to the local block level. Tunisia's Destourian Socialist Party has more than 1000 cells with an average of 100 to 400 members each, and operates effectively at the lowest precinct sphere of local politics. In addition, the party has formed close working alliances with the country's only labor union and has formed within itself an artisans' and shopkeepers' section, a farmers' union, a student group, a youth section, a scout organization for young boys, and a women's organization. Some of the older, successful parties, such as Mexico's PRI, have managed to transfer leadership and power to several younger generations without breaking the organizational continuity of the party. Effective modernization parties, such as Accion Demo-

cratic of Venezuela, provide social services for their members that go far beyond the mere mobilization of voters. A typical local office of one of these parties could be expected to provide information on jobs to an unemployed member, housing for a newly arrived person, or recreation for the member who wishes to spend his or her idle hours with friends.

But, if some political parties do more than their Western counterparts, many (perhaps most) do considerably less. Most organizations that call themselves parties in fact only faintly resemble what we would recognize by that name. Many are only the personal creations of a specific individual or family, and they will fade away after that person's death or loss of interest in politics. Many others have some ideological base, but lack the organizational basis to carry through the periods out of power. Most parties are underfinanced and understaffed, and they suffer from a lack of experienced personnel who can manage complex bureaucracies.

Probably the most significant difference between Third World parties and their counterparts in the First World is that Third World parties are not necessarily organized to organize and mobilize voters, to win elections, and to hold power for some recognizable political purpose. In perhaps a majority of the cases, Third World parties exist not to compete with other parties for votes, but to link the newly mobilized citizens to the modern segment of the multiple society. These parties operate in a noncompetitive situation. They are the only party permitted by law. A survey of the 112 nations in the Third World in 1975 shows that 35, or just slightly less than one-third of the total, permit only one official party to exist. Included on this list are major states as Egypt, Algeria, Tunisia, Kenya, the Philippines, Burma, and Zaire. Many others (the exact number would be impossible to determine) are legally multi-party states, but are *de facto* one-party systems because of the legalized dominance of one party over all the rest. Mexico is the best-known example of this phenomenon; other examples include Indonesia, Taiwan, and Costa Rica. In these systems, the dominant or single party exists not to mobilize the voters to win elections but, instead, to act as a communications and educational channel that hopefully will tie together the rural, traditional section of society with the modern, urban segment.[8]

Going beyond the political party, we find a wide variety of associational interest groups. For ease of discussion, let us categorize these interest groups according to whether or not the rationale for their existence is economic or not.

Generally, countries that are still relatively traditional in their economic and social makeup are also countries where the most active associational interest groups are those that cut across economic lines and are based on noneconomic criteria for membership. In many emerging African countries, urban neighborhoods are frequently organized by tribal or ethnic associations that exist to serve the social needs of their kinfolk recently arrived in the city from the countryside. According to Peter Lloyd, these ethnic associations assist recent arrivals to find housing and employment, incorporates them into a group that shares their culture and their language, and acts as an informal conflict resolution device for disputes between members of the association.[9] Local government ties with these associations will usually be limited to some sort of informal advisory status but, occasionally, the associations will assist the local municipal administration by acting as a law enforcement authority in the local neighborhood. Other traditional, noneconomic interest groups might revolve around criteria such as religion, language, or kinship patterns. One would expect that, as a society modernizes, the bases for such grouping should erode considerably; but the activity of distinct ethnic groups in American politics, such as the activity of people of Italian or Polish origin, should make us aware that noneconomic criteria for human association persist into even advanced states of modernity.

As a nation's economic system modernizes, it also becomes more differentiated; this means that its members begin to take on tasks and role assignments that are more and more specialized and that require specialized knowledge and working conditions. This is the basis for the growth of associational interest groups based on economic self-interest. Of these, the most important politically is the trade or labor union.[10] Trade unions in Third World countries differ substantially from their Western counterparts. Although Western (particularly American) unions concentrate on their economic needs first and leave formal political activity aside, in the Third World, trade union activity has become distinctly political, with little interest in pursuing a specifically economic approach. Because trade unions in the Third World are especially weak compared with Western unions, they rely much more on official or political party support and nurturance; such support frequently leads to control and political dominance.

The sources of trade union weakness in developing countries can be summarized quickly. The still-traditional state of the country's economy means that many, if not most, of the workers will be employed in jobs that are hard to unionize: subsistence agriculture, service tasks in urban areas (domestic servants, street vendors), and so forth. Rural farm workers are difficult to organize because of their geographical isolation. Consequently, trade unions rarely represent more than a small fraction of the workers in any given country. At least ten states in the Third World have no unions whatsoever, another dozen or so have only one officially recognized union to which few workers belong, and the remainder

[8] Henry Bienen, "Political Parties and Political Machines in Africa," in Lofchie, Chapter 9.
[9] Peter Lloyd, *Africa in Social Change* (Baltimore: Penguin, 1967).

[10] Bruce Millen, *The Political Role of Labor in Developing Countries,* (Washington, D.C.: Brookings, 1963). Everett M. Kassalow, "Trade Unionism and the Development Process in the New Nations: A Comparative View," in Solomon Barkin et al., eds., *International Labor* (New York: Harper and Row, 1967), pp. 62–80. Everett M. Kassalow, ed., *National Labor Movements in the Postwar World* (Evanston, Ill.: Northwestern, 1963).

The city of Caracas, Venezuela, must house a population of over two million, about one-fifth of the nation's total. Slum dwellings, called "ranchos," cover the mountains surrounding the city, and contrast sharply with the city's modern skyscrapers. The government would like to destroy the shantytowns and move the slum dwellers into the nearby high rise apartments, but the modern buildings cannot be erected fast enough to accommodate the city's exploding population.

have tiny, fragmented unions that represent 1 to 20 percent of the workers. To give some examples, the percentage of the work force represented by unions in Algeria is 17 percent; in India, 2.5 percent; in Colombia, 13 percent; and in Iran, Iraq, and Nicaragua, only about 1 percent.[11] A second source of weakness for Third World unions is their lack of regular financial support. Most of the workers in a lower-income area lack the means to contribute regularly to union treasuries; strike funds and other financial accoutrements of modern union activity must either be obtained from official sources, from sources outside the country (the competing American and Soviet-sponsored international trade union movements), or must be done without. In many countries, such as Zambia and Malaysia, prevailing ethnic or tribal allegiances cut across the working class and split the labor movement into quarreling factions. Add to these problems the lack of administrative personnel and the rampant graft and corruption within Third World unions, and one can see why the working class is only weakly represented, if at all, in these countries.

There is a second reason for the increased politicization of Third World unions; it has to do with the level of economic development of the country. During a country's early stages of development, there is a great need for investment capital, which can only be gotten from two places: either foreign sources must supply the financial aid through government loans or through private investment (both of which are distasteful to Third World governments), or there must be an economic surplus created within the country itself. If the latter strategy is adopted, the citizens of the country must be

[11] *The World Factbook: 1974* (Acton, Mass.: Publishing Sciences Group, 1974).

forced or persuaded to produce more than they consume, at least for the first decade or two of the development plan. This objective runs exactly counter to the rationale for trade unions, that is, to obtain increasing financial returns from the economic system for their members. This conflict is often referred to as the struggle between the consumption and savings imperatives of economic development. Although some economists assert that there is no necessary conflict between the two, most governments persist in their belief that there is such a conflict, and the only way to resolve the struggle is by persuading the working classes to accept a certain sacrifice for the initial period of the development effort. (Peasants are not usually affected by this call for sacrifice, since they produce and consume so little already that they could have little impact on development no matter what they do; most upper- and middle-income groups are likewise little affected, since their political power makes them immune to such government confiscatory taxation policies.) Obviously, few free and independent trade unions would accept such a bargain, and most union members would overthrow any leadership that tried to impose such an arrangement on the members. Thus, governments in developing countries must bring unions under their official jurisdiction in order to make them compliant members of the national development effort.

As a consequence of these factors, trade unions in the Third World are much more tightly controlled by political organizations than in the West. They are rarely free and independent in the sense that American unions are; instead, they are usually directly controlled by the country's Ministry of Labor, or they are merely a union sector integrated into the single or dominant political party. Either way, the trade union offers little opportunity to mobilize apathetic lower-income or working-class persons into political activity.

Roughly the same degree of underdevelopment in trade union organization is seen in Third World organizations that represent middle-class professional and business interests.

Perhaps as many as half the countries in the Third World report having something like a Chamber of Commerce but, in most instances, these business organizations are just small clubs that operate in the capital city. Only a few countries possess highly differentiated business sector interest groups that cover the entire range of a modernizing economy. Even in a relatively advanced country like Chile, where the private business sector is well represented by interest groups of long standing, only a minority of business leaders actually bother with the work of such groups, out of indifference, the press of business, or a feeling that political action is not likely to produce tangible benefits for business interests.[12] Because of their relatively high level of development, and because of the high degree of American business influence, Venezuela and Mexico have developed very large, well-financed, and well-organized business and manufacturing interest associations that have a great deal of influence with their respective governments. But these two countries are definitely in a tiny minority among Third World states.

The wealthy members of a nation's economy have ways of making their influence felt without the assistance of formal organizations or interest groups. Wealthy landowners, industrialists, and the representatives of foreign corporations are usually able to get the attention of the president or other top officials merely by virtue of their strategic location in the system, apart from any special organization representation they may enjoy. The wielding of influence by Western multi-national corporations such as Lockheed Aircraft or International Telephone and Telegraph to gain special favors in the developing world is already well known. Other examples of such foreign business intervention in Third World politics would be Gulf Oil Company's pay-

[12] Dale L. Johnson, "The National and Progressive Bourgeoisie in Chile," in James D. Cockcroft, Andre Gunder Frank, and Dale L. Johnson, eds., *Dependence and Underdevelopment: Latin America's Political Economy* (Garden City, N.Y.: Doubleday, 1972), pp. 201-206.

ment of $460,000 to Bolivian President Rene Barrientos from 1966 to 1969 to obtain special favors for their operations in Bolivia, or United Brands' payment of $1,250,000 to Honduran military dictator Oswaldo Lopez Arellano in return for exemptions from Honduran export taxes. Such tactics for gaining influence are equally well employed by the wealthy within the nation. Even governments that profess a radical and uncompromising hostility to the traditional business and agrarian élites of their countries are usually found to be doing business with them behind closed doors, reformist rhetoric to the contrary notwithstanding.

In addition to the groups already mentioned, there are at least three kinds of interest groups that span both economic and noneconomic criteria for membership; they must be treated in a special category: students, peasants, and neighborhoods. Student groups in all parts of the world came into prominence during the 1960s as the source of unrest and disorder, as well as the voice for radical changes in many societies. In a few countries, such as Korea and Venezuela, students came close to disrupting society sufficiently to bring about the downfall of the government. In Latin America, particularly, where the principal of the inviolability of a university campus had been used for generations to protect student protestors, the role of students in politics has been especially important. Many prominent Latin American political leaders, such as Fidel Castro of Cuba and Romulo Betancourt of Venezuela, got their start as leaders of student political groups.

In several countries, in addition, peasant groups or leagues have been formed to represent the needs and demands of the low-income, landless workers of the soil. Sometimes peasant leagues are created by government agricultural ministries or by political parties as mobilization devices to gain political support (as in Venezuela), or as administrative devices to assist in the implementation of land reform programs (as in Egypt). At other times, as in Brazil, peasant leagues have been formed essentially free of official control, in which case they are usually suppressed by government action. In either case, they are seldom the channel for the mass mobilization hoped for by Western observers.

Finally, in many cities there are neighborhood associations whose objective is to force government attention to persisting urban problems that they cannot solve by themselves: garbage collection, crime control, water, housing, paved streets, and so forth. In most Third World countries, but especially in Latin America and South Asia, a prime urban problem is that of the squatters, the illegal residents of urban slums or shantytowns. In cities like Lima or Caracas, the squatters have formed associations to establish some primitive organizational framework to administer their neighborhoods and to pressure the national government into granting them legal title to their lands. In many cases, where these associations have been careful to limit their demands to very narrowly stated aims and where they have been willing to resort to disruptive action to achieve their objectives, they have been reasonably successful.

ELECTIONS AND VIOLENCE IN THIRD WORLD POLITICS

At least at the level of symbolic rhetoric, most Third World governments have accepted the need to commit themselves to the principle of popular sovereignty as expressed through universal suffrage, mass voting, regular elections, free competition, and honest counting of the ballots. In many Third World countries, mass voting is not only encouraged, but coerced. A survey of the 28 nations of the Third World for which comparable data are available indicates that an average of 62.6 percent of their adult populations voted in elections held at some point during the middle 1960s. (The comparable figure for 20 Western industrial countries is 75.6 percent; for eight communist nations, it is 98.7 percent). And, as the data presented earlier indicate, only five

Helmeted riot police are seen in action quelling a protest demonstration against high prices and unemployment in Lahore, Pakistan. This demonstration took place in April, 1977. Although the government and the army attempted to prevent such assemblies and demonstrations, the continued political unrest added to Pakistan's economic woes throughout 1977. Such turbulence is typical of the tension and instability of politics in Third World countries beset by intractable economic problems.

Third World countries failed to hold elections sometime during the 1960s.

As one might suspect, however, the gap between symbolic promise and tangible performance is wide. Elections in the Third World have been notorious for the way in which the dominant political forces have suppressed opposition parties, coerced illiterate peasants and city workers into voting for the approved candidates, used "goon" squads to harrass political rallies and to disrupt campaign headquarters, and miscounted ballots or conveniently lost entire ballot boxes in hostile precincts. The list of violations of honest election principles could continue at length. Although few outside observers are in a position to attest to this, national elections in most Third World countries fall far short of offering the voter an honest choice between two or more candidates, each of which has an unfettered opportunity to campaign freely, to see that the ballots are counted, and to take power if victorious. On more than one occasion, in fact, the army has stepped in to nullify elections after the vote showed an unacceptable candidate on the verge of winning (as in Peru in 1962), or to declare certain political groups or parties to be illegal and, therefore, not entitled to present candidates (as in Argentina several times over the previous decade).

Even if elections were conducted in a spotlessly clean and scrupulous manner, we would still be concerned about the way in which the average citizen of the Third World views his or her role in elections or the electoral process. No matter how meaningful the elections might be, if they do not convey to the typical villager, peasant, or worker of the developing world a sense of efficacy, elections do not serve effectively the purpose of mobilizing traditional folk into a modern political process.

In his book on village life in Burma, Manning Nash describes the meaning of the electoral process for one set of Burmese villagers. The process began, observes Nash, with a visit by the village headman and the local patron, the village's richest man, to the national capital for a talk with the organizers of the Union Party. Upon their return to the village, the word was passed around the village that the patron, U Sein Ko, had decided to join the Union Party, and others from the village were expected to do likewise. The book to enroll new members was kept in U Sein Ko's house; aspiring members passed by the house for a ceremonial visit and cup of tea; this was followed by enrollment in the party. There were no campaign activities, and no mass enrollment effort, and only one "mass" meeting (attended by about 40 men of the village) at which U Sein Ko's son was chosen to head the local party organization. On election day, U Sein Ko's prestige and power as the local patron were sufficiently strong to mobilize 90 percent of the villagers to vote for the Union Party candidate. They voted not out of a conviction that they were influencing policy, but out of a complex set of traditional Burmese cultural mores: that society was organized around a local man of power, that followers joined this powerful figure to enjoy his protection from outside forces, and that voting for the Union Party candidate entitled the villagers to receive U Sein Ko's protection from government policies. Thus, we can see that voting plays a very special role in the lives of Burmese villagers, a role that may have little or nothing to do with the policy process or with politics, generally.

Violence in Third World politics also must receive special attention in the over-all treatment of mass political participation. There seems little doubt that, compared to the rest of the world, the developing countries of Latin America, Asia, and Africa suffer from high incidences of politically relevant violence such as riots, military coups, assassinations, guerilla war, and terrorism.[13] One important study of political violence from 1955 to 1961 ranked 74 nations on a scale of 0 to 700; 700 represented the highest amount of instability in any country. The 50 nations of the Third World averaged an instability score of 457.5, ten communist nations averaged 393.5, and the 24 nations of the Western bloc were scored at 277.3. That same study discovered a close relationship between political instability and level of modernization (as measured by a number of socioeconomic indices, such as mass media and health services) Modern nations had a mean instability score of 268, transitional countries scored 472, and traditional countries achieved a mean score of 470. Still another study of the period from 1961 to 1965 ranked 112 nations according to an empirical index called the Magnitude of Civil Strife (a complex indicator taking into account the number of events of political violence, their duration, and their intensity). The highest score was 48.7, and the mean for the entire sample was 9.08. The 80 nations of the Third World achieved a mean civil strife score of 14.3, the ten nations of the communist world

scored 4.9, and the 22 nations of the West averaged 5.3. During the 1975 to 1976 period, 37 nations in the Third World harbored significant insurgent activity, such as guerrilla war or terrorism, or contained at least one clandestine, illegal, opposition group.[14]

In Chapter 3, we discussed the psychological disturbances arising from object loss in rapidly changing societies, such as those we typically find in the Third World. Rapidly changing ideas about political participation also result in heightened levels of disorder and strife, primarily as a consequence of the uneven penetration of modern institutions into a society. Education, government propaganda, and the mass media are the first elements of modernity to impinge on the consciousness of traditional folk; their aspirations and expectations are raised thereby, and they begin to hope that they can achieve some improvement in their lot through government action. However, the other institutions of modernity that we have described—the political party, the associational interest group, the agricultural cooperative, the neighborhood association—all appear much later in the modernization process, and often they fail to appear at all. We have here the classic "revolution of rising expectations." Ideas about what people think they should be achieving in politics begin to outreach the institutions available to help them achieve these objectives. The results are frustration, anger, and aggression, and a generally increased level of political instability.

One should not conclude, however, that high levels of instability necessarily are associated with political reform. We have already noted that one of the most important features of the multiple society is the disjunction between the rural, traditional segment and the modern segment. This absence of an articulating link between traditional and modern is paralleled by a similar gap between those who have

[13] Ivo K. Feierabend, Rosalind L. Feierabend, and Ted Robert Gurr, eds., *Anger, Violence and Politics: Theories and Research* (Englewood Cliffs, N.J.: Prentice-Hall, 1972). The specific articles from this collection that are discussed are Ivo K. Feierabend and Rosalind L. Feierabend, "Systemic Conditions of Political Aggression: An Application of Frustration-Aggression Theory" (Chapter 9), and Ted Robert Gurr, "A Causal Model of Civil Strife: A Comparative Analysis Using New Indices" (Chapter 10).

[14] Based on a survey of the data in Arthur S. Banks, ed., *Political Handbook of the World: 1976* (New York: McGraw-Hill, 1976).

power and those who do not; this means that there seldom are linkages between political violence and the actual making of public policy. The high level of political violence witnessed in many Third World countries does not actually affect the prevailing political structures, because the violence takes place in a distant arena, sealed off from the centers of power. As long as the forces of law and order (the police and the army) remain loyal to the government, isolated outbreaks of rioting, terrorism, or guerrilla war can be contained remarkably easily without having much impact on public policy making. Of course, when the army *does* lose confidence in the regime in power, it is a relatively simple matter for it to intervene to overthrow the government and to install a military dictatorship. We will consider this phenomenon in detail in Chapter 5.

PATRON-CLIENT POLITICS: THE FAILURE OF INSTITUTION-BUILDING

Institutions are the key to increased political participation in rapidly modernizing societies. Yet, the record shows relatively few effective modernizing (and modern) institutional linkages between traditional, low-income peasants and urban workers, on the one hand, and the modern, nationalistic city élites, on the other. A mass mobilization political party in Mexico or Venezuela, the village institutes in Turkey, an agricultural cooperative in Pakistan, ethnic or tribal associations in Nigeria or Ghana: the scarcity of these few examples shows how thinly modernization is penetrating into the Third World in an institutional sense.

Why are so many Third World political leaders unable to build the institutional bridges out to the traditional folk of their countries? For one thing, many members of the modern, well-educated élites in developing countries cannot understand the ways in which traditional, lower-status people calculate the costs and benefits of their daily lives. The Westernized education received by the

modernizing élites has often blinded them to the essential rationality of the traditional style of life. They have forgotten, if they ever knew, the ways in which the elemental forces that play on the lives of traditional people impel them toward personal calculations that appear irrational to Western-trained observers. Often, the city élites in Third World countries cannot even speak the same language spoken by rural villagers; if they do share the same language, they do not speak similar dialects. In any case, communication of the simplest sort is rendered difficult, if not impossible. The urban, modern élites, in the shape of the visiting bureaucrat, planner, or agricultural extension agent, cannot empathize with, or even communicate with, the intended client.

Even where the bureaucrats of the national government are committed to a style of reform in the countryside that is intended to benefit the peasants, they frequently expect the peasants to respond to their plans as if some sort of modern class consciousness existed among the rural workers. When the peasants refuse to respond favorably to these plans and institutions, the bureaucrats become exasperated with their "backward" or "childlike" clients, and they impatiently decide to coerce the peasants into actions and decisions that are manifestly in their own interest. In Chile during the reformist regime of Salvador Allende, bureaucrats from the capital swarmed over the countryside intent on building a more modern and just social order. Land was to be expropriated from the large landowners and placed into collectives, to be worked communally by the peasants. The proceeds would be pooled and then redistributed equally, with a percentage going to the state to pay for the whole enterprise. Naturally, but to the surprise of the modernizing bureaucrats, the peasants would silently nod their assent to the project and then quietly go about the business of sabotaging the collectives. The bureaucrats were astounded at the lack of consciousness of their clients; frequently they were provoked into using coercion to motivate the peasants to act more according to their own rational interests (of course, as those interests were defined by the bureaucrats).[15]

As a consequence, élites cannot construct institutional arrangements that can induce, support, and reinforce modern behavior and attitudes. The characteristics of such arrangements, such as new farming techniques or novel methods for selecting a village chief, depend to a large extent on shared standards of rationality; these, in turn, derive in essence from the ideas of modernity. Remove these ideas, and the shared standards of rationality and the institutional arrangements will collapse because of the unwillingness of the people to internalize their lessons and to assimilate them into their daily lives. The problem is aggravated when the agents of social and technological change are merely temporary visitors in a rural area. A few months after bringing some innovation to the village, they may return to the comfort of the city, abandoning the villagers to their fate with the new equipment, seeds, medicines, or books. Small wonder that the villagers are reluctant to commit themselves to an unknown factor in their struggle to eke out a bare subsistence from the soil. Experience with the new miracle grains in Asia showed that the only farmers who were willing to adopt the new methods and seeds were those who were already wealthy and could afford to risk a bad crop. Those who lived perpetually on the edge of starvation were unwilling to risk any departure from the prevailing norms.

Traditional peoples in the Third World also lack what the nineteenth-century, French social observer Alexis de Tocqueville called the "art of associating together"; by this he meant the ability of people to join together in common enterprises. In traditional parts of the world, we find many people unwilling to join with others, especially if the others are not of their kin group or ethnic circle. After all, where everyone lives so close to the margin of survival, there is little reason to trust one another, especially in the context of a formal institution such as political party. In modern institutions, trust is derived from formal, impersonal features like laws, rights, obligations, and constitutional provisions. In traditional institutions, trust derives from personal familiarity, thereby limiting sharply the number of people who will meet the requirements of mutual trust in any consensus-based political organization.

Finally, and perhaps most important, reform governments in the Third World frequently fail to construct modernizing institutions in traditional areas because, in each case, some powerful traditional political force is present to resist such institutionalization. These traditional forces may be religious (priests, witch doctors, shamans), political (village chiefs), or economic (large landowners, peasants). Whatever the source of their power, these individuals resist modernizing institutions because they understand clearly that the introduction of these institutions into their community will undermine their power, their privileges (where they have them), and their accustomed way of life. Not surprisingly, they will fight back with the tools and weapons at their disposal, such as money, graft, bribes, rural insurgencies, refusal to implement the law, and voo doo and other ritualistic devices. And in most places in the Third World where this confrontation is taking place, the forces of tradition are winning, or at least holding their own.

As a consequence, mass local politics in the Third World has fallen under the control of numerous patron-client systems, or what John Duncan Powell calls "clientelist politics."[16] These patron-client relationships stand midway between the tribal chieftancies of the traditional, pre-colonial era, on the one hand,

---

[15] David Lehmann, "Agrarian Reform in Chile, 1965–1972: An Essay in Contradictions," in David Lehmann, ed., *Peasants, Landlords and Governments: Agrarian Reform in the Third World* (New York: Holmes and Meier, 1974), p. 109.

[16] John D. Powell, "Peasant Society and Clientelistic Politics," *American Political Science Review LXIV* (2) (June 1970), pp. 411–426.

and the modern, bureaucratic, rule-oriented authority relationships of urban, industrial politics. The patrons in question may be people of immense power, such as large landowners and priests; or they may be persons of modest influence, such as money lenders, ward bosses, and other kinds of intermediaries. Their clients may be poor, illiterate peasants, small shopkeepers, or even urban workers. But, however they are constructed and wherever they are, patron-client political systems are extremely important to Third World politics for several reasons: (1) they constitute the primary (and, often, the sole) channel for rural and urban poor to be involved in political activity; (2) they have great influence over the ways in which public policies are implemented at the local level; and (3) they are (or can be) valuable sources of information for modernizing élites who are attempting to formulate a policy to solve some recurrent problem. In the terms of this chapter, however, patron-client politics is most significant because of what it says about the failure of Third World élites to construct modernizing institutions to guide the newly mobilized citizen into productive and constructive political participation.

CONCLUSIONS: POLITICAL PARTICIPATION AND HUMAN DIGNITY

Mass populations in the Third World are not the inert and helpless "lumps of clay" as they are often depicted in Western literature. In some ways, citizens participate in politics to as great a degree as they do in modern, industrialized nations; in a few instances, they may even participate more than their Western counterparts. Yet this increased political participation does not translate evenly into public policies that are aimed at enhancing human dignity. It is almost as if there were a short circuit in the connection between mass participation and public policy in many developing countries.

In this chapter, we have identified the causes of this break in the link between participation and policy. The mass media were seen as an insufficient mobilizing agent because they fail to involve the citizen in an active role in the political process. The various institutions of political participation—parties, associational interest groups, and the like— exist only in fragmentary form and are often coöpted by the very government that they exist to influence. Even well-meaning reformist bureaucrats have difficulty in constructing the institutions of mass participation, for cultural and economic reasons that we presented earlier.

In the absence of these other channels for involvement, Third World citizens are mobilized (if that is the correct word in this case) by patron-client systems, or they are provoked by their frustration into unstructured violence. The aggressive features of political life in developing countries have been fully documented; they seem to stem from the unsettling experiences of change unrelieved by any opportunity for the citizen to intervene in the process of modernization. The patron-client system exists not to influence policy but, instead, to confer on a selected powerful few the privileges of an élitist society while maintaining the rhetoric of liberal democracy.

In sum, mass participation in Third World politics frequently fails to elicit progressive public policies, because there are few institutions whose purpose it is to transmit popular needs and demands and to link together the masses of the village and the slum with the national élites in the capital city.

Suggestions for Further Reading

Alba, Victor, *Politics and the Labor Movement in Latin America* (Stanford, Calif.: Stanford, 1968).

Davies, Ioan, *African Trade Unions* (London: Penguin, 1966).

Feierabend, Ivo K., Rosalind L. Feierabend, and Ted Robert Gurr, eds., *Anger, Violence and Politics: Theories and Research* (Englewood Cliffs, N.J.: Prentice-Hall, 1972).

Galenson, Walter, ed., *Labor in Developing Countries* (Berkeley: California, 1962).

Hodgkin, Thomas, *African Political Parties* (London: Penguin, 1961).

Huntington, Samuel P., *Political Order in Changing Societies* (New Haven, Conn.: Yale 1968).

———, **and Joan M. Nelson,** *No Easy Choice: Political Participation in Developing Countries* (Cambridge, Mass.: Harvard, 1976).

LaPalombara, Joseph, and Myron Weiner, eds., *Political Parties and Political Development* (Princeton, N.J.: Princeton, 1966).

Leiden, Carl, and Karl M. Schmitt, *The Politics of Violence: Revolution in the Modern World* (Englewood Cliffs, N.J.: Prentice-Hall, 1968).

McKenzie, William J. M., and Kenneth Robinson, eds., *Five Elections in Africa* (Oxford: Clarendon, 1960).

Millen, Bruce H., *The Political Role of Labor in the Developing Countries* (Washington, D.C.: Brookings, 1963).

Smith, T. E., *Elections in Developing Countries* (London: Macmillan, 1960).

Vega, Luis Mercier, *Guerrillas in Latin America: The Technique of the Counter-State* (New York: Praeger, 1969).

Weiner, Myron, *Party Politics in India: The Development of a Multi-Party System* (Princeton, N.J.: Princeton, 1957).

CHAPTER FIVE

Governmental Structures in the Third World

The historical, psychological, social, cultural, and economic features of a society provide the setting within which official governmental structures must operate. We have already seen the ways in which the setting of politics influences policies designed to increase human dignity. It is now time to examine some of the typical political institutions likely to be found in the Third World. We are concerned with uncovering links between kinds of formal institutions and levels of human dignity in a given country and across the Third World. Or, to put it another way, are the governmental structures that are typical of the Third World capable of undertaking policies that vigorously enhance human dignity in their societies? If not, how can we identify and explain major flaws in the political structures of developing countries?

POLITICAL IMPLICATIONS OF DELAYED INDUSTRIALIZATION

The majority of countries in the Third World possess what some scholars have called "regimes of delayed industrialization."[1] This

means that these countries typically began their industrialization process considerably after the nations of Western Europe and North America. The reasons for this delay, and its consequences, are central to an understanding of the prevailing Third World governmental structures.

Industrialization as a social process is never cheap. In fact, where the process has more or less run its course, the costs are seen to have been extremely high. While the costs of industrialization are always high, regimes vary widely along other important dimensions of the industrialization process, for example, which social classes will pay the costs, which will receive the benefits, and how rapidly the overall process will be carried out. The process of industrial growth seems to require a good deal of social coercion, but whether or not it explodes into revolutionary violence or class warfare depends on how a polity answers these questions.

The high costs of industrialization stem directly from the massive shifts in human values, attitudes, resources, and behavioral propensities that accompany the change from a preindustrial to an industrial society.[2] Income must be transferred from those who spend unproductively (on luxuries), to those

---

[1] Mary Matossian, "Ideologies of Delayed Industrialization: Some Tensions and Ambiguities," *Economic Development and Cultural Change VI* (3) (April 1958), pp. 217–228. This important article has been reprinted in several places, including Claude E. Welch, Jr., ed., *Political Modernization* (Belmont, Calif.: Wadsworth, 1967), pp. 332–334.

[2] Walt W. Rostow, *The Stages of Economic Growth* (Cambridge, England: Cambridge, 1960).

who will spend productively (on capital equipment). Current consumption must be held down in favor of future investment. Unproductive agrarian classes (peasants, mostly) must be encouraged or forced to leave their land and move to the cities, where they form the large pool of potential laborers.[3] The commercialization of agriculture and the shift of agrarian resources into food and away from export crops make possible the growing of enough food to maintain the urban working classes in a state of health and vigor adequate to make them productive workers. To cite Barrington Moore, the policy challenge of industrialization amounts "... to using a combination of economic incentives and political compulsion to induce the people on the land to improve productivity and at the same time taking a substantial part of the surplus so generated to construct an industrial society. Behind this problem there stands a political one, whether or not a class of people has arisen in the society with the capacity and ruthlessness to force through the changes."[4]

Nations that began their drive to industrialization relatively late must modernize under much more difficult conditions than the early industrial states like Great Britain or the United States. For the latecomers, internal social structures are not conducive to such far-reaching changes. Language, race, religion, class, and ethnic divisions present seemingly insurmountable obstacles to rapid development. Abroad, the special position enjoyed by the already-industrialized states blocks the developing countries from reaping the benefits of the international trade system. As traditional social structures and attitudes crumble under the strain of modernization, Westernized intellectuals agonize over some new kind of ideology that can guide their people toward a new brand of social cohesion. When industrialization is delayed, the tendency is for the process to take place in an atmosphere of intense feeling, hostility, passion, class and national prejudices, and little inclination to preserve the rights of the individual citizen.

Some late industrializers, including Russia, China, and Cuba, have chosen to deal with these obstacles by means of the model of development called (by political scientist A. F. K. Organski) the "Stalinist" alternative.[5] The stalinist regimes are characterized by the violent destruction of the premodern rural classes—both landed aristocracy and peasantry—and the accumulation of massive coercive power in the hands of an industrial élite. This élite uses its power to squeeze all possible surplus out of both the urban and the agrarian working classes, and to fuel the industrialization effort with this surplus. Peasants are driven from the land by collectivization, and the gentry by confiscation. Although the cost in terms of human suffering is high, the results of forced draft industrialization are impressive.

Most of the other late industrializers, including a majority of the countries of the Third World, have followed still another path to development. "Syncratic politics" is the term coined by Organski to describe this model, principally, it appears, to avoid using the more pejorative word "fascist." The chief characteristic of the syncratic model is how the government attempts to handle the inevitable conflict between the old landlord class and the rising industrialists. In liberal democracies, such as Great Britain, the conflict dissolved slowly as the agrarian sector modernized and became commercialized. In stalinist countries, the industrial élites smashed the antimodern classes, frequently using the peasants as shock troops against the landlords, only to dismantle the peasant class itself once the revolution was consolidated. In the syncratic model, however, agrarian interests were too powerful, or industrial sectors too weak, to permit either of these solutions. The result is a shaky compromise involving

[3] Barrington Moore, Jr., *Social Origins of Dictatorship and Democracy: Lord and Peasant in the Making of the Modern World* (Boston: Beacon, 1966).
[4] Moore, pp. 385-386.

[5] A. F. K. Organski, *The Stages of Political Development* (New York: Knopf, 1965).

completely different kinds of bargains, payoffs, and protective devices. In sum, syncratic politics refers to the style of governance that emerges in late industrializing countries when the agrarian class is too strong to be destroyed or converted by the industrial élite, and so must be brought into some sort of broad coalition to preserve the special premodern conditions of the countryside.

Although they are both members of their nation's economic élite, the landed aristocracy and the industrialists are actually divided from one another by a number of inescapable economic schisms. For one thing, agrarian and industrial élites frequently come from different regions of the country or are members of different ethnic, racial, linguistic, or religious groups. These noneconomic differences may aggravate emerging class distinctions. More important, the economic roles of the two classes are antithetical. Industrialists exist to save, invest, and produce; landlords exist to consume and to withhold resources from production. Urban élites value work and self-sacrifice; agrarian élites regard manual labor as demeaning. Industrialists need a large, mobile, well-educated, disciplined, and motivated work force, and will seek to lure farm workers into the cities to fill this need; landlords want to keep their peasant class docile, traditional, and poorly educated so that they will not wish to upset the clientelist system. The industrialists intend to squeeze the agricultural sector of its surplus production through taxation and to use the resources to advance the state's industrial base; the landlords quite naturally will try to resist being used in this manner.

In a few instances, the rural and industrial élites have managed to cover over their differences enough to cooperate in governing the country, usually through the mechanism of a semiparliamentary, authoritarian regime that, although strong, would still fall short of a military dictatorship. In most cases, however, economic crisis or foreign threat causes internal conditions to deteriorate; and, as the previously quiet lower classes clamor for change, the coalition loses its nerve and submits either to a syncratic party or to a military dictator who can impose order and establish the conditions necessary for industrialization to continue.

Once in power, a syncratic regime typically undertakes a set of reform measures designed to industrialize the country without disturbing the social structures of the countryside. Traditional territorial divisions, local peculiarities, and internal barriers to trade are suppressed, and strong central government agencies are put in charge of the nation's economic fortunes. The mass of citizens must be brought into the modern social order by means of the expansion of literacy and technical skills. Antimodern loyalties to region, clan, religion, or ethnic kin are over-ridden. Steps are taken to stimulate latent industrial potential. Government incentives, including protective tariffs, are used to aid native manufacturing. Where the private sector is unwilling or unable to invest in a needed project, the state itself will mobilize the needed capital. Since it appears that these early measures favor the industrial élite, a syncratic regime discovers it must now provide benefits to the other partner in the coalition. Agricultural élites are kept in the partnership through two types of policies. First, they are permitted a great deal of freedom to perpetuate their exploitation of the countryside, and the central government stands ready to suppress rural rebellion where it should occur. Second, by using the threat of revolution, the regime may convince the conservative, traditional élites that they have little choice but to side with the state in the struggle. Finally, industrial workers are kept under control by the enactment of increasingly liberal welfare measures and by the use of corporatist labor organizations that bind the urban proletariat into the very structure of the state economic system.

The special compromises struck by the syncratic state mean that the costs of industrial development are allocated much differently than in the liberal bourgeois or stalinist models. Since the landed upper classes are protected by the syncratic compromise, and their hold over the land is left unmolested, the surplus for reinvestment (forced savings) must come from some other source. Occasionally, these resources may be derived from foreign aid from one of the wealthy states in the international system, but this is a weak and insecure support on which to rest the industrialization policy. Eventually, the syncratic state must turn to the only remaining source of capital: the fledgling industrial sector itself. To cite Organski:

> Under a syncratic system, the savings for investment in industry are squeezed primarily out of the industrial sector itself, not gathered from the entire country. To a very large extent, the savings in the industrial sector are created by increases in productivity in the modern portion of the economy and by decreases in the living standard of the industrial proletariat.[6]

AYUB KHAN OF PAKISTAN: A SYNCRATIC REGIME

The 10½-year (1958 to 1969) military regime of Field Marshal Mohammed Ayub Khan of Pakistan offers a clear example of a syncratic regime in action.[7] The Ayub government took power in Pakistan in October 1958, following a period of prolonged instability, unrest, and violence under the former parliamentary system. The 1958 proclamation of martial law lasted for almost 4 years, until March 1962; Pakistan lived under martial law for 8 years between 1958 and 1971. During the period that Ayub was the chief executive of the country, Pakistanis had little access to open or free government; the executive branch of the government controlled all aspects of the country's political life. The 1962 constitution legitimatized one-man rule by placing all political functions—legislative, executive, and judicial—into the hands of Ayub.

[6] Organski, p. 139.
[7] Robert LaPorte, Jr., "Pakistan and Bangladesh," in Robert N. Kearney, ed., *Politics and Modernization in South and Southeast Asia* (New York: Wiley, 1975), pp. 122–135.

From 1958 to 1969, Pakistan's economy experienced a strong growth trend, with GNP rising at the average rate of 6 percent per year during the 1960s. A new business and industrialist class was fostered by government stimulus, but little was done for the urban proletariat or for the landless rural workers. An extremely small number of wealthy families continued to enjoy control of the growing industrial power of the nation, but income inequalities increased during Ayub's regime instead of diminishing.

The rhetorical dimension of Ayub's so-called "revolution" illustrates the syncratic governance style in action. In the case of land reform, the government responded to a critical problem by creating the Land Reform Commission in 1958. The Commission's report, issued in early 1959, contained only the mildest kind of recommendations for Ayub, but was still accepted by the President with minor changes. Few large landowners lost land, and few, if any, peasants received any. Apparently, Ayub was unwilling to risk losing support from the wealthy rural sector by imposing forced expropriation of agrarian lands. In other areas, such as equal rights for women, or education, far-reaching laws were passed, but little attention was paid to implementation or to the financial burdens of such legislation. The result was that a large set of unenforced (and probably unenforceable) laws developed that merely specified desirable goals, but left the question of how to reach them unanswered.

This gap between rhetoric and reality was not the product of ignorance or incompetence on the part of Ayub Khan and his colleagues; instead, it was the calculated effort on his part to build a governing coalition made up of both élites: the modernizing, urban-based, nationalists and the tradition-bound rural aristocracy. In the cities, Ayub not only sought to stimulate industrial development, but also turned government policy toward strengthening the army, both as a modernizing bureaucracy and as the ultimate arbiter of Pakistan's fate in any armed clashes. In the countryside, as we have seen, Ayub's rule was more notable for what it did not achieve than for what it did. The privileges of the landed élites were maintained and, perhaps, even strengthened.

Ayub was not without his opponents and, in the end, the disturbances caused by these opposition sectors unseated his government. The major forces against the regime were the disaffected intellectuals of the universities and the professions, religious leaders, the urban middle class, and the urban and rural workers. Toward the end of Ayub's regime, in 1968, these groups began to evidence their displeasures with the fact that they were being asked to carry more than their fair share of the development burden; the result was a series of street clashes between rioting workers and students and the army and police. By 1969, matters had worsened to the point that the army insisted that Ayub step down and allow a successor regime to try to restore order. Faced with these realities, Ayub resigned his office in March 1969 and appointed another general to take his place.

The syncratic political style is both a cause and a consequence of a social phenomenon we have noted before: the uneven penetration of modernization through various layers of a traditional society. On the one hand, uneven rates of modernization in a traditional society causes the rural élites to retain their stranglehold on the political system despite the progressive modernization of the industrial sector in the cities. At the same time, the syncratic state perpetuates this uneven penetration of modernity, simply because its very basis for existence is derived from reliance on two antithetical social groupings. For these reasons, the syncratic political style is an integral part of the central characteristic of Third World social, economic, and political systems today: their separation into dual societies, one modern, rational secular, urban, and nationalistic, and the other traditional, religious (or mystical), rural, and particularistic.

Binding together all of these features of Third World politics is a three-tier institu-tional arrangement that we can now consider in detail. At the top is what we will call (following Robert Gamer)[8] the major network. The major network consists of the power élite of the country, the national government ministries, the civil and military bureaucracy, and the industrial-entrepreneurial leaders. These individuals are almost always located in the nation's capital city, cut off from the vast majority of the country. The major network extracts political support, obedience, labor, and agricultural commodities from the general populace, with which they are linked by the second level of institutions, the many minor networks. The minor networks consist of the middle-echelon patrons, the leaders of patron-client systems both in the cities and in the countryside. These patrons receive personal rewards for their service that are adequate at least to maintain a satisfactory life-style. Below these minor networks the vast bulk of the population is found; it is usually unorganized and unrepresented in the power structure by any forces other than their patrons. The masses supply the national system with labor and with commodities, and they participate in the system more or less regularly by means of symbolic exercises like voting for similar candidates in rigged elections. The patrons maintain their clients in a state of commitment to the system by a variety of means that we will examine shortly.

MINOR NETWORKS: PATRON-CLIENT POLITICS

In the small remote Honduran village of Tocoa lives a very powerful man named Carlos Bascha. Mr. Bascha does not derive his power from any formal elective office, his ownership of large areas of land, or any special religious or ethnic status. Mr. Bascha is, instead, simply the freight agent for the Honduran national airline that operates (irregularly) a DC-3 flight into Tocoa; the flight

[8] Robert E. Gamer, *The Developing Nations: A Comparative Perspective* (Boston: Allyn and Bacon, 1976), Chapter 4.

links the town to the outside world. Tocoa was at one time situated on a rail line laid by the United Fruit Company many years ago. With the onset of a blight, the land in the vicinity was rendered useless for growing bananas, so the company took up the line, leaving Tocoa almost completely isolated from the rest of Honduras. All commercial activity, such as the movement of locally cultivated agricultural produce, depends on the air service provided by the government. Since Mr. Bascha controls that service, he rather completely controls the town. Preferential freight rates tie certain town influentials to his goodwill, and Bascha's general store (the only one in town) is allowed to dominate the village's local commerce. Mr. Bascha is, in our terms, a patron; the population of Tocoa is his clients.

In remote villages of Burma, Manning Nash reports, the patron may or may not be the elected village headman. In some cases, such as in the village of Nonwin, another man, more powerful than the headman, may be regarded as the local patron. In Nonwin, this local power, named U Sein Ko, was not only the richest man in the village, but the person everyone had to check with in case of any dispute or political question. His power derived from the almost mystical aura of *pon*, the Burmese concept of control, which implies one's possession of the ability to make others conform to his wishes. U Sein Ko had this ability, and no one else in the village did. Therefore the village population clustered around him to bask in the warmth of his power and to receive protection from it.[9]

Patron-client systems are very important features of urban politics in Third World countries as well. In large cities throughout the Third World, such as Lima or Caracas, the festering slums and improvised neighborhoods have produced squatters' associations to protect the land rights of the residents. These usually come under the jurisdiction or control of local patrons who defend the

interests of their clients and receive deference and respect (as well as more material rewards) from them in return. Several observers of the work of political parties in African cities have likened them to the big-city machines in the United States and other Western countries, especially as they operated before World War II. In Africa, these political machines rarely operate on the basis of ideology or political theory, but more often win their support as patrons win support from clients: by using an intricate mixture of coercion, prestige, material benefits ("spoils"), bribes, cajolery, and ceremony.[10] Other modern interest groups, such as labor unions, often find themselves infiltrated by tribal-based patron-client systems that use tribal, ethnic, and linguistic cleavages to fragment the unions and render them helpless. The presence of traditional patron-client relationships within their organizations explains the weakness of the otherwise powerful copper miners' union in Zambia or the rubber workers' union in Malaysia.[11]

Latin American specialist John Duncan Powell has observed that the patron-client system is marked by three characteristics: first, the tie between patron and client develops between two parties who are unequal in status, wealth, and influence; second, the formation and maintenance of the relationship depends on the reciprocal exchange of goods or services; and third, the development and maintenance of the system depends largely on face-to-face contact between the patron and his or her client(s).[12] In his study of Thailand, Clark Neher writes that

[9] Manning Nash, *The Golden Road to Modernity: Village Life in Contemporary Burma* (Chicago: Chicago, 1965), pp. 73-93.

[10] Henry Bienen, "Political Parties and Political Machines in Africa," in Michael F. Lofchie, ed., *The State of the Nations: Constraints on Development in Independent Africa* (Berkeley, Calif.: California, 1971), Chapter 8.
[11] Henry L. Bretton, *Power and Politics in Africa* (Chicago: Aldine, 1973), p. 258. See also Gordon P. Means, "Malaysia," in Kearney, p. 202.
[12] John Duncan Powell, "Peasant Society and Clientelistic Politics," *American Political Science Review LXIV* (2) (June 1970), pp. 411-425. See also Rene Lemarchand, "Political Clientelism and Ethnicity in Tropical Africa: Competing Solidarities in Nation-Building," *American Political Science Review LXVI* (1) (March 1972), pp. 68-90.

The ideal superior acts as a patron and is expected to protect, aid, complement, and give generously to those whose status is inferior. In return, the subordinate, or client, is expected to act deferentially to the superior, who is his patron. He is expected to perform tasks efficiently and with the least amount of trouble for his superior. The subordinate maintains his inferior position by not challenging the superior or undermining the latter's position.[13]

Patron-client relationships can be classified according to the kinds of values that pass in exchange. Those that are of greatest relevance to the political order involve power, trust, and loyalty. The clients of such a system support their patrons' choices for public office: in return they receive government services and personal security.

Patron-client systems are crucial to developing countries as links between the national, urban-based modernizing elites, on the one hand, and the mass of urban and rural laborers, on the other. Most patron-client systems can be viewed as existing at two levels. At the lowest level, in the rural village or the big-city neighborhood, clientelistic politics involves a relationship between large numbers of low-status persons and a single powerful patron, who defends the interests of his clients and who receives deference or more material rewards in return. This patron, however, is also a member of another, higher-level patron-client system, but this time as a client to a member of the national, urban élite. The intermediary depends on an élite patron to deliver special treatment to his or her clients, but the intermediary also provides valuable services to the urban élites, particularly by mobilizing the low-status clients for mass manifestations of loyalty to the regime, such as demonstrations and elections. Patron-client systems at the village or neighborhood level are institutions that lean backward toward tradition instead of forward toward modernity. At the lowest level of operation,

patron-client systems usually do not contribute to the modernization of the nation-state but, instead, detract from this process. In the case of patron-client links that tie intermediaries to national élites, however, the resources and values that are exchanged come closer to characterizing what we think of as modern politics: money, power, and all of the symbolic and tangible manifestations of these (votes, land, and so on).

Because of this dual nature, patron-client political systems can be regarded either favorably or unfavorably for their impact on the overall process of political development. Some observers, such as Robert Gamer, are quite critical of clientelistic politics; as they see it, such political processes always work a hardship on the mass of clients at the very bottom of the pyramid. According to this view, patron-client systems owe their origin to the uneven penetration of modernity through the several layers of a traditional social order. The modern nation-state has enough power and organizational ability to reach down into the traditional sectors to manipulate the masses and to mobilize them to perform the symbolic functions of politics, such as voting; but the two-way institutions that are truly indicative of modern politics—political parties and associational interest groups—are simply lacking in most Third World countries. In the absence of parties and interest groups, patrons are brought to the fore to facilitate communication (mostly of a top-down nature) between élites and masses. In the course of this communication process, however, the intermediaries extract their due (and more) from the exchange, and the minor networks end up receiving much less in terms of material well-being than they should. Accordingly, only the creation of truly modern, mass-based institutions such as political parties can do away with the exploitative patron-client systems and extend modernity all the way down to the very lowest level of society.

Another way of looking at the question, however, as exemplified by John Powell, holds that, at the middle-level of operation, patron-

[13] Clark D. Neher, "Thailand," in Kearney, p. 228.

client systems offer the potential for being transformed into modernizing institutions. Powell cites as an example the various peasant leagues that were created by the Venezuelan reformist political parties, primarily Accion Democratica. These leagues were not, at the outset, what we would regard as modern institutions. They were still operating on the basis of patron-client principles: unequal status; exchange of goods and services; obedience and deference; loyalty and security; face-to-face communications system; and so forth. Yet, by virtue of their reliance on these leagues for the mobilization of the peasants as potential voters, and as a consequence of their use of a vigorous land reform program in an attempt to attract peasant voters to their standard, the leaders of Accion Democratica transformed the clientelistic peasant leagues into modernizing institutions capable of linking the peasant (and, subsequently, the middle-class farmer) into the national political system in a way that meets the needs of the low-status members of the network.

The Venezuelan experience, although not unique, is certainly the exception rather than the rule. In the majority of Third World cases, low-status persons, whether in the city or in the countryside, simply have no other way to communicate with their government other than through their local patron. Transporation and communication gaps cause rigidity in the links between the government and its people; the absence of mass-based, modernizing institutions such as parties and interest groups likewise contributes to blocking effective communication. For good or ill, in most developing countries, patron-client systems, the minor networks of Robert Gamer, are almost the only indication that the nation and the mass of citizens are connected.

MAJOR NETWORKS: THE DOMINANT EXECUTIVE

The cornerstone of the American system of government is symbolized by the phrase "separation of powers." During the Republic's formative years, the new American colonial elite was so eager to prevent government from abusing the rights of the citizens that they devised a simple formula for keeping the central government weak: divide power and authority into so many hostile and competing institutions that the constant struggle between and among these agencies will occupy their attention and drain their resources so that there will be little of either left over to direct toward the average citizen in private life. John Taylor, a noted liberal writer of the period, expressed the thought this way.

> . . . Power is divided by our policy, that the people may maintain their sovereignty; . . . Our principle of division is used to reduce power to that degree of temperature, which may make it a blessing and not a curse . . . We do not balance power against power. It is our policy to reduce it by division, in order to preserve the political power of the people, . . .[14]

But it fell to James Madison, the principal author of the Constitution, to give us the classic argument in favor of separation of powers, which is contained in *The Federalist*, Number 51.

> But the great security against a gradual concentration of . . . powers in the same department consists in giving to those who administer each department the necessary constitutional means and personal motives to resist encroachments of others. . . . Ambition must be made to counteract ambition. The interest of the man must be connected with the constitutional rights of the place. . . . If men were angels, no government would be necessary. If angels were to govern man, neither external nor internal controls on government would be necessary. In framing a government which is to be administered by men over men, the great difficulty lies in this: you must first enable the government to control the

[14] John Taylor, *Inquiry into the Principles and Policy of the Government of the United States* (New Haven, Conn.: Yale, 1950), pp. 356, 171. Cited in John C. Livingstone and Robert G. Thompson, *The Consent of the Governed*, 3rd ed. (New York: Macmillan, 1971), p. 163.

governed; and in the next place oblige it to control itself. A dependence on the people is, no doubt, the primary control on the government; but experience has taught mankind the necessity of auxiliary precautions.[15]

Indeed, much of American political history can be regarded as a struggle between and among Madison's "auxiliary precautions": the various states against the national government, the legislature against the President, the courts against each of the others, and so on.

Because the principle of separation of powers is so deeply embedded in the American political system, it may seem strange to note that few other countries in the world share our aversion toward centralizing power in the hands of a single institution or person. Among the Third World countries, almost none of them have political institutions and constitutional structures that were inspired by a desire to divide powers among several competing agencies or sources of authority. In Latin America, for example, the Spanish and Portuguese tradition of centralized power in a monarchy was transmitted to the New World in undiluted form; there it was amalgamated with the indigenous political systems, which were similarly inclined toward centralization of power.[16] In Africa and Asia, the native, precolonial political systems were usually of the centralized and unified type; the introduction of European power did nothing to alter this inclination. The practice of direct rule employed by France, Holland, and other continental colonial powers lodged power in the mother country; British indirect rule merely confirmed authority in the local rulers (tribal chieftains, village headmen, and so on) who had been the beneficiaries of centralized power for centuries. Thus, the countries of the Third World came to independence and began

their drive to development with little in the way of historical preparation for, or appreciation of the benefits of, governance by means of separation of powers.

At the same time, Third World leaders confronted problems quite different from those faced by Washington, Madison, Hamilton, and Jefferson. Where the new country of America came into being determined to free the individual from government interference and, thus, to reduce government power, the new states of the Third World find that they must *increase* government power in order to meet the critical problems created by the dual processes of industrialization and modernization. Instead of limiting government's power, what the élites of the Third World want to do is break the substantial constraints on their power so that they might better cope with the social and economic difficulties of which America's founding élite could not have been even dimly conscious.

Finally, in the industrialized West, we have a tendency to look at government not as a party to a given dispute, but as the reconciler of conflicting interests, the ultimate recourse for the resolution of conflict. This view depends, however, on the prior existence of a rich and accessible network of modern institutions that are essentially outside government: political parties, interest groups, and many different kinds of voluntary associations, such as the Rotary or the Kiwanis. These institutions are notably lacking in most Third World countries. Voluntary associations are almost completely unknown in many developing countries; where they do exist, they are weakened by the traditional mistrust with which such associations are viewed by low-status individuals in poor countries. Parties and interest groups are frequently controlled by the government itself, and they are used not to channel messages upward from the populace, but to channel commands and rhetoric downward from the regime. In this context, government becomes more than a reconciler of interests; it becomes a party to the dispute. Consequently, there is great pressure

[15] Alexander Hamilton, John Jay and James Madison, *The Federalist* (New York: Modern Library, 1937), p. 337.
[16] Claudio Veliz, "Centralism and Nationalism in Latin America," *Foreign Affairs*, 47 (1) (October 1968), pp. 69–83.

on the government to adopt a unified position, to employ decision-making techniques that accelerate action and suppress dissent. The result is an inclination to over-ride whatever institutional separation of powers there might have been to begin with.

The notion of separation of powers actually has two different meanings. The first meaning has to do with the separation of powers within the policy-making body of government. Regardless of the form of government may take, there are three more or less distinct functions that must be performed in the course of the policy process: legislation (the adoption of general principles and statement of general goals); execution (the translation of these principles and goals into politically acceptable actions); and adjudication (the judgment of the fairness of the application of the general principle in specific cases where a party is thought to be damaged). In the United States, we like to think of these three functions as being assigned primarily to the three corresponding institutions: the Congress, the President, and the Supreme Court. (In reality, the dividing lines are much fuzzier in practice than they are in theory). But, in the Third World, they tend to be performed by the same institution or, in some extreme cases, by the same individual. That phenomenon we call the principle of *executive dominance*; in the struggle among and between competing institutions of government, in the developing world it is the executive power that has won.

Let us consider some concrete manifestations of the executive dominant system in the Third World. Most observers of politics regard an independent legislature or parliament as the surest check on the power of the executive. A survey of the 112 Third World nations in 1976 reveals that in 46, or more than 40 percent, the legislative branch has been summarily dismissed, dissolved, or suspended indefinitely. In many others, the legislature consists solely or largely of persons appointed by the President or military ruler. In instances where the legislature is freely elected, it usually has such little real power that it is reduced to the task of ratifying the decisions made by the executive power.

Another indicator of executive dominance is the degree to which incumbents manipulate or suspend the constitution, or engage in other electoral irregularities, in order to remain in power beyond the end of their legally prescribed term of office. In 1976, at least 43 Third World countries were operating either without any constitution, or with their basic law suspended or bypassed by the executive. And 48 percent of the countries (54) have experienced significant electoral irregularities, or even no elections at all in a few cases, during the period from 1960 to 1976.

Not all examples of executive dominance are extralegal or unconstitutional. Many Third World executives enjoy extraordinary powers as a consequence of a constitutional grant of authority. The 1962 Republic of Tanganyika Act provides that "except as may otherwise be provided by law, in the exercise of his functions, the President shall act at his own discretion and shall not be obliged to follow advice tendered by any other person." Following this broad grant of authority, President Julius Nyerere has acted unilaterally to end discrimination against non-Africans in the civil service; unite Tanganyika with Zanzibar (creating Tanzania); introduce a one-party state, making the Tanzania African National Union the sole legal party in the country; break diplomatic relations with Britain in 1965; and create completely new agencies, such as the Village Resettlement Agency (1963), where a conventional bureaucracy could not accomplish goals set for them.[17] Other Third World executives enjoy similar powers. The President of Brazil can (constitutionally) appoint state governors and the mayors of municipalities, remove from citizens their right to participate in politics, and dissolve the Congress if it disagrees with his decisions.

The Prime Minister of Singapore has im-

[17] R. Cranford Pratt, "The Cabinet and Presidential Leadership in Tanzania: 1960-1966," in Lofchie, pp. 96, 112, 116.

posed one-party rule, jailed political opponents and held them for years without trial, closed down newspapers, and otherwise suppressed public dissent, and all within the boundaries of the constitution.

Executive dominance is also reflected in the relatively high degree of administrative centralization that exists in most Third World countries. Not only does the nation's chief executive dominate legislative and judicial colleagues at the national level, but the concentration of administrative power in the hands of the national government means that he also dominates local, provincial, or municipal governments.

In his excellent analysis of local administration in Thailand,[18] Clark D. Neher has identified three separate but closely interrelated patterns of authority that apply to local populations in that country. The territorial or provincial administration, which receives its power and resources from the central government in Bangkok, is the most powerful of the three systems. Briefly, this administrative system consists of the Minister of Interior, 71 provincial governors, and 530 district officers. The Minister of Interior appoints, removes, and transfers both the provincial governors and the district officers; these subordinate officials are, consequently, responsible to the Interior Minister in all that they do. All major decisions are referred to the Minister for his personal attention. The provincial governors are powerful only in a sort of derivative sense, meaning that they have no resources themselves, but derive power from carrying out central government decrees. District officers' authority seems to be restricted primarily to the supervision of the Ministry's local employees and to the filling out and submission of an almost endless number of forms and reports. The second pattern of authority consists of some 50,000 villages that, in turn, are clustered into about 5000 communes for some limited purposes of self-government. Each village elects a headman who, as we saw

in the example drawn from Burma earlier, may have considerable social and economic power in addition to his formal political authority. But the actual powers of the village and commune are restricted to making arrests in criminal cases, settling petty disputes and quarrels, submitting reports and information to higher authorities, and deciding how to spend the meager sums distributed to the villages from the central government. The third pattern of authority, called local self-government units, is the weakest system of the three. It consists of provincial councils, municipal councils, and sanitation districts. The first two bodies are purely deliberative institutions; all substantive policy decisions remain in the hands of the central government. Sanitation districts are charged with responsibilities in fields such as garbage collection, street paving, street and house lighting, slaughterhouse regulation, water and sewage facilities, and health centers. These units are notoriously inefficient and lack adequate funds for their many operations.

Most local authority in Third World countries lies effectively in the hands of the national governments, primarily in the various ministries of interior and their subordinate units. In instances where local units actually have authority, however, a serious lack of resources prevents them from taking advantage of this constitutional delegation of power. Henry Bretton reports that local self-government in many African countries is hampered by a lack of locally obtained and locally expended funds.[19] Local governments either do not have the authority to collect their own taxes or, if they do have such authority, they lack the trained personnel to apply the authority efficiently. In addition, where power resides so solidly in the national government and local governments lack the financial resources to cope with local problems, the obvious strategy for patron-client systems is to bypass the local administrators and go straight to the pertinent ministry in the capital. Such a

[18] Neher, pp. 233–237.

[19] Bretton, pp. 141–145.

In 1973, Chile's armed forces, traditionally reluctant to intervene in politics, overthrew the elected government of Marxist Salvador Allende and established a military dictatorship. Since that time, outside observers and the supporters of democratic government in Chile, have been concerned about the deterioration of the state of human rights in that country. Apparently, the armed forces of many Third World countries are not willing to sit by idly while constitutional regimes search for ways out of mounting economic problems.

development further weakens local government and strengthens the central administration's ties over local patrons in a vicious circle of progressive local debilitation. This sort of circumstance seems to be a significant reason why state governors and municipal mayors in Mexico are bypassed by local patrons and interest group leaders, who feel that the only place their problem can be handled is in Mexico City.

MAJOR NETWORKS: THE MILITARY BUREAUCRACY

As noted earlier, one meaning of separation of powers involves the division of the legislative, executive, and judicial functions of the policy-making process among three separate institutions. The second meaning involves separating the institutions that make policy from those that implement it: the civil and military bureaucrats that put the political decisions into effect. It is usually assumed by observers of Western democracy that the individuals who administer or implement policy must be separated from those who make policy because of the need to identify clearly the lines of political responsibility. At least in theory, those who make policy are somehow to be more or less directly responsible to the electorate, who can judge the policies and change them if they desire, simply by electing a different group of policy-makers. Bureaucrats, on the other hand, are invulnerable to voter pressure, so they are not supposed actually to make policy but, instead, should simply apply the decisions of the political officials in successive specific cases. To the degree that bureaucrats, either civil or military, stray across the line from policy implementation to policy making, they are acting in an antidemocratic fashion, because they are putting into effect policy decisions over which the sovereign public has no control.[20]

Problems connected with the operations of the civil bureaucracy in the Third World (corruption, lack of training, clientelism) will be discussed in Chapter 6. In this section, we concentrate on the intervention of the armed forces into the policy-making process in the developing world.

It is true that, on occasion, some democratic governments in the Third World have welcomed military intervention in politics in order to restore order to political life. Yet, in the larger sense, military intervention in civilian politics constitutes a major barrier to Third World political development. Military intervention in politics has been a major problem of Latin American governments ever since the nineteenth century. During the 36-year period from 1930 to 1965, there were 106 illegal and unscheduled changes in the head of state in Latin America; all but a tiny portion of these changes were initiated and carried out by the military, although frequently with civilian support and encouragement. There were many observers, however, who believed that the nations of Africa and Asia that became independent after World War II would be spared this dismal history and would demonstrate that civilian constitutional regimes could meet the severe problems of development in a stable and responsive manner, without succumbing to military rule. Such hopes have been destroyed by military coups in most of the countries in Africa, the Middle East, and Asia and by continued military rule in 41 of them (nearly 48 percent of the total). Table 5.1 indicates the extent of military intervention throughout the Third World. These data show that a coup or attempted coup occurred once every 4 months in Latin America

(from 1945 to 1972), once every 7 months in Asia (1947 to 1972), once every 3 months in the Middle East (1949 to 1972), and once every 55 days in Africa (1960 to 1972)!

The degree of military rule in effect in the Third World today attests to the instability and ineffectivenss of civilian regimes since World War II. As Tables 5.2, 5.3, and 5.4 indicate, military rule is spread evenly and thickly across all four regions of the Third World. In Table 5.2, we see that in 33 nations, officers of the armed forces actually occupy the position of chief executive, usually without leaving active military service. Africa and Latin America are the two regions most susceptible to this sort of institutional decay, but it is not unknown in the Middle East or Asia, either. In Table 5.3, we see that an additional 24 countries have military establishments that, although not actually occupying the seat of power, exercise substantial influence in areas besides those traditionally assigned to the armed forces. In many of these countries, such as Jordan, the nonmilitary rulers must assume that a military coup attempt is being plotted virtually constantly; all of these nations' leaders are fully aware that any deterioration in public order or the financial status of the nation could bring the military into control. In some states, such as Burma, Indonesia, Egypt, and Guatemala, the incumbent regime is headed by a former military commander who rose to power at the head of a coup, then resigned his military status to be elected more or less democratically to be the chief executive of a newly established constitutional order. These two categories of military rule together account for 57 nations in the Third World, or about 51 percent. The percentage of Latin American states in these categories is 61 percent; the percentage of states in the Middle East is 53 percent; in Africa, 52 percent; and in Asia, 35 percent.

One can learn almost as much about Third World politics by studying countries in which the military is not dominant; for this, we can turn to Table 5.4. We can see that 47 Third

[20] Fred W. Riggs, "Bureaucrats and Political Development: A Paradoxical View," in Joseph LaPalombara, ed., *Bureaucracy and Political Development* (Princeton, N.J.: Princeton, 1967), Chapter 5.

TABLE 5.1
Military Coups in the Third World for Selected Periods, 1945–1972

	Successful	Unsuccessful	Total
Latin America (1945–1972)	53	28	81
Asia (1947–1972)	21	21	42
Middle East (1949–1972)	41	42	83
Africa (1960–1972)	32	46	78
Total	147	137	284

Source: Gavin Kennedy, *The Military in The Third World* (New York: Scribner's, 1974), Appendix A.

TABLE 5.2
Third World Nations in Which Armed Forces Occupy Executive Position, circa 1976 ($N = 34$)

Latin America (9)	Middle East (4)	Africa (18)	Asia (3)
Argentina	Algeria	Benin	Afghanistan
Bolivia	Iraq	Burundi	Bangladesh
Brazil	Libya	Central African	Thailand
Chile	Yemen Arab	Republic	
Ecuador	Republic	Chad	
Haiti		Congo Republic	
Honduras		Equatorial	
Panama		Guinea	
Peru		Ethiopia	
		Ghana	
		Madagascar	
		Mali	
		Niger	
		Nigeria	
		Rwanda	
		Somalia	
		Sudan	
		Togo	
		Uganda	
		Upper Volta	

TABLE 5.3
Third World Nations in Which Armed Forces Occupy Position of High Influence, circa 1976 ($N = 23$)

Latin America (7)	Middle East (6)	Africa (5)	Asia (5)
Colombia	Egypt	Cameroon	Burma
Dominican	Jordan	Gabon	Indonesia
Republic	Morocco	Lesotho	South Korea
El Salvador	Oman	Sierra Leone	Pakistan
Guatemala	Syria	Zaire	Philippines
Nicaragua	Turkey		
Paraguay			
Uruguay			

TABLE 5.4
Third World Nations in Which Armed Forces Occupy Position of Low Influence, circa 1976 ($N = 47$)

	Latin America (10)	Mid. East (8)	Africa (15)	Asia (14)
1973 population less than 2 million ($N = 26$)	Bahamas	Bahrain[a]	Botswana	Bhutan[a]
	Barbados	Kuwait[a]	Gambia	Brunei[a]
	Costa Rica	Qatar[a]	Liberia	Fiji
	Grenada	United Arab	Mauritania	Maldives
	Guyana	Emirates	Mauritius[a]	Nauru[a]
	Jamaica	Peoples	Swaziland[a]	Tonga[a]
	Surinam	Democratic		West Samoa[a]
	Trinidad and	Republic		
	Tobago	of Yemen		
1973 population more than 2 million ($N = 21$)	Mexico	Iran[a]	Guinea	India
	Venezuela	Saudi Arabia[a]	Ivory Coast	Malaysia
				Nepal[a]
		Tunisia	Kenya	Papua New
			Malawi	Guinea
			Rhodesia	Singapore
			Senegal	Sri Lanka
			South Africa	Taiwan
			Tanzania	
			Zambia	

[a] Indicates traditional monarchy ($N = 12$).

World states have so far managed to escape military rule or, as in the cases of Mexico and Venezuela, have actually produced civilian regimes that have defeated military insurgents. Of these 47 countries, however, 26 are quite small (population of less than 2 million in 1973) and consist largely of former British island colonies (Bahamas, Trinidad and Tobago, Jamaica), and very underdeveloped traditional monarchies (Swaziland, Tonga, Bhutan). Of the 21 states that have a population of more than 2 million in 1973, and that have also escaped military rule, three (Iran, Saudi Arabia, and Nepal) are autocratic, traditional monarchies, two are the white minority regimes of Rhodesia and South Africa, and most of the remainder have illiberal civilian regimes that have achieved a poor record in the field of human rights. (See Chapter 7.) Thus, of the entire range of 112 Third World nations, only a comparative handful (Mexico, Venezuela, Sri Lanka, Tanzania, Kenya, and Tunisia) can be said to have faced successfully the challenges of governing a large, rapidly developing country under a more or less open and constitutional process and, at the same time, have managed to avoid giving the military a reason and an opportunity to intervene.[21]

A brief review of the massive literature on the role of the military in Third World politics reveals that the following points have been advanced to explain the intervention of a nation's armed forces into politics.[22]

1. A sharp decline in the prestige of the government, or of the ruling political party, causing the regime to use increasing amounts of physical coercion to maintain order and to stress the imperative of national unity in the face of crisis, leading consequently to a suppression of dissent.

2. Schisms between or among political leaders, causing military commanders to doubt the continued ability of the civilian regime to govern effectively.

3. A low probability of external intervention by a major world power or by neighboring states in the event of a coup.

4. "Contagion" from military coups in neighboring countries.

5. Domestic social antagonisms, most obviously occurring in countries governed by a minority group (Ibos in Nigeria, Arabs in Zanzibar).

6. Economic crises, leading to "austerity" policies affecting the organized, urban sectors of society (labor unions, civil servants).

7. Corruption and inefficiency among governmental and party officials, or a belief that civilian officials are on the verge of "selling out" the nation to some foreign group (Peru, against Belaunde; Chile, against Allende).

8. A highly rigid class structure that makes military service the only possible avenue for a poor boy to move from low to high status.

9. A growing belief among the military that they are the only social class with enough discipline and enough commitment to modernization to move the country out of its traditional ways.

10. Foreign influences. These could include the military representatives of foreign governments, experiences gained in foreign wars (the Colombian battalion in Korea) or in foreign train-

[21] Eight of the 112 nations in the Third World were either too new or too unstable in 1976 to fit into one category or the other without question. In addition, some readers may disagree with the subjective judgments that placed a given country in one category or another. I have tried to give civilian rulers the benefit of the doubt where possible, so, if anything, some countries could be moved from low to high military influence (Venezuela is one example).
[22] Claude E. Welch, Jr., "Cincinnatus in Africa: The Possibility of Military Withdrawal from Politics," in Lofchie, Chapter 10. See also Robert P. Clark, *Development and Instability: Political Change in the Non-Western World* (Chicago: Dryden, 1974), pp. 185–186.

ing centers, or foreign aid in the form of equipment and weapons.

11. Defeat of the military in a war with another country, especially when the military are convinced that the civilian government betrayed them by negotiating disadvantageous peace terms or by mismanaging the war effort behind the front lines (Bolivia, in the 1940s).

Any one or any combination of these causes could constitute an impressive bill of particulars to lay at the doorstep of the ousted civilian government. No doubt, some military leaders have intervened in politics primarily (or even solely) out of a desire to advance personal prestige or power. The regimes of Idi Amin in Uganda or of Rafael Trujillo in the Dominican Republic seem to have brought to their respective countries not prosperity and peace, but suppression of human rights in the most brutal fashion, and economic stagnation, all for the greater glory of "The Dictator." The evidence seems to indicate, however, that the Idi Amins and the Trujillos are in the minority as far as military governments are concerned. The majority of military regimes in the Third World are in place not primarily because of a desire for personal power, but for the same reason people strive for political power anywhere: to improve the public sector's capacity to solve persistent and annoying (or even critical) problems.

And how well do military regimes perform that function? How effective have military regimes been in their search for economic prosperity and social order? One sort of evidence lies in both the life and the death of military governments. On the one hand, most military governments are most reluctant to give power back to civilian authorities, apparently on the assumption that the same circumstances that prompted their original intervention are still present; the civilians can simply not be trusted with power until the country's stability is assured. On the other hand, most military regimes end the way they

began: at the hands of another coup launched by a hostile faction within the military. Gavin Kennedy asserts that of all the precipitating factors that might bring the military into power in the Third World, the most important is simply that the incumbent regime is also a military government that gained power illegally. In other words, the more military coups a country has, the more it is likely to have. The first is the most difficult; they become progressively easier as the military become accustomed to holding power. But this observation also suggests that military governments rarely solve the problems they say motivated their entry into politics in the first place.

On the subject of the record of military regimes in stimulating economic growth, available data permit us to be somewhat more precise. Table 5.5 compares 92 Third World countries along the two axes of military influence and rate of growth of *per capita* GNP. This table reveals that nine military dictatorships achieved exceptionally good growth rates from 1965 to 1974 (over 3 percent annually), while 10 states did so under conditions of high military influence, and 17 did so in circumstances where the military have a low amount of influence. The respective percentages are: 27 percent of the military dictatorships; 42 percent of the regimes with high military influence; and 49 percent of the regimes with low military influence. By expanding our definition of "good growth rate performance" to include all countries with a rate higher than 2.0 percent annually, we obtain these percentages: military dictatorships, 42 percent; regimes with high military influence, 62.5 percent; and regimes with low military influence, 66 percent. Thus, while there seems to be little difference between regimes with significant military influence and those relatively free of such influence, both of these categories show better economic performance than states that operated under military regimes. To be sure, some military regimes achieved exceptionally good economic growth rates, although several of the performances could also be attributed to the basic

TABLE 5.5

Selected Third World Countries Compared According to Degree of Military Influence in Politics and Growth Rate of GNP/Capita, 1965–1974

Degree of Military Influence	Less than 0	0.00–0.99	1.00–1.99	2.00–2.99	3.00′
Military regime (34)	Chad (6) Equatorial Guinea Mali Niger Somalia Sudan	Benin (8) Burundi Central African Republic Ghana Madagascar Uganda Upper Volta Afghanistan	Chile (5) Haiti Honduras Ethiopia Yemen Arab Republic	Argentina (5) Bolivia Ecuador Peru Bangladesh	Brazil (10) Panama Algeria Iraq Libya Congo Republic Nigeria Rwanda Togo Thailand
High military influence (23)	Uruguay (1)	Egypt (5) Jordan Lesotho Zaire Burma	El Salvador (3) Morocco Sierra Leone	Colombia (5) Nicaragua Paraguay Syria Philippines	Dominican Republic Guatemala Oman Turkey Cameroon Gabon Indonesia South Korea Pakistan
Low military influence (35)	Bahrain (3) Senegal Zambia	Guyana (4) India Nepal Peoples Democratic Republic of Yemen	Kuwait (5) Qatar Mauritania Venezuela Guinea	Jamaica (6) Gambia Mexico South Africa Tanzania Sri Lanka	Costa Rica (17) Trinidad Botswana Liberia Mauritius Swaziland Saudi Arabia Tunisia Ivory Coast Rhodesia Malaysia Singapore United Arab Emirates Iran Kenya Malawi Taiwan

Source: Military influence—see Tables 5.2, 5.3, and 5.4. Growth rates—calculated from U.S. Arms Control and Disarmament Agency, *World Military Expenditures and Arms Transfers: 1965–1974,* (Washington, D.C.: USGPO, 1976).

Note: All growth rates are for the period 1965–1974 except the following: Guyana, Singapore, and Rhodesia (1966–1974); Botswana, Lesotho (1967–1974); Mauritius, Peoples Democratic Republic of Yemen (1968–1974); Equatorial Guinea, Swaziland (1969–1974); Bahrain (1971–1974); and Qatar, Bangladesh, United Arab Emirates (1972–1974).

strength of the economy (such as Brazil's rate of nearly 7 percent) or to enormous natural resources (Libya's rate of 7.5 percent). However, it appears that nations desiring to achieve a rapid rate of economic growth will not accomplish this goal by adopting a military form of government unless other economic, social, and political factors likewise favor rapid growth.[23]

CONCLUSIONS: GOVERNMENTAL STRUCTURES AND HUMAN DIGNITY

It seems that many Third World governments suffer from a number of important flaws that work to block them from making a maximum contribution to the enhancement of human dignity in their countries. Being comparative latecomers in the rush to industrialization, many Third World industrial élites have been too weak to absorb or defeat the traditional agrarian élites, so they have been forced to turn to the authoritarian rule of the syncratic regime, which manages to maintain order by refraining from attacking rural landlords and by suppressing mass demands for a better standard of living. Industrialization must proceed at a reduced pace because the rural élites oppose it and because the industrial sector has difficulty in financing its own development.

[23] This conclusion is supported by R. D. McKinlay and A. S. Cohan, "Performance and Instability in Military and Nonmilitary Regime Systems," *American Political Science Review*, LXX (3) (September 1976), pp. 850–865.

Whatever surplus there is must be extracted from the low-income city and village dwellers.

The ability of a syncratic regime to carry out this kind of policy depends largely on three sets of institutions, which have been considered in detail. The first set consists of the network of patron-client systems that link together the urban élites and the low-income citizens in a complex psychological bond that makes it possible for governments to ignore mass demands without provoking mass rebellion. The second set is the nation's dominant executive, the president and his circle of advisors and experts. Aided by both constitutional grants and extraconstitutional seizures of extraordinary powers, the chief executive can rule without serious challenge from outside interests or groups, as long as the patron-client systems remain intact and as long as he can effect the industrialist-landlord coalition that supports the syncratic regime. Behind many of these regimes, however, stands the third set of institutions, the military, ready to intervene to restore order if the constitutional government should prove unable to govern. The comparative frequency of military interventions in politics in the Third World reflects the continuing inability of civilian, constitutional regimes to break through the barriers of syncratic politics and to master the industrialization process. Levels of human dignity are unlikely to rise greatly in countries where these three institutions remain powerful and unchallenged.

Suggestions for Further Reading

Anderson, James N. E., ed., *Changing Law in Developing Countries* (New York: Praeger, 1963).

Ashford, Douglas E., *National Development and Local Reform: Political Participation in Morocco, Tunisia and Pakistan* (Princeton, N.J.: Princeton, 1967).

Burke, Fred G., *Local Government and Politics in Uganda* (Syracuse, N.Y.: Syracuse, 1964).

Braibanti, Ralph, ed., *Political and Administrative Development* (Durham, N.C.: Duke, 1969).

Janowitz, Morris, *The Military and the Political Development of New Nations* (Chicago: Chicago, 1964).

Johnson, John J., ed., *The Role of the Military in Underdeveloped Countries* (Princeton, N.J.: Princeton, 1962).

Kennedy, Gavin, *The Military in the Third World* (New York: Scribner's, 1974).

LaPalombara, Joseph, ed., *Bureaucracy and Political Development* (Princeton, N.J.: Princeton, 1967).

Lieuwin, Edwin, *Arms and Politics in Latin America* (New York: Praeger, 1960).

————, *Generals vs. Presidents: Neomilitarism in Latin America* (New York: Praeger, 1964).

Lloyd, P. C., ed., *The New Elites of Tropical Africa* (London: Oxford, 1966).

Park, Richard L., and Irene Tinker, eds., *Leadership and Political Institutions in India* (Princeton, N.J.: Princeton, 1959).

Sherwood, Frank P., *Institutionalizing the Grass Roots in Brazil: A Study in Comparative Local Government* (San Francisco: Chandler, 1967).

Tinker, Hugh, *Ballot Box and Bayonet: People and Government in Emergent Asian Countries* (New York: Oxford, 1964).

————, *The Foundations of Local Self-Government in India, Pakistan and Burma* (London: London, 1954).

Younger, Kenneth, *The Public Service in New States* (London: Oxford, 1960).

CHAPTER SIX

Policy Making in the Third World

In preceding chapters, we have examined some important social, economic, and psychological dimensions of Third World political life, and we have discussed the major institutions and structures of Third World political systems. The capacity of Third World governments to enhance human dignity in their countries depends largely on how these various ingredients come together to form an effective and creative policy process. The term policy-making process refers to the series of steps taken by a government to solve problems, make decisions, allocate resources or values, implement policies and, in general, to do the things expected of them by their constituents. We cannot appreciate the connections between levels of human dignity and politics until we have analyzed the nature of the policy process in a typical Third World setting.

There is obviously some risk involved in making generalizations about more than 100 different political systems in an area of social behavior that is so poorly defined. This chapter offers an outline of a policy-making process that many observers think characterizes most governments in the Third World, regardless of their social and economic circumstances or their colonial heritage. The principal components of this process derive largely from the nature of traditional society and personality, from the scarcity and unpredictability of funds needed to carry out government policy, and from a shortage of modernizing institutions to assist governments in the making and implementing of public policy choices.

POLICY-MAKING IN THE THIRD WORLD: AN OVERVIEW

Several years ago, Yale University economist Albert O. Hirschman published the first of a series of books and articles in which he attempted to outline what he understood to be the major reasons that developing countries so frequently fell short of their goals, particularly in the field of economic well-being. Based on his experiences as an economic advisor to the government of Colombia and a number of in-depth studies made in other Latin American countries, Hirschman's analysis eventually focused on what he terms the "failure-prone policy process" in the less developed world.[1]

Hirschman begins by considering the fundamental problem of less developed countries:

[1] Albert O. Hirschman, *Journeys Toward Progress: Studies of Economic Policy Making in Latin America* (New York: Twentieth Century Fund, 1963). Albert O. Hirschman, *The Strategy of Economic Development* (New Haven, Conn.: Yale, 1961).

the inability to make decisions that will induce development (specifically, development
of the economy). For Hirschman, the prevailing inability of development élites to make
these decisions can be traced back to certain psychological and social structural inadequacies that inhibit the decision-makers
of the country from bringing to bear the
needed amount of knowledge and commitment
to make the proper judgments about the allocation of resources. In the face of this recurring inability to meet development problems,
struggling groups within the society begin to
grow desperate at their failure to penetrate the
decision-makers' attention screen, and they
attract attention to their problems. As the
problems become more and more aggravated,
groups are pushed toward acts of violence in
order to attract attention. The consequence is
usually an impulsive policy decision, taken in
the heat of debate or passionate confrontation,
without adequate understanding of what is required to solve the problem. The result, not
surprisingly, is failure.

The fatal flaw, according to Hirschman,
now appears in the decision-making styles of
developing countries. Instead of learning from
their mistakes, Third World élites typically
compound the problem by what Hirschman
calls *"la rage de vouloir conclure,"* a phrase
taken from Flaubert, which means (approximately) "the mania for wanting to be
done with it." At the point of recognizing
failure, a great cry arises from the country's
intellectuals, who call for a comprehensive,
total attack on the problem. Earlier solutions
are decried for being piecemeal, partial, fragmented, less than total, and generally inadequate. "Fundamental" change must be introduced; anything less will certainly fail. The
reformist élites of the country cannot tolerate
any further delay in attacking the problem.
Now, very few countries possess governments
with the policy-making apparatus adequate to
the task of producing a comprehensive program dealing with a major issue in a span
of months; and certainly the Third World
countries are more poorly equipped in

Steel production in this mill in São Paulo, Brazil, is impressive. Yet, production of steel in Brazil almost never
reaches predicted levels. Repeated failures of major programs or projects to achieve their goals or targets are
depressing to the morale of Third World technicians and
political leaders. Government legitimacy must be won
through performance, and the failure of many Third
World regimes to meet their own stated goals makes them
appear incompetent in the eyes of their own citizens.

this regard than most other governments.
Therefore, calls for comprehensive solutions
are met in the only possible way: by introducing policy solutions from abroad. The history
of Third World attempts to solve domestic
problems is littered with examples of poorly
related solutions borrowed from the industrialized states. Successful policy solutions
like the Tennessee Valley Authority have been
copied all over the Third World to solve problems in agrarian reform, flood control, land
reclamation, power generation, pest control,
and many other issues for which that
particular policy tool may be inappropriate.
Likewise, international agencies like the
World Bank and the International Monetary
Fund are frequently called on to send
professional advisors to struggling Third
World countries to prescribe an instant
remedy to their centuries-old ills.

The failure-prone nature of the Third World
decision-making style continues to exhibit itself in what occurs next. Not only do the
foreign solutions usually fail to resolve the immediate problem, but their very use tends to
have an adverse effect on future efforts. For
one thing, the nation's intellectual resources
are prevented from acting on a local problem

as long as some foreign "miracle" is being developed. Anyone who has worked in the field of solving public policy problems knows that before a person can really solve a problem, he or she must interact with the problem, become immersed in its very nature, and come to know the problem intimately. There must be, to quote Hirschman, "that long confrontation between man and a situation" before creativity emerges. By introducing foreign solutions on a poorly thought out "crash" basis, Third World élites deprive themselves, and their intellectuals, of any chance to master the problem on their own terms. In addition, the continued failure to solve a given problem begins to sap the morale and weaken the resolve of a national political cadre. They begin to believe that they merit the title "failure-prone," they deprecate the national style, and they either escalate the ideological battle considerably, or "drop out" by resigning themselves to mediocrity or going into self-imposed exile. Each time this sequence is repeated, it erodes the scant supply of problem-solving talent with which Third World political leaders have to work. The long-term consequences of failure-prone politics are to lead the country into a vicious circle of one disaster after another, until some authoritarian force, usually the army, steps in to impose discipline on the nation and attempts to insure the people that they are in control of their destiny once again.

POLICY-MAKING IN THE THIRD WORLD: GOALS, ACTIONS, OUTCOMES

Setting Goals

The policy-making process begins with the setting of goals. For the average American, the idea of setting national goals is alien, since our system of separation of powers and our cultural predeliction against long-range planning obscure the setting of goals in our government. There is, for example, no single document in the U.S. government that could be called "National Goals for 1976." The closest thing we have to that would be the federal government budget for any given fiscal year. Similarly, we do not have any single agency responsible for devising the nation's goals for a specific period. The closest agency to this would be the Office of Management and Budget (OMB), located within the Office of the President. The ability of OMB to influence the structure of our national political goals derives almost entirely from the OMB role as the coordinator of the Executive Branch's budget proposal, which is sent to the Congress for approval each year. Without doubt, the United States is moving inexorably toward central planning and the formal setting of national goals. Probably before the end of the century, even the U.S. government will adopt formal goal-setting procedures for its operations. As of the middle 1970s, however, we are practically the only country of any significance that still believes that single sets of national goals should not be imposed on our heterogeneous population.

In the Third World, in contrast, there is usually very great emphasis placed on goal-setting exercises and planning agencies.

In Mexico, for example, according to Anderson and Cockcroft, there are four national goals: political stability, economic growth, public welfare, and Mexicanization.[2] The goal of political stability consists of three components: that basic institutions are viewed as legitimate by the population; that decision-makers are regarded as having the right to make binding decisions for the polity; and that the mode of transferring power from one person to another is accepted by most people. Economic growth in the Mexican context means approximately what it means elsewhere: an increase in the industrial productivity of the nation and in per capita GNP. The public welfare goal involves the raising of the material and cultural level of the country's

[2] Bo Anderson and James D. Cockcroft, "Control and Cooptation in Mexican Politics," in James D. Cockcroft, Andre Gunder Frank, and Dale L. Johnson, *Dependence and Underdevelopment: Latin America's Political Economy* (Garden City, N.Y.: Doubleday, 1972), pp. 221–225.

masses, especially in the rural sector. Mexicanization refers to the policy of gaining control of the major corporations and other economic activities in the country either for private Mexican citizens or for public agencies.

Morocco's first Five-Year Plan for 1960 to 1964 listed two chief goals: to lessen the country's dependence on foreign technicians, capital, and markets; and to integrate the traditional sectors into the national economy.[3] These two broad goals led to the establishment of these specific programs: to increase the number of technicians and other qualified personnel by emphasis on education and training; to stimulate traditional agriculture by giving top priority to agricultural reform and the introduction of modern technology into the rural areas; to establish basic steel and chemical industries by promoting private investment if possible, but by state intervention if necessary; and to facilitate the implementation of the plan by reforms in government administration and organization and by the Morocconization of the civil service. This last objective appears to have much the same meaning as Mexicanization has for Mexico: gaining control of national agencies for national personnel.

Pakistan's first Five-Year Plan (1953 to 1958) listed these major objectives: to achieve the greatest increase possible in national income and the standard of living; to increase health, education, housing, and social welfare services "justified primarily on grounds other than increasing the national income"; to improve the nation's balance of payments by increasing exports and import substitution; to increase opportunities for useful employment; and to increase rapidly the rate of development in East Pakistan and other relatively less developed zones of the country.[4] Although the first four objectives presented problems that were primarily technical in nature, the fifth objective—showing favoritism toward the relatively less developed East Pakistan—was the subject of intense controversy. Incidentally, the controversy was never resolved, and East Pakistan seceded from the rest of the nation in 1971 to form the new nation of Bangladesh.

Where are goals typically formulated in Third World countries? In a very few instances, such as in Mexico, nations with very strong "official" political parties may employ the inner councils of the party to discuss alternate goals and to formulate the final list for state action. In an equally small number of traditional monarchies, like Saudi Arabia or Iran, goal setting amounts to little more than an expression of personal convictions of the monarch and his closest advisors. However, in most Third World republics, central economic and social planning agencies have been created and charged with the task of setting goals for public policy-makers to follow. In a 1965 study, Albert Waterston lists central planning institutions in over 100 Third World independent nations and soon-to-be independent colonies.[5] Although the degree of sophistication and state control obviously vary considerably from one example to another, the list of Third World countries at least formally committed to some kind of central planning is clear evidence of the strength of the idea of rational government ordering of a society's priorities.

Planning in the Third World has usually followed one of three models, depending on the colonial heritage of the country, the type of planning used by the former colonial mother country and, most important, the specific economic and social structures in the developing state.[6] At one end of the spectrum are the states that engage in detailed central planning of both the private and the public sectors of

---

[3] Albert Waterston, *Planning in Morocco* (Baltimore: Johns Hopkins, 1962), pp. 28–29.
[4] Albert Waterston, *Planning in Pakistan* (Baltimore: Johns Hopkins, 1963), pp. 44, 102.

[5] Albert Waterston, *Development Planning: Lessons of Experience* (Baltimore: Johns Hopkins, 1965), Appendix III.
[6] John C. Honey, *Planning and the Private Sector: The Experience in Developing Countries* (New York: Dunellen, 1970), Part I.

the economy. Typical of this style is India, whose civil servants were strongly influenced by the Fabian socialists under whom they studied in England. India's brand of socialism is rather unconventional, since over 90 percent of the country's business enterprises remain in private hands. This means that the government must undertake to set detailed goals and objectives for the businesses in the private sector if the overall goals of the national economic plan are to be realized.

At the other end of the planning spectrum lie the states that are basically committed to reliance on the private sector to achieve the broad goals of the national economy. These countries, of which Malaysia, Iran, Pakistan, and the Philippines are the best examples, typically restrict their planning to the formulation of the broadest goals possible (called "macroplanning"). Thus, a planning document in one of these countries might set as a goal the achievement of an increase of 3 percent in per capita income over the next year, without specifying exactly how such a goal is to be accomplished. Then the plan is augmented through budgetary and other procedures to grant special incentives to the private sector to undertake projects whose overall result will be the fulfillment of the national plan goals. Accordingly, the state does not become involved in direct industrial activity unless there is clearly no alternative and unless the project in question is badly needed. Another feature of macroplanning is its tendency to encourage and rely on regional planning institutions. As in Malaysia, the national plan is frequently little more than the regional plans collected under one cover.

In the middle of the planning spectrum are the countries that have adopted the French consultative planning method; these include Chile (before 1970), Tunisia, Tanzania, and Morocco. The French method of planning involves careful consultation between the public sector's planning officials and representatives of the private sector. As a result of this planning style, private industry and commerce leaders leave the consultations knowing (and

accepting) what is expected of them in the way of investment and production decisions. The state, for its part, undertakes to provide support for economic activities conventionally not financed by private industry: social infrastructure such as roads and schools, large projects that cannot pay for their costs of construction, such as huge dams, and so forth.

Regardless of the exact model followed by planning agencies in Third World countries, these nations have exhibited a serious tendency to set unrealistic goals, which frequently are followed by failure and a decline in public morale. Hirschman has observed that government decision-making can fit into one of two categories: either capabilities outrun motivation (the technical solution to a problem surfaces before the problem become critical), in which case the goals adopted are usually within the reach of government power; or motivation outruns capabilities (as when a problem becomes critical rapidly), in which case the outcome is usually failure. Goal setting in the Third World tends to be of the second type, thus helping to account for the failure-prone political style noted earlier.

Brazil, according to an old saying, has a great future—and always will have! Brazilians are accustomed to seeing their government plan in a dreamlike confidence about the realizability of grandiose projects. It almost seems as if the enormous size of the country has encouraged its leaders to imagine that they accomplish miracles. Recent press reports coming out of Brazil reveal, however, that several key projects are seriously behind schedule, contributing even more to disbelief and cynicism in the Brazilian and foreign private economic circles.[7] In 1970, for example, Brazil announced that it would increase steel production from 5.4 million ingot tons to 20 million ingot tons by 1980. Shortly thereafter, the goal was raised to 24 million tons, and then to 35 million tons by

[7] Bruce Handler, "Brazil: Big Projects but Big Delays," Washington *Post,* July 20, 1976.

1985. Actual performance has been disappointing; 1975 figures show steel production reaching 8.3 million tons. Most observers now admit that the goal of 35 million tons was totally beyond the country's capacity. Another fantastic project envisioned by Brazilian planners has been the Northern Perimetral Highway, a space-age highway intended to link Brazil's northern Amazon region with Venezuela, Colombia, and Peru. Construction was begun in 1973, and completion was promised by 1977. But, in the middle of 1976, only 400 miles of the highway's 2600-mile length had been completed, and construction was proceeding so slowly that the jungle was reclaiming parts of the completed roadway. But, as Brazilian Finance Minister Mario Henrique Simonson was quoted as saying, "It's better to plan for too much than for too little. If your original goals are too high, you can always change your plans. But, if they're too low, progress could become strangled." Perhaps the minister would be correct were it not for the serious blows to national confidence and morale that are suffered each time the government defaults on a promise.

Another example is the huge Helwan steel mill in Egypt. Begun in 1955 by a West German firm, the Helwan iron and steel works was nationalized by the Egyptian government in 1961. As a consequence, Egypt has needed continued aid from the Soviet Union to complete Helwan, to expand it, and to keep it running in the face of mounting operation and maintenance problems. Total capital investment in Helwan, one of the largest industrial enterprises in the Middle East, has reached $1 billion. Despite Egypt's political break with the Soviet Union, there are still 500 Soviet technicians working at Helwan, now supplemented by a team of consultants and advisors from U.S. Steel and from the United Nations.

All of these foreign advisors are needed simply because nothing ever seems to go right at Helwan. Originally designed to be producing 1.5 million tons of steel products by 1976, the plant's current output is more like 500,000 tons. Although export sales reached $21 billion

in 1975, Egypt spent more than that amount on imports—coal, spare parts, vehicles, and other equipment—needed to keep the plant running. Egyptian iron ore has a very high salt content, which corrodes the plant's machinery. Although Helwan has its own plant for converting coal into coke, the coal must be imported, and it is frequently delayed in the country's snarled port facilities. Staffing is a huge problem. There are 20,000 workers, far too many for the plant's needs, but political considerations make layoffs impossible. Low salaries make it difficult to retain middle-level managers and engineers. Many managers spend more time in their offices than they do supervising operations on the plant floor. Alleged corruption and kickback deals have caused plant supplies to lag behind requirements. Improper use of equipment causes much breakage and many maintenance problems. One piece of expensive equipment, designed to last 10 years, was broken in 4 days at Helwan. Finally, the Egyptians depend almost completely on foreign capital and technology to make the plant function properly. In an effort to reduce the cost of importing coal, Egypt has tried to convert some of the equipment to run on natural gas, which the country has domestically. Amoco Oil Company has run a pipeline to the plant, but cannot complete the task because U.S. law inhibits American companies from participating in projects funded by the Soviet Union. The USSR, for its part, refuses to connect the pipeline to plant facilities because of its running feud with Egyptian President Anwar Sadat. And Helwan stumbles along consuming more wealth than it produces.[8]

The Third World inclination toward the setting of unrealistic goals has its economic disadvantages in that it distorts the efficient allocation of resources; but, from our vantage point, the most disturbing consequences of this tendency are political and psychological.

[8] Thomas W. Lippmann, "Egypt's Large Steel Plant Is Economic Embarrassment," Washington Post, October 11, 1976.

Most Third World governments lean on shaky popular support under the best of circumstances. Few governments in the developing world enjoy such popular acclaim that they can maintain their legitimacy in the face of repeated failure. Thus, when failure comes, as it inevitably must if goals are set unrealistically high, one serious effect is to weaken mass confidence in their ruling élites.

Why do Third World political élites set such high goals for themselves and for their political systems? A review of the policy-making literature in developing states suggests at least four reasons. First, political debate in the Third World is carried on with such intensity and fervor that appeals to moderation have little impact. The role of inspirational, charismatic leaders was highly useful during the struggle against the colonial masters, when a lethargic populace had to be roused into heroic actions to gain national (and personal) liberation. But, once independence is obtained and the state must settle down into the routine of managing complex economic and social problems, charisma loses its utility. Legitimacy must be based on real achievement, and regimes based on inspiration and promises do not long survive, as the fate of Sukarno of Indonesia or Nkrumah of Ghana can attest.

A second source of unrealistic goal setting derives from the general non-Western cultural inclination to deal in the comprehensive and the total, leaving the marginal and the partial to the pragmatic (but, they say, the unprincipled) Western capitalists. I recall leading a seminar on incremental decision-making before a group of middle-level bureaucrats in a Latin American country. After the seminar, one participant remarked, "All those ideas are fine for an Anglo-Saxon; but we Latins need a more complete and well formulated way of thinking." Such cultural predilections certainly reinforce the already present institutional tendencies toward global and grandiose projects and goals, or toward what some call "grand design politics."

Third, unrealistic goals are established largely because decison-makers lack reliable information on which to base their calculations. The problem of insufficient information is partly derived from inadequate data-gathering services and national statistical agencies. Too often, bureaucrats in developing countries simply cannot obtain complete and reliable data. Even more symptomatic of political underdevelopment, however, is the way in which empirical data are distorted for political purposes. In nations where the population is narrowly balanced between competing and hostile tribal or ethnic groups, such as Lebanon or Nigeria, even outwardly simple statistical exercises such as conducting a national census become the cause of much concern, lest the new data reveal that the balance of demographic power has shifted. In Nigeria, this fear became so great that in 1975 the military dictator, Brigadier General Murtala Ramat Muhammad, simply declared the 1973 census to be inoperative and proclaimed that the 1963 census would be used henceforth for planning purposes. A similar example can be seen in Pakistan, where the first Five-Year Plan (1955 to 1960) was drafted on the assumptions that (1) GNP would rise by 20 percent during the period; (2) population would increase 7.5 percent (a rate of only 1.5 percent annually); and (3) consequently per capita GNP would grow 12.5 percent. As Waterston reports, according to the Deputy Chairman of the Planning Board, it was believed that population was actually growing much faster than 1.5 percent, but that it was felt that the growth rate of population had to be understated in the plan in order "to keep despair away."[9]

A fourth and final cause of incorrect goal setting involves the suppression of dissent in most Third World regimes. In a recent study of foreign policy decision-making in the U.S. government, Irving Janis discovered that our policy-makers were most disposed to make serious errors of judgment whenever the social cohesion of the group imposed a sort of

[9] Waterston, *Planning in Pakistan*, p. 46, footnote 29.

dissent-free atmosphere over the deliberations, in such a way that contradictory opinions were suppressed, often by those who held them.[10] Janis labels this phenomenon "groupthink." Any group that is wrestling with a particularly complex problem should take pains to insure that dissent is protected and encouraged, even institutionalized, in order to avoid as many errors as possible. In most Third World regimes, however, just the opposite is true. Dissent is suppressed and ideological conformity is imposed during all stages of decision making. The certain consequence of this practice is to lead the government into making numerous errors of judgment and into setting unreasonably high goals.

Taking Actions

Clearly our discussion about the setting of unrealistic goals would not be necessary if Third World governments somehow found the ability to carry through with their plans and to implement the policy choices they have made. Yet, when we come to this second phase of the policy-making process, we find that many Third World governments must operate under administrative economic and political constraints that virtually guarantee failure at the point where the policy is applied to the society.[11]

The first kind of constraint on Third World policy actions comes from the administrative sphere. Here we note the numerous problems connected with the administration of development plans and specific projects: long delays in execution of the plan (some plans, such as those of Pakistan, were not put into effect until the plan period is more than half over); increased costs over the projected costs, because of delays and inflation; inferior

construction; low yields on investment; unnecessary dispersal of resources among a number of small and uncoordinated projects; and so forth. There are at least three sources of administrative confusion and incompetence. The first is the most obvious: the lack of trained experts to administer the complex programs and projects so vital to economic development. This severe shortage of expertise brings on poor project preparation, especially in crucial areas such as economic feasibility (cost-benefit) studies, and engineering supervision of the project once under way. A second problem stems from the lack of political support for civil servants and bureaucrats. From Tanzania, for example, we have the report that the cabinet officials were so opposed to the basic provisions of that nation's first Five-Year Plan that, even after the plan had been put into effect, they fought for, and secured, major changes in the program; the changes benefited their ministries, but eroded the administrators' enthusiasm for the plan. A similar phenomenon was observed in Pakistan, where the planning agency's own analysis for the reasons for plan failure began by accusing the political élites of failing to enforce the plan's provisions. Finally, we must again note the casual way in which Third World bureaucrats manipulate statistical data to conform to political requirements. This point brings to mind the story told by the American political scientist and State Department official, Roger Hilsman, at the time of America's involvement in the Vietnam war. During the early years of that struggle, Americans were still trying to develop statistical indicators to measure our progress in the war. To which one of the Vietnamese generals replied, "Ah, les statistiques! Your Secretary of Defense [Robert McNamara] loves statistics. We Vietnamese can give him all he wants. If you want them to go up, they will go up. If you want them to go down, they will go down."[12]

The second kind of constraint on policy im-

---

[10] Irving Janis, *Victims of Groupthink* (New York: Houghton Mifflin, 1972).

[11] On this general subject, see Immanuel Wallerstein, "The Range of Choice: Constraints on the Policies of Governments of Contemporary African Independent States," in Michael F. Lofchie, ed., *The State of the Nations: Constraints on Development in Independent Africa* (Berkeley: California, 1971), Chapter 2.

[12] Roger Hilsman, *To Move a Nation* (Garden City, N.Y.: Doubleday, 1967), p. 523.

plementation is an economic one, the severe lack of funds available to pay for the many projects and programs that all Third World governments would like to establish. Immanuel Wallerstein has shown that in virtually every independent nation in Africa, expenditures have exceeded receipts at least in the long run (more than 2 or 3 years). Even where some sort of windfall makes new revenues available unexpectedly, as with the negotiation of new arrangements between the Zambian government and the international copper companies, increased needs absorb the new revenues as fast as they become available. Even oil-rich states like Venezuela and Iran find themselves in financial straits only 3 years after the oil embargo and the rise in oil prices brought them close to the point of luxury for Third World countries.

There are only a limited number of sources from which a development-minded élite can extract the money needed to pay for their programs. The industrialized states such as the United States and countries in Western Europe can provide official, government-to-government loans or grants; but these sources attach significant conditions to this money, and such "strings" usually infringe on the power of the developing nation. No Third World nation likes to find itself in the situation of India, where 30 percent of the entire income of the third Five-Year Plan was to come from foreign aid. Many Third World countries have sought financial relief by controlling the sale of export commodities, either by administering these sales entirely through some sort of export marketing board (as with cocoa in Ghana), or simply by levying an indirect tax on the exported items. In extreme cases, such as those of oil in Venezuela or copper in Chile, the exporting country's government will actually nationalize or expropriate the commercial, mining, or industrial enterprises, so that all foreign exchange from export sales will accrue to the government. Dependence on foreign sales of raw materials is a shaky source of support for government policy, since prices are so volatile that it is dif-

ficult to predict far in advance what exactly government revenues are likely to be. Furthermore, many Third World countries are based on monocultural economies, meaning that one single commodity or product dominates the export picture. Fluctuations in the price of that commodity can have disastrous effects on the nation's over-all economy.

When a development élite turns to their own national resources, the picture is not too bright. Some governments have chosen to avoid the problem of insufficient funds by simply creating money to pay at least their domestic bills. In cases like that of Chile in the 1960s, inflation was used by the government to avoid a clash between economic sectors that were not predisposed to compromise. Inflation was a substitute for taxation and expenditure of real resources. As recent events in Chile testify, that kind of policy cannot be maintained for long without tragic results. Only a regime that already maintains a reputation with its people for honesty and legitimacy can afford to run budget deficits and to meet the difference in created money. Governments that do not enjoy legitimacy with their people, or with significant disadvantaged sectors, do not usually have this option. In addition, inflation by creating money at home does not solve the equally severe problem of shortage of foreign exchange, which a government needs to purchase greatly needed imported items for industrial and agricultural modernization.

Thus, development regimes are led to consider the most critical of all financial alternatives: how to levy taxes on private and corporate income. As compared with the typical industrialized country which annually extracts between 25 and 30 percent of its GNP in taxation, the less developed states of the Third World usually manage to take out between 8 and 15 percent in this manner.[13] As might be expected, the typical Third World

[13] Nicholas Kaldor, "Will Underdeveloped Countries Learn to Tax?" *Foreign Affairs 41* (2) (January 1963), pp. 410–419.

government's inability to tax income properly stems from several defects in the political and economic systems: the highly unequal distribution of income, combined with the close connection between income distribution and political power; the regressive nature of most Third World tax systems (tax rate goes *up* as income goes *down*); the tendency for the wealthiest sectors of Third World economies to derive their income from inaccessible sources, such as rents and land; and the bureaucratic inadequacies that make levies such as land taxes easy to evade.

This last observation brings us around finally to a consideration of the political constraints of policy implementation, which will be subsumed under Gunnar Myrdal's phrase, "the soft state."[14] According to Myrdal, all underdeveloped countries are, to one degree or another, "soft states." This means that they suffer from social indiscipline, which manifests itself in deficiencies in legislation and, in particular, in law observance and enforcement; a widespread disobedience by public officials of rules and directives handed down to them; and often their collusion with powerful persons and groups whose conduct they should regulate. In the word of Singapore's Minister for Foreign Affairs and Labor, S. Rajaratnam, what we have is government by "kleptocracy." In specific terms, the "soft state" includes corruption, racketeering, bribes, payoffs, smuggling, kickbacks, black market profits, arbitrary enforcement of the law, lax or nonexistent enforcement of the law, and abuse of power, especially on the local level.

Before we discuss the specific causes for the "soft state," we must immediately discard two erroneous notions. The first is that political corruption in the Third World has something to do with the form of government. Actually, many Third World regimes are "soft," lax, and corrupt, regardless of whether the chief of state is a military dictator or an elected president and whether parties and press function freely or are suppressed. The second erroneous idea is that political corruption has something to do with inferior standards of morality. The morality of Third World citizens and public officials is about what it is in most political systems, and probably higher than the public morality exhibited by political bosses in some of America's larger cities. If we want to understand the causes of political "softness" in developing countries, we must learn to look for it in the nature of political power in a less developed political system.

For one thing, we must attempt to put ourselves into the place of the citizens of most Third World countries. Often, low-status and low-income persons from these countries, whether they live in urban or rural areas, have grown up in an environment where the government was feared, or hated, and rightly so. In many cases, the pre-colonial administrations were only slightly benevolent dictatorships; and their successors, the colonial regimes, only exceeded their predecessors in the extent to which they could abuse power. Manning Nash's description of politics in a remote Burmese village is significant in this regard.

> . . . *Government [to the people of Nondwin village] is one of the five traditional enemies, along with fire, famine, flood and plague. . . . From the days of arbitrary demands from the royal city to the British colonial administration, through the Japanese occupation and the civil disorders following independence, political power in the shape of government has been something alien, demanding, and usually capricious or enigmatic. Government is identified with the unrestricted use of force. Nondwin villagers seek means to avoid or subvert the force of government, except when there is a local man who also has the kind of power that governments are thought to have.*[15]

The effect of this ancient tradition of mistrust

[14] Gunnar Myrdal, *The Challenge of World Poverty* (New York: Vintage, 1970), Chapter 7.

[15] Manning Nash, *The Golden Road to Modernity: Village Life in Contemporary Burma* (Chicago: Chicago, 1965), p. 75.

of government is to encourage local villagers to look the other way when smuggling or bribery occur, and to engage in passive resistance when the national government enters their village. It seems as if peasants the world over have learned much the same kind of defense against government intruders: stare at the bureaucrats with a passive, noncommittal look, and then wait for them to leave, secure in the knowledge that nothing of consequence will really change, for good or ill.

A second cause for political corruption in the Third World can be traced to the administrative style of many of these countries. Despite a notable lack of real political power and authority, Third World governments have legislated an attempt to enforce an amazing array of official restrictions and regulations that amount to an open invitation to bribery and payoffs. In Burma, the state attempts to control most retail merchandising by requiring merchants to sell their wares through state-run stores. However, visitors to the official stores find them virtually empty, while street vendors outside a few feet away display a wide variety of consumer goods—all illegally sold, of course. The customary insistence on a seemingly endless series of forms, permits, licenses, and other devices allows administrative discretion at a very low level; this encourages bureaucrats to take advantage of the helpless business people or consumers. In addition, many Third World countries try to regulate citizen behavior by offering financial subsidies for certain kinds of private decisions—rental of an apartment, for example—which burdens the administrative apparatus and offers further opportunity for abuse. Add to this apparatus the notoriously low salaries earned by civil servants in poor countries, and you have a situation open to abuse, corruption, and bribery. Some of the worst offenders appear to be foreign multinational corporations, which regard the bribes they pay to public officials as a normal cost of doing business in the Third World.

A third cause of the soft state lies in the highly unequal distribution of political power in the Third World. We have already seen that Third World governments frequently make use of the syncratic style of governance as they attempt to modernize and industrialize their countries without seriously altering the privileges and special powerful status of the traditional sectors of the country. This effort leads, in turn, to the promulgation of laws, decrees, and proclamations that are more honored in the breach than in the observance. Third World regimes have enacted numerous laws intended to reform the land tenure patterns of their countries, curb abuses of power, grant security of property to peasants, establish a minimum wage for urban laborers, or provide free health care for the poor, and so on. What happens to these laws? As Myrdal makes clear, most of the provisions of these laws are designed to please either low-status interest group representatives or foreign governments trying to urge local reforms before external assistance is granted. But the really powerful of the country know that the law will contain enough escape provisions, or loopholes, so that they themselves need never feel the adverse impact of the law. Despite the radical sounds emanating from many national capitals in the Third World, little in the way of radical change ever really takes place because of the élites' ability to block effective enforcement of the law. Thus, we see a growing gap between the symbolic pronouncements of the political leaders and the tangible significance of the regime's actions. There is not a government in the world that does not distribute at least a little symbolism instead of tangible benefits to its people. That is, no government has enough control over real goods (money, food, housing, health care) that they can distribute a satisfactory quantity to each person; so each government has to concentrate on making its people feel happy instead of enjoying material well-being. All governments do this, but the evidence suggests that Third World governments do it more than most other political systems. Again, as in the case of unrealistic goal setting, the real difficulty arises from a growing class consciousness of low-income persons, who are coming to realize that one cannot live on symbols indefinitely, and that eventually governments must turn to the real issues of power, wealth, and their unequal concentration.

One final point needs to be made regarding corruption in the soft state. It appears as if the real hidden cause of political softness and public immorality in the Third World lies in the comparatively underdeveloped state of countervailing powers in these societies. Perhaps the chief characteristic of Third World power systems is the relative lack of power anywhere in the system. Coercion, force, and authoritarian rule are all present in abundance, but power is a genuinely scarce commodity. Little power exists outside of the local-level patron-client networks and the international influences, which bear on the national network from both sides. (This theme will be examined in greater detail later.) But, at the national level, individuals are not organized into collectivities that can exercise power efficiently. There are few freely operating opposition political parties or independent judiciary systems. Most legislatures are of the "rubber stamp" variety; interest groups are primitive, and are mostly under the control of the government itself. Press freedom is rare. In other words, there are few checks on the unrestrained and abused power of a dominant executive (civil or military) and its representatives. Laws are made or unmade and enforced or unenforced, not according to some master guide, such as a constitution, but according to the whim of the administrator and the special access enjoyed by traditional élites. The founders of the U.S. system did not assume that political leaders were especially moral people. The opposite seems true, because they created the system in such a way as to pit one force against another, each with enough power to defend itself, and none with enough power to overwhelm the others. Through the years, that system has been subjected to many threats, but the essential soundness of the principle appears to have emerged intact. This lack of a system of countervailing powers

paradoxically encourages Third World leaders to try to accumulate more and more force and authority; it is paradoxical because even as they violate their own laws and abuse their own supporters to gain more power, in the long run they condemn themselves to further weakness and softness.

Evaluating Outcomes

To complete the picture of the failure-prone policy-making process, we examine how Third World governments evaluate the outcomes of their policy choices. We will find that the defects of the first two stages of decision-making (setting goals and taking actions) are compounded by an inability to evaluate policies quickly and accurately, to locate mistakes, and to remedy those errors in order to avoid serious adverse consequences.

Several concepts are particularly useful here. We have already encountered the idea of feedback, information about past or present system performance that can be used to improve future system performance. Feedback in the political context means any information about the impact of past and present policy choices; it also means to make new and different decisions about policy directions. When feedback is lacking political systems in an environment of rapid change cannot respond to mistakes quickly enough to avoid their adverse consequences. When certain environmental factors, such as population change by means of a percent increment each year instead of by a fixed quantity (for example, population growth of 2 percent per year instead of 1 million persons), we say that these factors are growing exponentially. In contrast to linear growth, when the increments are always of a fixed quantity, exponential growth makes quantities grow surprisingly fast, because the base for growth expands itself so rapidly. Third World political systems are particularly vulnerable to exponential growth because of their poor facilities for evaluating policy outcomes (feedback), their penchant to make mistakes in the first place, and their limited resources to rectify their errors once detected. When environmental factors change so fast that a mistake cannot be detected until it is too late to avoid its adverse consequence, we say that the system is in a condition of "over-shoot." When overshoot is experienced often enough in enough sectors of the society, to a strong enough degree, the policy-making mechanism of the system collapses under the burden of repeated failures. This is the situation facing many Third World governments today.

We have already discussed some of the characteristics of Third World societies and political systems that contribute to an inability to evaluate policy outcomes. Certainly the limited communications media available in less developed systems inhibit the free flow of information that is so vital to policy-makers in attempting to understand their own societies. Third World governments' policies to constrain a free press also play a key role in undermining their own self-analysis efforts. Political culture, especially in the mass of urban and rural poor, is another important obstacle faced by developing governments. In examples drawn from countries as far apart as Burma and Chile, we have already noted the prevailing peasant response to mistaken policies advanced by bureaucrats from the national government: "They rarely say no (writes David Lehmann); they prefer to nod their heads in agreement, so that the long-winded officials will depart soon, and so that they can continue to pursue their interest in their own way."[16] No government can evaluate its own policies as long as the supposed beneficiaries of these policies remain mute about their defects.

But of all the causes of poor policy evaluation in the Third World, perhaps the most serious is, again, the institutional flaw in developing political systems. There simply are not enough autonomous associations and institutions at work in Third World societies, obtaining information about the impact of policies on their members, assessing the costs and benefits of this impact, and communicating this information to public officials. The policy evaluation tools that have become so familiar to American observers—"think tanks," university research facilities and laboratories, and investigative journalism—are virtually unknown in the developing countries. And the more conventional feedback mechanisms, such as political parties and interest groups, either are fragmented, not trusted by their constituents, or controlled or ignored by the government. Robert Scott, for example, points out that most Latin American governments have found it exceedingly difficult to respond to the multiple dislocations brought about by rapid social and economic change, because of their lack of accurate information about their societies.[17] Most governments in that region have discounted the benefits to be derived from nurturing and encouraging a multi-party system stocked with reform-minded, modernizing political parties. Instead, they have preferred to proceed on the institutional basis of an expanded bureaucracy (civil and military), and the artificial creation of captive interest groups, representing industry, commerce, and agriculture, at a minimum. Yet, Scott continues, these awkward and stilted feedback mechanisms simply are not up to the demands of rapid development. Bureaucrats, whether civil or military, tend to see development where there is none, and they have the "data" to prove it. Even in countries where interest groups are nominally independent of government control, as in Chile before 1970, as Dale L. Johnson reports, the majority of the business sector declined to participate in their interest group's activities; they felt the group to be ineffective and too subservient to govern-

[16] David Lehmann, "Agrarian Reform in Chile, 1965–1972: An Essay in Contradictions," in David Lehmann, ed., Peasants, Landlords and Government: Agrarian Reform in the Third World (New York: Holmes and Meier, 1974), p. 109.

[17] Robert Scott, "Political Parties and Policy Making in Latin America," in Joseph LaPalombara and Myron Weiner, eds., Political Parties and Political Development (Princeton, N.J.: Princeton, 1966), pp. 365–367.

ment dictates.[18] Finally, where the government sets out to create feedback institutions, as in Pakistan's "Basic Democracies" experiment, the regime's opponents quickly learn that dissent within the controlled institutions is permitted only up to the point where it begins to be effective. In other words, the institutionalization of dissent is done more for theatrical purposes than for the purpose of obtaining badly needed information about the state of affairs in remote areas. (The proof of this flaw lies in Pakistan's inability to sense the depth of grievances in East Pakistan until it was too late, and secession was inevitable.) The Tanzanian example seems particularly typical; I cite Cranford Pratt at length.

> *[Other than the National Executive Committee of the ruling TANU Party,] there were few other ways for the government to inform itself of popular reactions to its proposals. Parliamentary discussion was none too vigorous and members were very cautious with any criticism they might wish to make of government policies. The newspapers were either controlled by the party or were extremely timid. The trade union movement had been brought increasingly under tighter government control. Within both the civil service and the party bureaucracy the upward flow of information on popular reactions to government policies was sporadic and inadequate.[19]*

I conclude this section of the analysis by citing Myron Weiner on one of the key differences between developed and less developed political systems.

> *A modern political system has no single mechanism, no single procedure, no single institution for the resolution of conflict; indeed, it is precisely the multiplicity of individuals, institutions and procedures for dispute settlement that characterizes the modern political system—both democratic and totalitarian. In contrast, developing societies with an increasing range of internal conflict, typically lack such individuals, institutions and procedures. It is as if mankind's capacity to generate conflict is greater than his capacity to find methods of resolving conflict; the lag it clearly greatest in societies in which fundamental economic and social relationships are rapidly changing.[20]*

CONCLUSIONS: POLICY-MAKING AND HUMAN DIGNITY

As a generalization, let us conclude this analysis by outlining the consequences of the Third World policy-making style: unrealistic goals, ineffectual and under-financed actions, and poorly evaluated outcomes. Policies designed to enhance human dignity often suffer from the tendency of many Third World states to swing wildly back and forth between two polar extremes, the conservative and the radical approaches, drawn here in abstract and general terms. In this analysis, we follow the work of Immanuel Wallerstein on styles of governance in Africa.[21]

The conservative regime, according to Wallerstein, desires above all to maintain a relatively open economy and national society. This has usually meant keeping the country within the zone of some international currency (dollar, pound, franc), maintaining few economic restrictions such as import quotas, tariffs, or controls over the transfer of capital, and permitting (and encouraging) foreign private capital investment. At home, agitation from the left has been suppressed, and human rights have not flourished. As the years pass, the initial difficulties of the conservative regime stem from its growing international

[18] Dale L. Johnson, "The National and Progressive Bourgeoisie in Chile," in Cockcroft, Frank, and Johnson, pp. 201–206.
[19] R. Cranford Pratt, "The Cabinet and Presidential Leadership in Tanzania: 1960–1966," in Lofchie, p. 100.

[20] Myron Weiner, "Political Integration and Political Development," *The Annals*, Vol. 358 (March 1965), p. 60.
[21] Wallerstein, pp. 28–32. See also James D. Cockcroft, "Last Rites for the Reformist Model in Latin America," in Cockcroft, Frank, and Johnson, pp. 118–119.

problems, with consequent pressure on the government's budget. Declining prices on the world market for the country's raw materials exports cause the nation's foreign exchange situation to become critical. Much of the national income is spent on imported luxury items, worsening the nation's balance of payments, and not contributing to domestic production. Free transfer of capital leads to capital drain or "flight," typified by the opening of Swiss bank accounts by the country's élite. Steady expansion of the nation's educational system produces too many over-educated persons for the small number of jobs available in the contracting economy, but the government finds that it cannot do anything to reduce school enrollments. Universities become centers of agitation against the government's hiring policies. Unemployment grows, particularly among the urban lower classes and the young intellectuals, creating an explosive coalition of disaffected masses and restive articulate leaders. Foreign interest in supporting the government declines, either as a result of lessening international tensions (the decline of the Cold War) or because of the decline in the return on foreign investment on domestic enterprises. In the face of growing unemployment, rising prices, and declining government services, the lower classes begin to believe charismatic leaders who offer them simplistic explanations for their plight. In Latin America, these leaders may come from universities or from the trade union movement; in Africa, from tribal leadership positions; and in Asia, from plantation unions or from the élite professions (law, medicine, journalism). Popular pressure on the government provokes considerable suppression of individual rights and reshuffling of the cabinet, but the basic causes of the government's discomfort—economic cramp, magnified by international pressure—refuse to go away. As popular rebellion grows, the armed forces are provoked once again to enter the political arena, less for their own benefit (although military budgets *will* increase, once they take power), but more out of a growing realization

that the civilian leaders cannot set things aright.

Wallerstein's typical radical regime begins with an entirely different set of assumptions. Instead of openness in the economy and polity, they seek to close off the national system from disturbing and imperialistic influences. At the international level, this means breaking ties with the former colonial country's currency zone and establishing strict currency controls. Heavy constraints are placed on imports, currency transactions, and the movement of convertible currencies abroad. Internally, while the growing commercial and industrial bourgeoisie has been limited in its development, private foreign investment has not been inhibited until it became apparent that such investment was working against the best interests of the nation. Then, it has usually been confiscated or expropriated by the government, sometimes with compensation (oil companies in Venezuela), sometimes without adequate compensation. In the international political sphere, the radical regime usually adopts an anti-Western, neutralist position, supporting the national liberation movements in the still-colonized areas of the Third World (southern Africa, especially), and radical opposition parties in conservative states. Internally, the one-party state comes into being, and dissent from the right is suppressed. Human rights are denied, as they were by conservative regimes. Despite the many differences between radical and conservative regimes, however, their undoing commonly comes from the same place: growing budgetary deficits, combined with inflation and economic policies that alienate key political groups. In the case of radical regimes, budget deficits grow because of the desire to spend larger amounts to provide needed social services, as well as to create employment. With sufficient jobs, the urban working classes are kept relatively quiet. The problem comes from the taxation side of the equation. In order to pay for growing government programs, the regime tries to tax the traditional and progressive élites, the cash-crop farmers, the urban middle class, and the urban workers. Government bureaucrats are asked to do more with less in the name of fiscal austerity. Luxury imports are restricted, leading to higher domestic prices for inferior goods and angering the middle class. The leftward shift of the government brings about economic retaliation from the West, as manifested by pressures by the World Bank, the International Monetary Fund, and the U.S. government. Foreign sources of capital begin to dry up. Once again, the dreary picture of instability is displayed. Rising costs, declining incomes, loss of governmental control over events, and so forth, all lead to growing unrest, disorders, turbulence, the threat of even more radical policies from the far left and, at last, intervention by the armed forces.

And, so, for the past two decades, the nations of the Third World have swung back and forth between these two alternative governance styles. Sometimes the period between regimes is marked by military government; sometimes the military takes power permanently and attempts to establish its own style or approach to meeting the nation's problems. The exact sequence of events or the exact labels on all the key participants are not important. What does matter is that each regime lacks the sensory mechanisms necessary to let it know when disaster looms, in enough time to pull back from mistaken policies. What we see are a series of experiments in failure, as the Third World oscillates from conservative to radical, and back again, never finding its own solid path to development, and failing to emulate the models from the First and Second Worlds.

Suggestions for Further Reading

Dror, Yehezkel, "Public-Policy-Making in Avant-Garde Development States," *Civilisations* XIII (4) (1963), pp. 395–405.

Heidenheimer, Arnold J., ed., *Political Corruption* (New York: Holt Rinehart and Winston, 1970).

Hirschman, Albert O., *Journeys Toward Progress* (New York: Twentieth Century Fund, 1963).

———, *The Strategy of Economic Development* (New Haven, Conn.: Yale, 1958).

Honey, John C., *Planning and the Private Sector: The Experience in Developing Countries* (New York: Dunellen, 1970).

Ilchmann, Warren F., and Norman Thomas Uphoff, *The Political Economy of Change* (Berkeley: California, 1969).

LaPalombara, Joseph, ed., *Bureaucracy and Political Development* (Princeton, N.J.: Princeton, 1963).

Mason, Edward, *Economic Planning in Underdeveloped Areas* (New York: Fordham, 1958).

Montgomery, John D., and William J. Siffin, eds., *Approaches to Development: Politics, Administration and Change* (New York: McGraw-Hill, 1966).

Riggs, Fred, *Administration in Developing Countries* (Boston: Houghton Mifflin, 1964).

Waterston, Albert, *Development Planning: Lessons of Experience* (Baltimore: Johns Hopkins, 1965).

————, *Planning in Morocco* (Baltimore: Johns Hopkins, 1962).

————, *Planning in Pakistan* (Baltimore: Johns Hopkins, 1963).

Wraith, Ronald, and Edgar Sompkins, *Corruption in Developing Countries* (New York: Norton, 1964).

CHAPTER SEVEN

Political Performance in the Third World

Politics is a struggle under the best of circumstances; but the Third World does not enjoy the best of circumstances, or even anything approaching the best. Nevertheless, the political life of a community must go forward, for better or worse. The pressure of events is relentless. Our concern as students of comparative politics is to assess the degree of success or failure experienced by Third World regimes in responding to these pressures.

Inquiries such as this are always susceptible to distortions caused by ethnocentrism, or the disposition to judge foreign groups by reference to one's own cultural and political customs, institutions, and standards. We have examined Third World governments as they allocate four values: power, well-being, respect, and enlightenment. Although the simple listing of these four values may seem objective enough, the way in which we interpret each of the four may make a great deal of difference in our findings. Consider, for example, the value of respect. In the industrialized democracies of Western Europe and North America, respect means the guarantee of individual human rights against the pressure of the group or the coercion of the state. In countries inspired by Marxist or Maoist philosophy respect may mean comradeship or the feeling of being accepted by the rul-

ing group. In many Third World countries (but by no means all), Western norms of individualism are less important. In these countries, respect may mean the domination of one ethnic group by another, or the prestige enjoyed by the government in international or regional organizations.

As we go about the task of applying the four-value framework to political performance in the Third World, we must try not to define values and goals solely by Western norms. Many developing countries have adopted the goal structure of modern, industrialized nations, even if only superficially or partially. Yet, in most instances, the transfer of Western values took place under duress or coercion, when the recipient colony could not defend itself and its culture against European influence. Understandably, many Third World leaders are caught uncomfortably between their desire to match the economic and political power and well-being of the industrialized nations, on the one hand, and their need to return to the cultural tradition that characterized their peoples before the arrival of the Europeans. The result has been the emergence of mixed traditional-modern philosophies and ideologies to guide the new nations of the developing world. In the 1930s, Victor Raul Haya de la Torre of Peru began to articulate the doctrine of *aprismo* in an attempt to link together the urban, modernizing élites of his country and the poor Indian villagers of the remote interior. Similarly, Julius Nyerere in Tanzania has espoused Ujamaa socialism as the best way to combine traditional village communal values with the benefits of the modern welfare state. Whether any of the mixed ideologies will survive their founders cannot be known this early. At this juncture of history, we can only note the dangers of ethnocentrism, observe the efforts of Third World leaders to define their own goals in terms they can relate to, and then use these same goals as yardsticks against which to measure their performance.

GOALS, ACTIONS, OUTCOMES: POWER

We begin our discussion of political performance in the Third World with the value of power, because of the central role of power in any plan to maximize or distribute any of the other values. Possession of power is, by itself, no guarantee that individuals or governments will really try to enhance human dignity in their societies. But, without power, no individual or government can do much to advance this goal.

Power in the Third World can best be visualized as existing in three more or less separate realms: the international, the national-modern, and the local-traditional. Most national governments in Latin America, Asia, Africa, and the Middle East are caught in a squeeze between two largely autonomous power centers, neither of which is much interested in promoting the power of the national regime. One power center lies outside the Third World: the governments of the developed nations (both the industrialized democracies of the West and the communist states); the private, multi-national corporations located primarily in Western Europe and North America, many of which are richer and more powerful than entire nations in the Third World; and the international institutions that represent the industrial countries (the United Nations, and its subordinate agencies; the International Monetary Fund; the World Bank; and the many separate institutions that control the marketing of raw materials). As long as the international economic, military, cultural, and political systems continue to intrude into their national arenas, the Third World's latitude for reform will be defined by what the international system will permit.

The other competing source of power is just as much an obstacle to national development as the international system, but it usually is harder to locate and identify. This second power center consists of the traditional élites of the countryside and the patrons of both the city and the village, who manipulate their clients to protect them against an encroaching national government. We have already discussed the agents, money lenders, plantation owners, slum bosses, local chieftains, village heads, and the many other petty political powers, each guarding his or her province from the national authority, each benefiting from the respect and privilege received from clients.

In view of the fact that both the international and the clientelistic power sources are in agreement about the necessity to limit the power of the national government, it is not surprising that we occasionally find them in alliance to undermine a particular reformist élite, or to weaken its policies that are designed to strengthen national power. Examples of these alliances are difficult to find in the open literature, since they are usually clandestine and are denounced by the government as illegal when they occur. Nevertheless, there are enough cases openly admitted to suggest that such alliances are fairly common in the Third World. Agencies of the U.S. government, for example, have entered into working relationships with local traditional élites to weaken or unseat reform-minded national regimes on several occasions in Latin America

(Chile, Peru, Guatemala). Return to Chapter 2 to review the arguments about the reasons behind such actions. Here, however, we simply want to illustrate the informal ties that exist between the international power triad (national governments, multi-national corporations, international institutions) and local patrons and other traditional leaders. Together and separately, they render many progressive, reformist regimes in the Third World powerless to carry out their intended transformations of their societies.

Accordingly, the first order of business for reform-minded élites in the Third World must be to concentrate on the accumulation of power at the national level. In the first instance, this means seizing the institutionalized power of the state; and, in the second, it means securing that power and expanding it to reach into areas of the country and the society previously beyond the control of central authority. Power has been seized in the Third World in one of the following ways. A few regimes still in existence can trace their legitimacy back through previous rulers, handed down to them by inheritance. These include the traditional monarchies of Iran and Saudi Arabia. The fate of Ethiopia reveals what happens to this fast disappearing type of political order if it delays modernization too long. In a second type of regime, also represented by comparatively few cases, the present rulers were handed power peacefully by the departing colonial regime. A few such regimes, such as that of Kenyatta in Kenya or Nyerere in Tanzania, are still in power; the great majority have been removed one way or another by successor regimes. Still another way of achieving power is through violent revolution against a stubborn colonial authority, as in Algeria and Indonesia, and (much earlier) in most of the states in Latin America. For most Third World countries, however, the transfer and acquisition of power have now settled down into one of two techniques: either peacefully, through democratic procedures, including open elections (Venezuela, Mexico, Costa Rica, Sri Lanka), or violently and extralegally, often through a military coup, but also through a civilian seizure of power (as in India, prior to the 1977 elections).

Once in power, however, most Third World regimes find that they must devote major resources to the task of remaining there. Of course, simply staying in power is not enough to enable a government to enhance human dignity. The regime must accumulate enough extra power so that some may be diverted to making badly needed changes in the country's society, economy, and culture. Although different strategies are used by different regimes to accumulate power, in essence they all boil down to one significant fact: virtually all of the country's leaders, and most of its mass population, must regard the incumbent regime as having the authority to make decisions on behalf of the entire nation, or the coercive force necessary to require acceptance of these decisions, or both.

Power in this sense can be thought of as a commodity. Power can be exchanged or traded, like money; and it can be taken from one person or group and given to another, like land. In the short run, however, it can not be increased in absolute terms for an entire society. As a regime increases its power, the power of other groups in society, or outside its boundaries, must decline by an approximately equivalent amount. If, for example, the government of Peru were to develop the country's industrial base sufficiently to be relatively impervious to the international economy, then the power of the International Monetary Fund to influence Peruvian politics would decline accordingly. Internally, as the power of the government of India to set a national policy regarding languages increases, the power of various minority linguistic factions must be reduced by the same degree. To the extent that national governments succeed in accumulating and consolidating power, they do so only by influencing competitors to relinquish their power and to transfer their loyalty to the central regime. This is the goal with regard to power.

For regimes that lack control over tangible resources, reliance on the charismatic leader quickly becomes a cornerstone of policies designed to increase power.[1] Charisma has been defined as the ability of a person to make others feel more powerful in his or her presence.[2] In politics, charisma involves a complex psychocultural relationship between a leader and the masses who are led to believe themselves more powerful simply by being in the presence of the great ruler. The entire process then feeds back into itself; the ruler, by enjoying the enthusiastic support of the mass of followers, does indeed become capable of great things, and can lead the country on to high achievements.

Charisma has several functions in a developmental setting. Aided by the apparatus of modern mass communications, the charismatic leader bypasses the traditional bosses, chieftains, and heads of the local areas, and reaches out to enter the consciousness of the low-income and low-status citizens who previously were shielded from national politics by their patrons. Thus armed, the charismatic leader can persuade the masses to undergo sacrifices, to unite in national movements to carry out grand schemes, and to feel themselves part of a larger enterprise: the work of a nation. On the foreign scene, a charismatic leader personifies the nation in its relations with other states, and can, when necessary, direct the sentiment of the people against foreign enemies or to meet external threats.

If the individual leader is not particularly well endowed with charisma, a frequently used substitute is leadership through ideology. Many people in the developing world live in a confusing state of rapid change. One way to secure their support and loyalty is to make rapid change understandable and rational to them. An ideology, in its cohesive and comprehensive picture of the world, makes sense to the populace and enables them to grapple with a world that is more and more threatening. Moreover, the leadership, as the custodian of the official ideology, is given the authority to carry the ideological prescriptions out to their logical, policy conclusions.

Child psychologists tell us that one of the most important early tasks of a mother is to make a child's deprivations and frustrations understandable and rational in a world that the child does not at first grasp. Ideologies and charismatic leaders do much the same sort of thing for illiterate and poor citizens in rapidly changing societies. If the élites perform this function effectively, the masses respond by following them, by obeying their orders, and by quietly enduring the sacrifices imposed on them.

Regimes that rest their power on the personality of a single leader or ideology are in a weak position; individual leaders grow old and die, and ideologies lose their significance in the face of rapid change and repeated crisis. Reforming élites that would endure in power must turn their attention to ways to institutionalize their rule. To institutionalize a particular political phenomenon such as power means to depersonalize it, to embed it in a regularized set of interactions and activities that are identified with the name or label of an organization, and not with the name of an individual. Any mass of politically aware people must be given a feeling that the enterprise in which they are engaged has a life of its own, that it existed before they joined it and, most important, that it will persist after they have left, so that their contributions will not have been in vain. In the United States, political leaders seek to identify themselves and their followers with the ancient sages and leaders of another era (Jefferson and Jackson among the Democrats, Lincoln among the Republicans) to give members of both parties a

[1] This discussion leans heavily on Howard W. Wriggins, *The Ruler's Imperative: Strategies for Political Survival in Asia and Africa* (New York: Columbia, 1969).
[2] David McClelland, "The Two Faces of Power," *Journal of International Affairs XXIV* (1) (1970), pp. 29–47.

sense of the historical ties that bind them not only to earlier generations, but to future ones as well.

Institution building also has to do with predictability and reliability. Feelings of unpredictability and discontinuity often characterize politics in newly created nations. There is little tradition of the essence of politics: how power is transferred, how ordinary citizens can relate to political leaders, what kind of morality one can expect from élites, and so forth. Political organizations, in performing the same tasks over and over, lend predictability to the political process; and the people soon learn what to expect from élites and from their fellow citizens.

Institutions can also improve communications in a society. Rulers can transmit messages to subordinates and hence to mass followings, and they can be reasonably certain that the message that was sent will be the one that arrives. At the same time, the channels of communication are available for the masses to respond, either through acceptance or through protest and dissent. Leaders are well advised to pay attention to the reverse flow of information through institutions, since these channels are likely to be the only ones available.

With comparatively few exceptions, political parties, interest groups, and the other institutions of a modern, developed polity have simply not emerged in the Third World. Where they have emerged, as in Venezuela, Tunisia or Sri Lanka, progressive political leaders have made good use of them to pursue policies that consolidate the power of the ruling élite and also enhance the level of human dignity of the masses of the society. Where they have not emerged, regimes rarely last long enough to embark on fundamental reform, or they are so preoccupied with mustering coercive force to suppress dissent that there is little in the way of resources, energy, or time left to devote to bettering the lot of their citizens.

No regime can endure long if it depends solely, or even largely, on the charismatic charm of a single leader or on the organizational strength and flexibility of a party. At some point, regimes must try to alter certain aspects of the political environment, either inside the country or abroad. At least four kinds of policies have been used by developing regimes in their quest for power: economic development; expansion of participation; encouragement of ethnonationalism; and foreign relations.

Economic development is one of the most important policies for the maintenance of a regime in power. In societies where many people live at or near subsistence levels, expansion of the over-all economic "pie" is a prerequisite for distribution of income or wealth to the poor. Monuments, sports stadia, or public works symbolize the presence and the strength of the regime. Communications and transportation media not only facilitate movement of people from the countryside to the cities and, thereby, throw off the domination of the local patrons, but they also permit extension of central governmental authority into previously inaccessible regions. National industrial strength enables a developing country to resist international economic pressures, especially as they affect its balance of payments and rate of inflation. Certainly, policies of economic development have their drawbacks; it is difficult to finance their costs, and benefits appear only after a long waiting period. But few regimes can last for long if they do not have the industrial and agricultural potential for material well-being in their countries.

A second kind of public policy designed to consolidate a regime's power involves the expansion of political participation. Several of the more progressive élites in the Third World have come to power supported by sectors of the population that previously had been politically inactive. The new regime has reached down into the inert layers of traditional society and awakened groups that had never tried to exert their influence before. The regime must then reinforce the inclination of these new groups to participate by being genuinely responsive to their needs and wishes. Where this has happened, as with the peasants in Venezuela or rural villagers in Sri Lanka, the political system undergoes a genuine transformation, and it is never quite the same again.

At times, however, the mobilization of new actors in the political drama takes on an ugly overtone; regimes may seek to take advantage of smoldering ethnic animosities to secure their power position in society. By pitting one ethnic group against another, or by representing themselves as the protectors of formerly oppressed ethnic groups, regimes may purchase some time in the race to develop and modernize their countries. We have already seen that ideologies are used at times to help define "the enemy" and, quite often, that "enemy" turns out to have a different skin color, speak a different language, or worship a different god. The cost of such policies can only be excessive. The hatred and hostility generated by ethnonationalistic chauvinism may produce solidarity behind the regime for a time; but it is a weak reed on which to rest an entire national government.

Finally, the international environment offers two different kinds of resources that can be directed toward securing domestic power. First, tangible resources, particularly money and military aid, can be of great use to an economic and a political development effort, especially if the donors of such aid can be kept at arm's length. Some developing nations have found that they can form regional alliances, free trade associations, or raw materials cartels, and they thereby come to one another's aid in staving off the threat of Great Power interference in their economies. In addition, the international system offers many important symbolic resources to a struggling, young regime. Membership and a speaking platform in the United Nations and related agencies are taken as proof of the nation's acceptance as an equal member of the world community. Foreign enemies can also be conjured up to provide justification for solidarity behind the regime. These foreign enemies may be industrial states, like the United States, or they may be regional neighbors that profess differing ideologies (Kenya and Uganda, for example) or that claim the same territory (Peru, Bolivia, and Chile). Although this facet of the international system may turn out to be a disadvantage if hostilities flare into real war (as Indonesian President Sukarno found out in his confrontation with Malaysia), a sort of psychological "mini-Cold War" may actually help to consolidate political power on both sides of the border.

With so many state actions available to accumulate and consolidate power at the national level, it is remarkable that in the middle 1970s, 15 to 30 years after the Third World came into being, there is still so little real national power in the region. There remains an abundance of coercive force and personal abuse of power, but the stable, progressive development of power is still a slippery goal that eludes more Third World regimes than have mastered it. Numerous case studies presented here and in other books and articles attest to the continued dominance of the international system in the economies of developing states.[3] There is less firm evidence of the continued power of patrons and anti-modern élites; but the fate of radical reformers such as Chile's Salvador Allende or the leaders of the Palestinian Liberation Organization reveal that the forces of the status quo retain their stranglehold over development policies throughout most of the Third World. Several countries seem to have broken through these obstacles to develop strong, flexible, sources of power that are independent of the international and local spheres. Venezuela, aided by its enormous oil deposits, or Sri Lanka, with its relatively high level of education, or Tanzania, with its extraordinarily astute leader, lead the way, But few of their fellow Third World states follow.

[3] James D. Cockcroft, Andre Gunder Frank, and Dale L. Johnson, *Dependence and Underdevelopment: Latin America's Political Economy* (Garden City, N.Y.: Doubleday, 1972).

GOALS, ACTIONS, OUTCOMES: WELL-BEING

After the seizure, accumulation, and consolidation of power, the next important goal of most developing countries is to enhance the value of well-being. The principal distinguishing feature of the Third World is its grinding and dehumanizing poverty, accompanied by high infant mortality rate, malnutrition, unemployment, lack of housing, social disintegration, and illiteracy. To combat its poverty, almost without exception, nearly every government in the Third World, "radical" or "conservative," must be committed to improving the well-being of its citizens. To achieve this goal, these states must solve the problem of underproduction in industry and agriculture.

The industrial goal of most developing states is twofold: to increase the amount of inputs available to the industrial sector (capital, energy, raw materials, trained labor, infrastructural improvements such as roads and telephone service); and, second, to increase the number of outputs received per unit of input (to increase the productivity of the various production factors). In addition, Third World states would like to channel industrial production away from the extraction of raw materials and toward the manufacture of finished goods; away from industrial systems that were designed with Western societies in mind and toward systems more in keeping with local traditions and resources; away from the manufacture of Western-influenced goods and toward the production of goods that will satisfy real (not manipulated) native demand.

To accomplish these objectives, Third World governments have a wide variety of alternate policy choices available: the regulation of national currency and foreign exchange; the expropriation of private property for public uses; the control of monetary flow and currency levels; propaganda efforts to exhort the citizens to sacrifice for the industrial effort; the power to levy tariffs on imported goods, to tax (or to exempt from taxes) certain industries or firms, or to create money and credit; investment in social and economic infrastructure (roads, electric power, potable water); granting of credit and technical assistance to productive enterprises; direct investment in productive activity; negotiation of contracts with foreign businesses; and price stabilization of major export commodities.[4]

Governments across the entire ideological spectrum try to stimulate industrial production through many of the same public policies.[5] In India, the nation's industrial sector is divided into three spheres: industries reserved for public ownership (mostly strategic industries such as iron and steel, and public utilities); industries in which private capital is expected to supplement public investment (machine tools, drugs, aluminum, transport); and industries reserved for the private sector and guaranteed against national expropriation. Even though India professes to be a socialist state, 90 percent of the nation's industrial productivity remains securely in private hands. The Indian government, through its central economic planning mechanism, seeks to direct private investment decisions in directions desired by the government. However, the government's paramount position in the country's financial and credit institutions, together with the conventional governmental monopoly of certain taxing and spending functions, means that much stimulation of industrial growth occurs in the form of traditional incentives, including the licensing of new industrial facilities, the potential for assuming management of facilities if conditions warrant, and the control over supply, distribution, and price of the company's

[4] Charles W. Anderson, *Politics and Economic Change in Latin America: The Governing of Restless Nations* (Princeton, N.J.: D. Van Nostrand, 1967), pp. 64–65, Table 1.

[5] This is based on John C. Honey, *Planning and the Private Sector: The Experience in Developing Countries* (New York: Dunellen, 1970), especially Chapter 6. See also Stanley A. Kochanek, "India," in Robert N. Kearney, ed., *Politics and Modernization in South and Southeast Asia* (New York: Wiley, 1975), pp. 86–89.

production. The Indian government also gives incentives in the form of tax "holidays" to firms it desires to attract to the country, and otherwise provides substantial advisory services for prospective industries. Finally, because of the nation's recurring severe balance-of-payments problems, India has had to apply sharp restrictions on imports, contributing thereby to national industrial development through import substitution.

Third World countries have access to a sufficient variety of policy instruments to attack the problems of industrial underproduction. Yet, as worldwide industrial production statistics for the past decade reveal, Third World achievements in industrialization have been mixed.[6] The period from 1960 to 1973 was generally a good one for industrial production around the world. Manufacturing rose more than 9 percent annually for the entire world, but the developing countries actually achieved a higher growth rate than the developed market economies of the West: 11.3 percent for the Third World, 8.3 percent for the West. Spurred by this advance, GNP for the planet grew by more than 7 percent annually; the rate was 6.2 percent in the developing states. However, the rapid population growth of the Third World offset much of this gain. Per capita GNP grew worldwide at the rate of almost 4 percent; 4.6 percent in the Western industrial nations; and only 3 percent in the developing countries.

Regional figures sustain the general conclusions. Manufacturing increased at substantial annual rates in specific regions of the Third World: 11.2 percent in Africa; 10.8 percent in Latin America; 18.9 percent in the Middle East; and 10.9 percent in Asia. High population growth rates reduced GNP per capita increases, however, along these lines: 2.4 percent in Africa; 3.2 percent in Latin America; 5.9 percent in the Middle East; and only 2.2 percent in Asia. For the 92 countries in the Third World for which comparable data

are available, only 36 demonstrated GNP per capita growth rates higher than 3.0 percent, 16 showed growth rates between 2.0 and 2.99 percent, and 40 nations struggled along with growth rates that ranged from negative to 1.9 percent. (See Table 5.5.) Despite major increases in industrial production, high rates of population increase mean that per capita GNP in the Third World will double in 20 to 30 years (except in the oil-rich Middle East).

The second half of the problem of poverty lies in agriculture. Here, Third World regimes begin with what seems to be a fairly simple overall objective: to increase the food supply available to their people, to avoid famine, to lower rates of malnutrition and, generally, to raise over-all levels of health and physical well-being in their populations. There are, however, two competing strategies for accomplishing this broad objective.

The first strategy, which emphasizes the continued interrelationships between the developing world and the dominant international economy, is based on the maintenance of the agricultural status quo in the Third World. According to this dependence strategy, the Third World will continue to cultivate export crops such as bananas, coffee, sugar, and cocoa. The foreign exchange gained from these over-seas sales will, in turn, be used to purchase food supplies, principally wheat and rice, from the major international sources: the United States, Canada, Australia and (to a much lesser extent), Argentina. In times of crisis, Third World recipients of food can assume that the world's grain exporting nations will give them free food or sell it to them at highly subsidized prices, not necessarily out of humanitarian concerns, but in order to guarantee high returns to their own farmers, who constitute a powerful domestic interest that must be treated kindly. The dependence strategy has a few good features. It insures that food prices will be kept low in the urban areas of the Third World; hopefully, these low prices can be subsequently translated into social peace and support for the incumbent regime. Foreign business enterprises that own

---

[6] The following is based on the United Nations *Statistical Yearbook* for 1974.

plantations are also reassured that they will be treated fairly and profitably.

By all measures, however, the costs of the dependence strategy outweigh the supposed benefits. For one thing, the strategy practically guarantees that the nation's rural areas will remain backward, not only economically but socially and politically as well, without the financial incentives that accompany production for the national market. Inflation in the grain exporting countries means that the purchase price for wheat and rice will continue to rise, draining the Third World of badly needed foreign exchange. Finally, oscillating prices on the world's raw materials markets mean that secure income cannot be predicted, and national economic planners in developing countries must be prepared for foreign exchange shortfalls from year to year. The results of all of these factors in recent years have been growing food shortages, starvation, and malnutrition on a planet that theoretically could support 40 billion people at an acceptable level of caloric intake.

Confronted with the defects in the dependence strategy, more and more Third World countries, principally Mexico, Brazil, India, Pakistan, and the Philippines, have now turned their attention to a strategy of self-sufficiency. Most, if not all, Third World countries were at one time food exporters, or they at least produced enough food for their

The plenary session of the 1976 meeting of the United Nations Educational, Social and Cultural Organization (UNESCO) convened in Nairobi, Kenya. At this meeting, Third World representatives sharply criticized the news media from the industrialized countries for their biased reporting of events in developing countries. Plans are going forward to restrict the access of foreign media representatives to Third World countries and to form a Third World news Agency that will report the positive aspects of political and economic life in the developing world.

own needs. Many would like to return to that status, and some actually show promise of being able to do so. The self-sufficiency strategy requires an increase in the productivity of land presently under cultivation, as well as bringing new lands under cultivation. For political and technological reasons, the second objective is proving to be more difficult to accomplish than the first. Some presently cultivated land is being used for nonfood export crops; but to bring that land into food production would put the government on a collision course with powerful foreign commercial enterprises, such as United Brands (bananas) and the various international coffee companies. Under-utilized haciendas contain much land kept out of production either because of the cautious mentality of the owner or the absence of sufficient price incentive; to bring it into production would require policies aimed at breaking the power of the landed gentry. There is much land lying in remote areas of many Third World countries that is essentially untouched; to bring it under the plow would require enormous investments in infrastructural improvements (especially roads and irrigation) and other agricultural technologies. One authority on the subject estimated that more than $46 billion would be needed to modernize 50 million hectares of arable but unused land in India. At this same expenditure rate, more than $700 billion spread out over 30 or more years would be required to bring all arable land in developing countries under cultivation.[7] (To put this sum into perspective, remember that the same amount is spent on military purposes by NATO and the Warsaw Pact countries in less than 2 years.)

For these reasons, most developing countries have concentrated their efforts on increasing the agricultural productivity of each unit of land already being used for the cultivation of food. To put into context the actions taken to reach this goal, we must understand the na-

ture of the development process in agricultural production. Generally, agricultural development takes place in four relatively well-defined stages. Each step represents a definite intermediate goal that must be reached and passed through in order to make subsequent stages feasible. The first stage, traditional agriculture, was marked by reliance on conventional hand-wielded implements, rudimentary cultivation and ground-breaking practices, and rainfall for water. Land cultivated this way typically yields less than 1 metric ton of rice per hectare. Most of rural Africa and substantial parts of Latin America (especially in the Andean and Central American mountains) are still farmed in this manner. The second stage is characterized by the introduction of land improvement through irrigation and drainage, the enhancement of soil nutrients through improved incorporation of organic materials, and by better timing of crop production through improved cultivation techniques. Rice yields typically reach 2 tons per hectare. Nearly all of South and Southeast Asia and much of the remainder of Latin America fall into this category. In the third stage, scientifically developed techniques are introduced, thus raising rice yield to the range of 2.5 to 4 metric tons per hectare. During this stage improved varieties of seed, fertilizers, pesticides, and improved storage and transportation facilities, are introduced. Very few countries in the Third World (Taiwan, Malaysia, Mexico, with Venezuela and Brazil soon to enter) are in this category yet. Finally, during stage four, institutional and structural reforms are introduced, thus changing the very nature of agricultural production. Institutions such as research and development laboratories, credit banks, farmers' cooperatives, tractor stations, and farm extension services begin to dot the countryside, making improved food production a regularized and institutionalized matter instead of a question of providence and good weather. Countries fortunate enough to achieve this stage typically produce as much as 6 tons of rice per hectare, and often more. Only South Korea

[7] Roger Revelle, "The Resources Available for Agriculture," *Scientific American 235* (3) (September 1976), pp. 165–178, especially p. 172.

has reached this stage among Third World countries.[8]

The actions required for a developing country to move its agrarian sector from stage two to stage three are contained in the handy but over-worked phrase, "the Green Revolution." Ever since 1970, when Norman Borlaug won the Nobel Peace Prize for developing a miracle strain of wheat that promised food self-sufficiency to developing countries, the Green Revolution has been looked to for salvation for hungry millions. Actually, the Green Revolution is simply a summary term for the many different scientific and technological advances that were being introduced into farming in several developing countries at that time. Foremost among these innovations were the new, high-yield strains of rice and wheat that allowed farmers to irrigate and fertilize their crops to degrees never before possible. But, as many farmers came to understand, the Green Revolution consists of a more or less complete "package" of techniques, each of which must be applied efficiently and in conjunction with the others. The absence of any of these other significant factors could erode the grains brought about by the miracle strains of rice and wheat. These additional technologies include: improved fertilizers (which, because of their petroleum base, made for increased imports from the oil exporting countries); wells, pumps, ditches, and embankments for better irrigation; improved harvesting and cultivating machinery; improved facilities to store, transport, and market the additional output; and new pesticides to keep down the rodents and other pests that infested the fields. In addition, certain social factors had to be present as well. The nature of cultivation of the miracle strains required more labor, and for a more regular period of time; so the character of rural employment had to change. Finally, because the investment required to acquire all of these innovations was substantial, progressive farmers had to be guaranteed a satisfactory return on their investment which, in turn, meant the introduction of guaranteed high prices, or subsidies, or both. In any event, major government intervention in both the rural areas and the urban markets seemed inevitable.[9]

To what extent have these government policies succeeded in actually raising the level of food production in the Third World? Certainly, no one can doubt that some amazing achievements have been recorded by certain individual countries. India, for example, one of the leading exponents of the Green Revolution, has raised its rate of increase in farm output from 2.5 percent during the period from 1947 to 1965 to about 3.3 percent during the 1965 to 1971 period, and prospects are for a jump to 5 percent during the 1970s. Pakistan, another important Asian agricultural state, increased its rice and wheat production from 1966 to 1967 by more than 30 percent to 1968 to 1969. From 1966 to 1970, production of rice in Asia as a whole rose from 232.4 million metric tons to 260 million metric tons; wheat rose from 61.8 million metric tons to 71.4 million metric tons. Similar advances were registered in maize and barley.

Nevertheless, when taken as a whole, the record of the Third World in food production has been poor, and it is probably going to get worse before any improvement is noted. Let us consider gross production indicators from 1963 to 1973. During this 11-year span, world food production climbed at an average annual rate of 2.8 percent, in the developing countries, the rate was slightly lower: 2.5 percent. In Africa, the worst record was compiled, 1.5 percent annually; Latin America and Asia registered increases of about 2.5 percent; in the Middle East, production climbed about 3 percent. These increases, however, do not take into account population growth. World food production per capita from 1963 to 1973

[8] W. David Hopper, "The Development of Agriculture in Developing Countries," *Scientific American* 235 (3) (September 1976), pp. 197–205.

[9] Zubeida Manzoor Ahmed, "The Social and Economic Implications of the Green Revolution in Asia," *International Labour Review, 105* (January-June, 1972), pp. 9–34.

remained almost stable: an increase of 0.6 percent. In the developing world as a whole, per capita food production actually *declined* by two tenths of 1 percent, as a result of Africa's disastrous record (−1.0 percent) and relative stability in the other three regions. Of the 71 developing nations for which data are available from 1953 to 1971, food production failed to keep pace with population growth in 24; in 17 more nations, growth in food production fell short of the increased demand for food (a combined result of increased population and rising personal incomes). Thus, in only 30 nations from this sample did food production manage to equal population growth and increased demand. Even in Mexico, where Borlaug developed the miracle strains of wheat, the Green Revolution appears to have run its course, but population growth continues at the rate of 3.5 percent. Where Mexico was actually exporting wheat, corn, and beans from 1966 to 1969, by the early 1970s, the country had to import between 15 and 20 percent of its basic food grains. Despite almost heroic measures in some countries and continued effort in most of the rest, population growth is eroding what little increase in food production there is in the Third World.

GOALS, ACTIONS, OUTCOMES: ENLIGHTENMENT AND RESPECT

Third World governments generally accord a higher priority to power and well-being policies and goals than they do to enlightenment and respect. The relative poverty of the Third World in both power and material comfort dictates that any progressive government must attend to these needs first, relegating enlightenment and respect goals to a second level of importance. Where enlightenment and respect policies do receive great attention, it is usually to serve the goals of power and well-being first. Only secondarily do policies bearing on enlightenment and respect have any intrinsic worth.

We will shortly examine some data regarding the performance of Third World regimes in the fields of enlightenment and respect. Be aware that we have entered areas of human behavior that resist quantitative analysis. We will look at some numerical indicators of performance, but treat all such data with a certain degree of skepticism. At best, the data reflect general orders of magnitude instead of precise levels of performance.

Enlightenment

In a different context (see Chapter 3), we have already considered what Third World governments attempt to do in the field of enlightenment in order to increase the value of national power. Turn back to the section of control and censorship of the mass media of communications; you should realize now that what Third World regimes intend with their policies is to manipulate the media to advance the cause of national unity, integrity, loyalty, and legitimacy. In the conclusions from Chapter 3, we found that the majority of Third World governments exercise some form of control over their nation's news media, especially in radio, film, and television. Even in the print media, newspapers and magazines, many Third World regimes exert what amounts to de facto censorship powers in an effort to shape the information given to the mass population.

The fate of Mexico City's great newspaper *Excelsior* in 1976 illustrates the unmistakable trend toward increasing government control of the news media in the Third World. In July 1976, a splinter faction of dissidents and toughs took over the cooperative-run newspaper, while Mexico's President Luis Echeverria looked on with disinterest. For many months, the world-famous and prestigious *Excelsior* had been carrying on a running feud with the Mexican government, not only for the paper's criticism of government policies, but also because of its attacks on the military dictatorships that came to power in Chile and

Uruguay during the early 1970s. From late 1975 to the middle of 1976, the Mexican government lashed out at the *Excelsior* editor-in-chief, Julio Scherer Garcia, and his staff, for allegedly undermining public confidence in the government through its attacks. In June, a mob of slum dwellers was bussed by the government to a 90-hectare property owned by the newspaper; they began to squat illegally on the land. Government officials refused to take action to evict them. Matters worsened until the tumultuous meeting of July 8, when a gang of thugs shouted down the Scherer supporters in an illegal meeting of the *Excelsior* cooperative; they threatened Scherer with bodily harm if he did not leave the newspaper's building. Once evicted from the premises, Scherer was removed from his position, and the paper passed into the control of pro-government editors and reporters. Scherer's subsequent efforts to launch another newspaper in Mexico City have been harrassed by government agencies, which have denied Scherer the newsprint he needs to start printing. In effect, all free press criticism of the Mexican government has been stifled by the *Excelsior* coup.[10]

Third World governments have demonstrated resolutely that they have the power to close down critical newspapers and magazines internally, but they have still not been able to do much about the persistent criticism emanating from the international wire services and other news agencies, such as Reuters or United Press International. During 1975 and 1976, many developing countries, led by Mexico, began to urge the creation of a Third World news agency, to be based in Mexico City. This new agency would foster the publication of news reports favorable to the Third World, in order to counteract the bad impressions left by the critical international news agencies. In October 1976, the issue came to a head at the meeting of the United

Nations Educational, Scientific and Cultural Organization (UNESCO) in Nairobi, Kenya. At the UNESCO meeting, Third World delegates sought to pass a resolution that would go beyond the "news pool" idea, and they asserted that governments "are responsible for the activities in the international sphere of all mass media under their jurisdiction," a proposition that runs exactly counter to the notion of press freedom. Regardless of how that particular issue is resolved, Third World regimes are determined both to silence criticism of their policies and to see to it that positive and favorable press accounts of national politics are made available to their people.

Such policies toward the news media will have the effect of promoting national unity and, thereby, of strengthening national governments; but such policies will also concentrate power into fewer and fewer hands. As the opposition élites that formerly occupied positions of responsibility in the media are forced out and replaced by government representatives, power will be redistributed toward a single national élite that is directly beholden to government agencies. The prevailing trend in the Third World is to undertake policies in the field of enlightenment that will encourage the growth of power at the national level, but that will also distribute that power even more unequally than had previously been the case.

Our consideration of enlightenment policies that have a bearing on well-being must obviously lead us to look at educational policy in the Third World. Third World élites have been greatly influenced by the very favorable effects of large expenditures on public education in developed countries. Despite the obvious differences between the economic and cultural environments in developed and less developed countries, Third World leaders are convinced that they can make massive improvements in the economic potential of their countries by investing heavily in the human capital of their society, and that means invest-

[10] Armando Vargas, "The Coup at Excelsior," *Columbia Journalism Review*, (September/October 1976), pp. 45–48.

Bodies, bearing placards, hang from the gallows in downtown Damascus, Syria, September 1976. The three men (and an accomplice who was killed) had seized a hotel the day before and held hostages before they were captured by Syrian troops. Thousands of people crowded to within 50 yards of the hanging, the first held publicly in Damascus since the 1965 execution of an accused Israeli spy.

ing in education. Table 7.1 illustrates the level of effort being made by selected Third World governments in the field of education. These 12 governments spend between 2.5 and 7.1 percent of their GNP and between 10.8 and 31.2 percent of their national government budget on education. (The respective mean percentages are 4.4 percent and 19.3 percent.) These figures indicate that education has only a slightly lower priority for Third World countries than national defense has for the United States.

Beyond the bare statistics of educational expenditures lie several major areas of dispute over educational priorities. Boiled down to its essentials, the dispute amounts to a difference of opinion whether to stress low-level education to raise literacy rates, or high-level education to provide the managers and skilled professionals to run a developing economy. To some degree, the dispute changes focus, depending on the relative stage of development of a given country. Nations that are still rather backward and traditional are faced with a major problem in communications; no matter

how much they spend on the electronic media (radio and television), there are still many significant kinds of information that can only be communicated by the written or printed word. In an urban setting, well over half of all information is conveyed by written media, according to one study by a communications expert.[11] A society that enjoys general literacy among its adult population possess the potential for a completely different kind of economic and social organization, one that emphasizes bureaucratic rule-making, the transmission of formal, written messages, and one that can rely on the performance of routine tasks efficiency by individuals with a minimum of personal supervision. The drive for adult literacy in developing countries goes far beyond the need for an individual citizen to be able to read a newspaper. It has an impact on the organizational potential of a society. Inasmuch as we have repeatedly stressed the need for Third World countries to

[11] Richard L. Meier, "The Measurement of Social Change, in *Proceedings of the Western Joint Computer Conference,* San Francisco, 1959.

TABLE 7.1
Performance of Selected Third World Countries in Education, circa 1971–1973

Country	Percent of total population enrolled in schools	Percent of GNP devoted to education	Percent of central government budget devoted to education
Tanzania	8.1	3.8	15.0
Ivory Coast	14.6	7.1	31.2
Ghana	16.7	4.6	19.8
Sri Lanka	18.9	4.1	12.2
India	10.7	2.5	23.2
Indonesia	12.5	2.7	18.9
Mexico	24.1	3.0	12.0
Venezuela	23.3	4.7	24.4
Peru	26.6	4.3	22.5
Tunisia	21.4	6.0	22.7
Egypt	17.0	5.8	18.6
Syria	21.1	3.9	10.8

Source: United Nations *Statistical Yearbook,* 1974 and 1975.

enhance their institutional power, both politically and economically, we see that increased literacy is an indispensable component of this approach.

In Table 7.2, we can see the result of literacy policies in the 12 countries we have selected for detailed examination. Obviously, many of these figures are rough and unreliable, especially those for the earlier period. Nevertheless, very few countries exhibit any remarkable breakthrough in literacy. Those nations, like Sri Lanka, that enjoyed high literacy rates two decades ago improved slightly on their performance. A few, like Tunisia, managed to double their percentage, but the very low point of departure means that they are still basically an illiterate nation for most purposes. The remainder demonstrated either slight improvement, stagnation, or (in the case of Peru) actual deterioration in literacy rates. Despite massive infusions of

technical assistance and capital into literacy programs, rapid population growth, especially among the rural and urban poor, robs the policy of much of its impact.

At the opposite end of the spectrum are the advocates of policies that would stress upper-level training to prepare people to staff a complex society and its institutions. Here, the data are clearly inadequate and are merely suggestive of the magnitude of the problem. In the United States, for example, approximately 1.25 percent of the total population is employed as a scientist, engineer, or technician, while about 0.3 percent of the population works in fields that deal with scientific research and development. In typical Third World countries, the figures are likely to be about a tenth of these levels. In India, a country relatively well endowed with educational facilities, scientists and enigineers constitute about 0.25 percent of the total

TABLE 7.2
Changes in Literacy Rates in Selected Third World Countries, circa 1955–1960 and 1974

Country	Literacy Rate 1955–1960	Literacy Rate 1974
Tanzania	18	15–20
Ivory Coast	20	20
Ghana	23	25
Sri Lanka	75	82
India	28	29
Indonesia	43	60
Mexico	65	65
Venezuela	65	74
Peru	60	45–50
Tunisia	16	30
Egypt	27	40
Syria	35	40

Sources: For 1974: *The World Factbook: 1974* (Acton, Mass.: Publishing Sciences Group, Inc., 1974). For 1955-1960: United Nations *Statistical Yearbook: 1964*; also, Charles Taylor and Michael Hudson, *World Handbook of Political and Social Indicators*, 2nd ed (New Haven, Conn.: Yale, 1972), pp. 232–235.

population, while research and development tasks occupy 0.017 percent. In Ghana, comparable figures are 0.2 percent and 0.04 percent. The same holds true for most Latin American countries.[12]

The gravity of the problem is clear to all interested observers, but policy solutions are consistently falling short of success for several reasons. For one thing, upper-level training of this sort has been found to be extremely expensive, especially when compared with lower-level, primary grade education. Whereas

[12] Calculated from data in the United Nations *Statistical Yearbook: 1975.*

in the United States, post-secondary education may cost, per pupil, about twice what it costs to educate a student in the primary grades, in developing countries the data indicate that the ratio may be 1:40. Pressed by the scarcity of funds, Third World governments may succumb to the apparent bargain they purchase by investing in primary education. A second problem stems from the relatively great prestige of higher education in fields like the humanities, law, and the social sciences, while what developing countries need are students in fields like the physical and natural sciences, engineering, and agronomy. The distortion in university enrollments often means that many students flood the market in law and humanities and become disgruntled when they fail to find employment. The interaction of an expanding educational system and a stable or contracting economy brings about the third problem in educational policy: the phenomenon of the "brain drain," or the migration of highly trained professionals from developing countries, where they are needed in theory but where there are often too few real jobs available, to the more highly developed markets of Europe and North America. Finally, we must note the effects of educational policy on equality in the Third World. As Charles Elliott points out, Third World educational programs frequently aggravate the tendency toward differentiation, whereby a certain few individuals are chosen to move up the social, economic, and political ladder by means of a highly selective policy that relegates the vast majority to a continued life of poverty. Educational policies as they are implemented in the Third World usually skew the distribution of income and power even more than would be the case if the government allowed market forces to operate freely. Government loans and scholarships, decisions about where to build schools, teacher assignments, informal ties to certain racial or religious groups that smooth their access to educational resources, and other policies operate to accelerate the rise of a very few individuals, at the expense of leaving behind the great bulk of their fellow citizens.[13] We find that educational policies emphasize growth, while operating to accentuate inequity.[14]

Respect

During his campaign for the Presidency and, subsequently, in the opening months of his administration, Jimmy Carter moved quickly to make clear the concern of the U.S. government over the plight of political prisoners and over the fate of human rights generally, not only in the Soviet Union, but also in many Third World states. The expressions of concern were not limited to rhetoric; foreign military assistance was reduced or eliminated entirely if the recipient was judged to be in violation of human rights (and if the aid reduction did not adversely affect America's defense posture). Some of the Third World countries affected were Uruguay, Ethiopia, and Chile. Others, such as Brazil, rejected continued American aid if it was to be accompanied by lectures about human rights.

Few policy areas are as difficult to assess as those having to do with human rights violations, and the difficulties are compounded when the region of concern is the Third World. Let us consider first the problem of information. We must recognize the extreme sensitivity of most governments to matters of this sort. Are governments really interested in evaluating policy outcomes or in measuring political performance, in this field? Past experiences and common sense suggest that they are not. Nearly every state in the Third World is a signatory of the United Nations Declaration on Human Rights, yet many of them systematically violate that Declaration. Most governments are reluctant to admit any

deviation from their professed goals and objectives; can we expect any less when the issue of concern is so controversial and sensitive? Then there is the problem of unbiased news reporting in the Third World. Most of the information that we have about human rights violations in the Third World comes from one of two sources: Amnesty International and other international human rights reporting agencies; and Western news agencies. Both of these agents of information have come under fire for extreme biases in their reporting. Critics of Amnesty International complain that it only criticizes right-wing dictatorships, such as Chile and Argentina, and never (or seldom) charges left-wing regimes with suppression of human rights. On the other side of the ledger, as we have already seen, so many Third World governments have complained of reporting by the Western news agencies (such as United Press International and Reuters) that they are moving to replace these services with a Third World news network. In such an emotion-charged area of human relations, can we ever expect to obtain information that would meet scientific standards for objectivity, methodological rigor, and verifiability? The answer seems highly doubtful.

Even if the information problem could be solved, however, we must still deal with the philosophical question of how to interpret news about Third World violations of human rights. Are these events really all that uncommon? We know that many countries that now enjoy a democratic tradition once suppressed dissent and freedom of political thought in the interest of public order and economic progress. Is the Western tradition entirely applicable here? Perhaps the poverty and illiteracy of many Third World countries work to make freedom of political expression an unacceptable luxury at this stage of their development. And, are there no long-term benefits to be derived from the near-term suppression of human rights? At one time or another, nearly every country on earth, including our own, has denied free expression to certain groups of

[13] Charles Elliott, *Patterns of Poverty in the Third World* (New York: Praeger, 1975), Chapter 9.
[14] Many of these issues are discussed in greater detail in Bert F. Hoselitz, "Investment in Education and Its Political Impact," in James S. Coleman, ed., *Education and Political Development* (Princeton, N.J.: Princeton, 1965), Chapter 16.

people in the interest of increasing or preserving the well-being of the remainder.

For their part, many Third World leaders claim that human dignity can be guaranteed and protected without building the intricate structure of institutions and laws that characterize the Western approach to human rights. On the contrary, they argue, many Western traditions actually work to deny individuals their rights in a developing setting. Political parties, for example, only aggravate conflict and institutionalize class strife; while elections polarize opinion and foster disunity, when what the country needs is an integrating force. A free press merely serves to enflame passions; while irresponsible demogogues take advantage of free speech to whip up the masses, and provoke them to rebellion. Many non-Western societies, such as Indonesia, place greater emphasis on mass, public consensus as a prelude to decision-making than they do on dissent and adversary proceedings so important to pluralist democrats in the West. Most important, many Third World leaders assert that public order is required to preserve private rights. Those who would dissent and who would disrupt the public order must be suppressed in order to protect the rights of those who are loyal to the state.

We may admit the validity of more than one approach to this most complex question, but we may not retreat into ignorance and fuzzy generalizations about human rights. Instead, what we have attempted to do here is survey several sources of information about the status of human rights around the world and categorize the various Third World regimes according to the actions they have taken in this field.[15] The reader must then determine for himself or herself what this information signifies in our overall appraisal of Third World political performance.

We will consider government policies that have to do with political rights, or the liberties that a person is thought to enjoy regardless of political opinion, partisan affiliation, or attitude. In order for a political system to be considered a democracy, three criteria must be satisfied. First, there must be safeguards for each individual to speak and to organize according to his or her political beliefs. Governments that seek to suppress these rights may censor or otherwise control the media of mass communications, imprison persons for their beliefs in the political realm, and infringe on the rights of representative assemblies (legislatures, parliaments, congresses) to articulate dissenting opinions. Second, in a democracy, safeguards must exist for the freedom of individuals to remove the existing regime through elections, and to replace it with one more to the liking of the people. Furthermore, this freedom must be protected through the creation of appropriate institutions, so that its exercise does not depend on the whim of a single individual. Regimes that intend to suppress these freedoms concentrate their policies on preventing free and open elections, on the prohibition of some or all political parties, and on over-riding the constitution by some extralegal procedure. Third, in a democracy, individual citizens must be able to live in peace, without fear that the state will terrorize them or allow others to do so for political reasons. Regimes that do not uphold these freedoms practice torture and other inhuman prison practices, and encourage vigilante-type groups to engage in illegal but unpunished, assassinations or dissenting political leaders.[16]

Tables 7.3 and 7.4 reveal findings about the extent of human rights violations in the Third World. In Table 7.3, for example, we see that

[15] Major sources of information include Arthur S. Banks, ed., *Political Handbook of the World: 1976* (New York: McGraw-Hill, 1976). Also, Amnesty International, *Annual Report* (annual), and other Amnesty International publications.

[16] This discussion is based on Rupert Emerson, "The Prospects for Democracy in Africa," in Michael F. Lofchie, ed., *The State of the Nations: Constraints on Development in Independent Africa* (Berkeley: California, 1971), Chapter 11. See also the important collection of studies in Willem A. Veenhoven, ed., *Case Studies on Human Rights and Fundamental Freedoms: A World Survey,* 2 vols. (The Hague: Martinus Nijhoff, 1975).

TABLE 7.3
Actions Taken by Third World Governments To Suppress Human Rights, 1971–1976

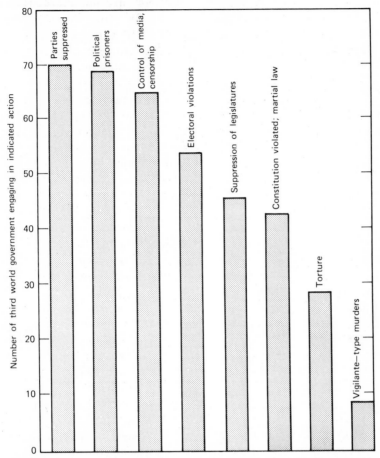

Number of third world government engaging in indicated action

- Parties suppressed
- Political prisoners
- Control of media, censorship
- Electoral violations
- Suppression of legislatures
- Constitution violated; martial law
- Torture
- Vigilante–type murders

Sources: Arthur S. Banks, ed., *Political Handbook of the World: 1976* (New York: McGraw-Hill, 1976). Publications of Amnesty International; Contemporary press reports.

during the early 1970s, 70 governments in the Third World (more than 62 percent of the total) had implemented policies to outlaw at least one political party, and many had prohibited all parties. Sixty-nine countries imprisoned individuals for expressing their political beliefs; 65 controlled or censored the mass media in some fashion; between 40 and 50 had violated their own constitutions and their own electoral laws; and 46 had dismissed or suspended their national legislatures. Finally, in 29 cases, prisoners were tortured to at

least a great enough extent to attract the attention of the international news media or of Amnesty International; in nine countries, illegal "death squads" carried out vigilante-type murders of opponents of the incumbent regime. Table 7.4 categorizes Third World nations by attaching numerical indicators to rights violation policies. In brief, countries were given one "point" each time they engaged in one of the six suppressive policies listed to the left of Table 7.3, and two "points" for each instance of the more serious policies

TABLE 7.4
Human Rights Violation Scores in the Third World, 1971–1976
(0 = no rights violations recorded; 10 = rights violations in every category recorded)

Not Ranked (3)	0 (18)	1 (4)	2 (10)	3 (12)	4 (19)
Angola	Bahamas	Bhutan	Bahrain	Dominican	Burma
Cyprus	Barbados	Mauritius	Brunei	Republic	Burundi
Lebanon	Botswana	Nauru	Cameroon	Gabon	Colombia
	Cape Verde	West Samoa	Comoro Island	Guatemala	Egypt
	Costa Rica		Congo Republic	Malawi	Kenya
	El Salvador		Honduras	Malaysia	Kuwait
	Fiji		Maldives	Mauritania	Lesotho
	Gambia		Nepal	Mozambique	Liberia
	Grenada		Sao Tome	Qatar	Madagascar
	Guinea-Bissau		Venezuela	Sierra Leone	Mexico
	Guyana			Sri Lanka	Oman
	Jamaica			Tanzania	Panama
	Papua			Zaire	Rhodesia
	Surinam				Somalia
	Swaziland				Syria
	Tonga				Tunisia
	Trinidad				Upper Volta
	United Arab				Yemen Arab
	Emirates				Republic
					Peoples
					Democratic
					Republic
					of Yemen

5 (18)	6 (14)	7 (7)	8 (4)	9 (2)	10 (1)
Afghanistan	Algeria	Bolivia	Brazil	Argentina	Uruguay
Bangladesh	Benin	Ghana	Chile	Uganda	
Ecuador	Central	Haiti	Iraq		
Guinea	African	Iran	Paraguay		
Ivory Coast	Republic	Philippines			
Jordan	Chad	Singapore			
Libya	Equatorial	Thailand			
Mali	Guinea				
Niger	Ethiopia				
Nigeria	India				
Peru	Indonesia				
Rwanda	Morocco				
Saudi Arabia	Nicaragua				
Senegal	Pakistan				
Sudan	South Africa				
Taiwan	South Korea				
Togo	Zambia				
Turkey					

of torture and vigilante-type murders. Thus, the highest score a nation could receive would be 10 points, indicating that we had found evidence of rights violations in every category of the study. The table shows that 18 countries had no record of rights violations, while four appeared in only one category, and 10 appeared in two. Thus, we can group together these categories and assert that 32 nations of the Third World were fairly respectful of human political rights. In the middle group, with scores of three, four, or five, are 49 countries; the extreme violators of human rights (scores 6 to 10) constitute fully one quarter of the entire group (28 countries). Careful inspection of the table will show, however, that most of the countries at the "democratic" end of the scale are very tiny islands, a large percentage of which were former British colonies (Barbados, Bahamas, Trinidad, Jamaica, and so on); the larger and more populous nations are clustered in the four, five, and six categories. Taken as a whole, the table shows that human rights violations constitute a significant problem in more than two-thirds of the entire group of 112 nations.

As suggested elsewhere in this textbook, many Third World regimes would attempt to justify their policies toward human rights by claiming that they make possible more rapid economic growth. In Table 7.5, we test that assertion by comparing economic growth records for 1965 to 1974 with a country's record in the field of respect for human rights. (Only 92 nations are dealt with in this table because of an absence of comparable data for the remainder.) Notice that, of the 28 nations that violated human rights extensively (scores 6 to 10 on Table 7.4), nine (or about one-third) had achieved GNP per capita growth rates higher than 3.00 percent. Of the 48 countries where human rights were violated only to a moderate degree, 19 (39 percent) attained a high growth rate. Of the 16 countries where human rights were respected, 8 (50 percent) achieved high rates of economic growth. Now, it is obvious that we cannot claim that one

phenomenon caused the other. Respect for human rights does not cause high growth rates, although *poor* growth rates *may* cause human rights suppression. Nevertheless, we believe that the data from Table 7.5 reveal that it is possible to achieve high rates of economic growth while at the same time guaranteeing the protection of human rights. That few Third World leaders accept this proposition is not only a mark of their lack of faith in the judgments and opinions of their people, but also an unfavorable sign of future developments for the Third World.

CONCLUSIONS: ENHANCING HUMAN DIGNITY IN THE THIRD WORLD

In the preceding pages, we have assessed the performance of the 112 governments of the Third World as they struggle to improve the level of human dignity in their countries. Not surprisingly, the record is a mixed one. Scattered throughout the developing world are significant cases of impressive success, and even of heroic triumph over the obstacles to development. In Venezuela, Sri Lanka, Tanzania, and Tunisia, among others, progressive governments have the development process in hand, and they have achieved this without serious suppression of individual freedoms. In other countries, including some that once offered great promise of success, the results have been decidedly negative, even bordering on disastrous. Uruguay, Uganda, Ghana, and Ethiopia typify these countries. In general, however, we simply do not know at this stage in their development how most countries will fare in the struggle. Many countries exhibit wide variations in performance from year to year, and most are highly vulnerable to factors beyond their control, such as the condition of the international economy or the weather. With the exception of the older countries of Latin America, most Third World states have not been independent long enough to demonstrate a "track record," so it is too

TABLE 7.5
Selected Third World Countries Compared According to the Degree of Violation of Human Rights, and Growth Rate of GNP per Capita, 1965–1974

Violation of Human Rights	GNP/capita Growth Rate				
	Less than 0.00	0.00–0.99	1.00–1.99	2.00–2.99	3.00+
Human rights violated to great degree (scores 6–10, Table 7.4) (28)	(4) Chad, Equatorial Guinea, Uruguay, Zambia	(5) Benin, Central African Republic, Ghana, Uganda, India	(4) Chile, Haiti, Ethiopia, Morocco	(6) Argentina, Bolivia, Nicaragua, Paraguay, Philippines, South Africa	(9) Brazil, Algeria, Iraq, Thailand, Indonesia, South Korea, Pakistan, Iran, Singapore
Human rights violated to moderate degree (scores 3–5, Table 7.4) (48)	(5) Mali, Niger, Somalia, Sudan, Senegal	(10) Burundi, Madagascar, Upper Volta, Afghanistan, Egypt, Jordan, Lesotho, Zaire, Burma, Peoples Democratic Republic of Yemen	(6) Yemen Arab Republic, Sierra Leone, Kuwait, Qatar, Mauritania, Guinea	(8) Ecuador, Peru, Bangladesh, Colombia, Syria, Mexico, Tanzania, Sri Lanka	(19) Panama, Libya, Nigeria, Rwanda, Togo, Dominican Republic, Guatemala, Oman, Turkey, Gabon, Kenya, Liberia, Malawi, Taiwan, Saudi Arabia, Tunisia, Ivory Coast, Rhodesia, Malaysia
Human rights respected (scores 0–2, Table 7.4) (16)	(1) Bahrain	(2) Guyana, Nepal	(3) Honduras, El Salvador, Venezuela	(2) Jamaica, Gambia	(8) Congo Republic, Cameroon, Costa Rica, United Arab Emirates, Trinidad, Botswana, Mauritius, Swaziland

Sources: Violation of human rights: see Table 7.4. GNP per capita growth rate: see Table 5.5.

early to make any firm judgments about their future.

As most Third World élites know only too well, however, many of the important determinants of human dignity look more like obstacles than opportunities. Power remains divided among three competing forces: local, tradition-bound élites, national governments, and powerful international agencies. Economic development is being advanced somewhat in the industrial sphere, but agricultural production has stagnated throughout the area, and exponential population growth threatens to erode progress in both sectors. Enlightenment policies dwell excessively on interference with the free flow of ideas, particularly when they offer criticism of the existing regime, while educational expenditures are too little and too late to keep up with the challenge of population growth. And a growing number of Third World regimes are leaning toward the denial of human rights in an effort (usually futile) to keep order and accelerate economic growth. In sum, the balance sheet of human dignity in the Third World looks mixed, but with signs of deterioration over the coming decade.

The preceding chapters have focused on the separate threads of Third World politics. It is time now to pull these threads together into a coherent picture to explain why many Third World countries find themselves in such difficulty today. Our explanation must deal with three factors: the environment, the individuals who occupy important political roles, and the structural setting within which the political drama is acted out. Just as the surface area of a rectangle is a function of the interaction of its length and width, so also is Third World politics a function of the interaction of these three factors. No single factor can be isolated as being of paramount importance; each interacts with the other two in both cause and effect relationships.

First, let us consider the environment. The historical experience of colonialism has left a residue of attitudes and institutions that has proven intractable. The international political and economic system works against the national interests of poor and developing states, quite apart from whether some evil force so wills it, or whether the system is some kind of mammoth practical joke played by impersonal forces on struggling Third World countries. The privileged role enjoyed by traditional élites is also a severe obstacle to more progressive policies at home. The comparative scarcity of natural resources (and of financial ones, too) has aggravated the disadvantage suffered by developing states who are late arrivals on the path to industrialization. At times, it seems that even the weather and other natural forces conspire against the world's poor countries, as droughts, monsoons, floods and earthquakes seem to affect most those nations and peoples that can least protect themselves against their force. In short, the environment within which the Third World must act is mostly unfavorable for the improvement of human dignity.

The human resources of the Third World also offer their share of obstacles to progress. Low levels of health, nutrition, and literacy come together to sap the working class of its strength and productivity, and thereby make it that much more difficult to launch a flourishing industrial effort with the necessary skilled labor. The prevailing personality structure that characterizes many non-Western societies seems ill suited to the requirements of incremental politics, compromise, joining with others for political gains, or valuing achievement. Many facets of the traditional personality do seem quite functional in the context of a struggle against colonial powers, where heroic measures and enormous sacrifice are called for, and compromise is equivalent to betrayal. But, once independence is won and the system settles into the day-by-day routine of meeting economic and social challenges, a new kind of personality is required, and traditional child-rearing and socialization procedures seem badly equipped to shape such a personality. In addition, dimensions of a society such as the way in which families rear their young are beyond the reach of most Third World governments. Changes in basic personality may occur, but they will take place more as the result of the gradual impact of economic modernization than they will as the outcome of intentional public policy. Finally, the heavy reliance of mass populations on charismatic leaders makes it correspondingly more difficult for these same leaders to build the institutions so necessary for a developing country. Again, the charismatic leader is very valuable during the anticolonial struggle, when public commitment must be raised to new heights. Eventually, however, charisma must yield to institutions as the motivating force for political change. Regretably, many charismatic leaders fail to sense the appropriate time to begin to ease the state to a new foundation, one that will outlast the revolutionary leaders.

These comments bring us to the structural dimension of Third World politics. Readers who have followed our arguments through the book must now realize that the institutionalization of political change must receive top priority from reforming élites. The reasons for this are spelled out in greatest detail in Chapters 4, 5, and 7. The institutional base left behind by colonial economics and politics contains both individuals and regularized relationships that resist and, eventually, undermine efforts to modernize and industrialize. Instead of dealing decisively with these antimodern forces, as has been done in both Western democracies or in communist states, most Third World governments have opted for a sort of shaky compromise, wherein the traditional élites are left alone, and modernization is pursued in only a part of the nation. Not surprisingly, the costs of change are than borne by those individuals who cannot protect themselves from bearing the burden: the urban and rural poor. The institutions that have come to the aid of these classes in other regions in the past, political parties and interest groups, are notoriously ineffectual in most Third World situations, and they often are even captive of the very regimes whose actions they exist to influence. This is not to say that every country in the Third World must now adopt the two-party system and create a chamber of commerce. The particular institutional network created within each country must be closely related to that country's peculiar social, economic, and historical background. But, absent the institutions to mobilize, organize and shape the collective behavior of the Third World's masses, and progress toward distribution of power, well-being, enlightenment, and respect will lag behind the expectations of the bulk of the population, with disastrous consequences.

WHY IS THERE SO LITTLE UPHEAVAL IN THE THIRD WORLD?

Given the massive discontent that we in the West sense in developing countries, why is there so little actual revolutionary change in these nations? This textbook has tried to make the argument that the majority of developing nations are not appreciably better off today than they were 10 or 15 years ago. Even worse, the small gains of development are distributed in a highly uneven manner, so that the average citizen of the Third World must surely note little real improvement in his or her life over the years. Yet, with few exceptions, there seems to be little support for radical change in these countries. Even in those few countries where radicalization has occurred, such as Cuba or Vietnam, the motivation was at least as much one of establishing national independence as it was raising the material standard of living of the mass of the people. Why do the poor of the developing countries accept their fate with so little resistance?

Several explanations have been suggested. Some Western observers point to the apathy, fatalism, and lethargy of the rural masses in traditional countries as a factor that robs them of the strength to rebel. Others claim that there is actually a great desire to rebel among the poor, but that the cultural obstacles to common causes prevents them from organizing to achieve their goals. Still others assert that there is actually a great deal of violence in politics in the Third World, but that the military and the police have so far been able to contain rebellion by sheer coercion and counter-terror.

Still another cause of mass acceptance of what seems to be a manifestly unjust social system exists. The central feature of this explanation has to do with the difference between symbolic and tangible politics. We begin with a quote by Robert Dahl, as he discusses ethnic politics in New Haven:

> Politicians who play the game of ethnic politics confer individual benefits like jobs, nominations, bribes, gratuities, and assistance on all sorts of individuals more or less according to ethnic criteria. But ethnic chacacteristics serve as a kind of comprehensive symbol for class and other criteria. Moreover, benefits conferred on an individual member of an ethnic group are actually shared to some degree by the rest of the group, for every time one member makes a social or economic breakthrough, others are likely to learn of it, to take pride in his accomplishment, and to find it easier themselves to achieve the same sort of advance. The strategies of politicians are designed to confer specific benefits on particular individuals and thus to win the support of the whole group.[17]

What Dahl is describing with regard to ethnic politics in New Haven is just another specific example of the more general social institution that Charles Elliott calls the "confidence mechanism." The confidence mechanism is any social practice or structure that permits real resources to be distributed unequally, but that does so in such a way as to convince those who lose that the system is essentially fair, and that they lost because of their own shortcomings. To cite Elliott, any confidence mechanism consists of these six characteristics: first, there must be competition among the members of a group for individual enrichment; second, only a few members of the group are chosen to benefit from the enrichment process; third, the process of selection is biased away from natural abilities or merit, and toward some ascriptive criterion, such as race or language; fourth, these selective biases are not obvious to those who compete; fifth, the system remains sufficiently open (at least to all appearances) so as to make the process seem legitimate to those who lose from it; and sixth, the overall process of enrichment is controlled by persons who benefit directly or indirectly from it.[18]

Murray Edelman has drawn our attention to the central role of symbols in any political system.[19] In poor countries, symbolic capability may be the key to regime survival. Symbols have their greatest value in politics as media to bestow the psychic benefit of a given policy on those sectors or individuals who do not receive any material benefit from the policy, and who did not have the opportunity to participate in its formulation. In other words, political symbols help a government make its people feel good about a policy that does not benefit them materially in any way. In developing countries where there are not many material benefits to distribute, symbolic politics (as administered by confidence mechanisms) takes on heightened importance.

Does this line of analysis suggest that people who benefit from politics only symbolically are being deceived or duped? More radical commentators of Third World politics would certainly answer in the affirmative. To these people, the lower classes are being bought off by essentially worthless symbols, such as racial or ethnic pride, and they must experience an increase in class consciousness in order to attract more tangible benefits to their lives. On the other hand, argues Dahl, who are we to denigrate another person's

---

[17] Robert A. Dahl, *Who Governs? Democracy and Power in an American City,* (New Haven, Conn.: Yale, 1961), p. 53.

[18] Elliott, *Patterns of Poverty.*

[19] Murray Edelman, *The Symbolic Uses of Politics* (Urbana, Ill.: Illinois, 1964).

values, which may include symbols instead of tangible goods and service. As he says,

> ... *terms such as benefit and reward are intended to refer to subjective, psychological appraisal by the recipients, rather than appraisals by other observers. An action can be said to confer benefits on an individual ... if he believes he has benefited, even though, from the point of view of observers, his belief is false or perhaps ethnically wrong.*[20]

After all, when people have lost all hope of gaining material rewards commensurate with thier efforts, can anyone deny them the right to take refuge in symbols? One of the lasting contributions of Freud to our understanding of human consciousness was to show that our

[20] Dahl, p. 52, footnote 1.

desires were inherently insatiable and, therefore, we must engage in psychological exercises to be able to live on a day-to-day basis with frustration and denial as our constant companions. Certainly, persons who have had their class consciousness raised and who are denied the sanctuary of symbolic gratification are frequently the fuel for the fires of revolution. Nevertheless, traditional identities based on race, religion, tribal affiliation, ethnic characteristics, or language are still powerful in the Third World. They should serve as a constant reminder to potential revolutionaries that the task of mobilization of the poor of their country has so far defied all but the most talented of leaders. Whether this continues to be the case or not is a secret locked in the minds and in the social institutions of the 2 billion people of the Third World.

Suggestions for Further Reading

Adams, Don, and Robert M. Bjork, *Education in Developing Areas* (New York: McKay, 1969).

Baranson, Jack, *Industrial Technology for Developing Economies* (New York: Praeger, 1969).

Carter, Gwendolyn, and William O. Brown, *Transition in Africa: Studies in Political Adaptation* (Boston: Boston, 1958).

Froelich, Walter, ed., *Land Tenure, Industrialization and Social Stability* (Milwaukee: Marquette, 1961).

Hoselitz, Bert F., and Wilbert E. Moore, eds., *Industrialization and Society* (Paris, UNESCO, 1963).

Livingstone, Arthur, *Social Policy in Developing Countries* (London: Routledge & Kegan Paul, 1969).

Marchal, Jean, and Bernard Ducros, eds., *The Distribution of National Income (London: Macmillan, 1968).*

Schultz, Thomas W., *Transforming Traditional Agriculture* (New Haven, Conn: Yale, 1964).

Schram, Wilbur, *Mass Media and National Development* (Stanford, Calif.: Stanford, 1964).

Sigmund, Paul E., ed, *The Ideologies of the Developing Nations* (New York: Praeger, 1963).

Veenhoven, William A., ed., *Case Studies on Human Rights and Fundamental Freedoms: A World Survey*, 2 vols. (The Hague, Martinus Nijhoff 1975).

Warriner, Doreen, *Land Reform and Development in the Middle East*, 2nd ed. (London: Oxford, 1962).

Wriggins, Howard W., *The Ruler's Imperative: Strategies for Political Survival in Asia and Africa* (New York: Columbia, 1969)

Photo Credits

Index